Edition KWV

Die „Edition KWV" beinhaltet hochwertige Werke aus dem Bereich der Wirtschaftswissenschaften. Alle Werke in der Reihe erschienen ursprünglich im Kölner Wissenschaftsverlag, dessen Programm Springer Gabler 2018 übernommen hat.

Weitere Bände in der Reihe http://www.springer.com/series/16033

Norman Kellermann

Searching for a path out of distance fares

A review of historical passenger railway
pricing and an agent-based simulation
study on possible fare amendments

 Springer Gabler

Norman Kellermann
ÖBB-Personenverkehr AG
Wien, Austria

Bis 2018 erschien der Titel im Kölner Wissenschaftsverlag, Köln
Dissertation, Freie Universität Berlin, 2014

Edition KWV
ISBN 978-3-658-23111-8   ISBN 978-3-658-23112-5   (eBook)
https://doi.org/10.1007/978-3-658-23112-5

Library of Congress Control Number: 2018955566

Springer Gabler
© Springer Fachmedien Wiesbaden GmbH, part of Springer Nature 2014, Reprint 2018
Originally published by Kölner Wissenschaftsverlag, Köln, 2014

This Springer Gabler imprint is published by the registered company Springer Fachmedien Wiesbaden GmbH part of Springer Nature
The registered company address is: Abraham-Lincoln-Str. 46, 65189 Wiesbaden, Germany

Geleitwort

Der Preis eines Gutes gehört seit jeher zu den wichtigsten absatzpolitischen Parametern eines Unternehmens und er bildet auch ein zentrales Element vieler theoretischer Konzepte in der Wirtschaftswissenschaft. Im Gegensatz dazu ist den Prozessen des Preismanagements, d. h. der aktiven Gestaltung und Durchsetzung von Preisen in Unternehmen und am Markt, in der Marketingwissenschaft bislang nicht die gleiche Bedeutung zugemessen worden. Dies kann vielleicht auch als Erklärung dafür angesehen werden, dass – zumindest in einigen Bereichen – das in der Praxis anzutreffende Preismanagement wenig professionell gehandhabt wird mit der Folge, dass nicht alle Erlöspotenziale ausgeschöpft werden. Dies scheint insbesondere für das Pricing im europäischen Eisenbahn-Personenverkehr zu gelten, wo über Jahrzehnte ein überwiegend auf Tarifkilometern basiertes Preisregime dominant war.

Der Verfasser des vorliegenden Buches vermutet nun, dass diese Tatsache das Ergebnis eines pfadabhängigen Prozesses ist, weshalb der erste Teil des Werks auch der Überprüfung dieser Annahme gewidmet ist. Hierfür zieht er eine große Anzahl empirischen Materials unterschiedlichster Provenienz heran, das er in mühevoller Arbeit gesammelt und analysiert hat. So wird dem Leser ein überaus detailliertes und gleichzeitig sehr anschauliches Bild von der Entwicklung der Preissetzung im europäischen Eisenbahn-Personenverkehr vermittelt. Dabei wird zunächst deutlich, dass es zu Beginn der Entwicklung keineswegs sicher war, dass sich die kilometerabhängige Tarifierung als Standard durchsetzen würde, sondern dass es sehr wohl alternative Formen der Preisgestaltung gab. Ausgehend hiervon identifiziert der Verfasser die selbstverstärkenden Kräfte, die zur Herausbildung des Pfads und schließlich zum Lock-in geführt haben. Letztlich hat der Erfolg des entfernungsbasierten Standardtarifs die – zu der Zeit staatlichen – Bahnbetreiber in diese Situation getrieben, weil das Schienennetz grenzüberschreitend wuchs, das Entgelt leicht zu kalkulieren war und hierzu komplementäre Güter und Vertriebswege entstanden, die dessen Akzeptanz und Durchsetzung zusätzlich beförderten.

Entscheidend für den Nachweis einer Pfadexistenz ist aber nicht nur das Aufdecken selbstverstärkender Effekte, sondern auch das Aufzeigen der (potenziellen) Ineffizienz des Lock-ins. Auch diese kann der Verfasser mittels einer schlüssigen Argumentation belegen. Letztlich zeigt sie sich in den unzureichenden Reaktionen der Branche auf das Eintreten der Wettbewerbstechnologien Auto- und Flugverkehr, der damit verbundenen Verschlechterung ihrer Position im intermodalen Wettbewerb sowie dem dadurch wiederum bewirkten stetigen Rückgang des Marktanteils des Personenverkehrs auf der Schiene.

Wie könnte nun das System des Schienenpersonenverkehrs aus dieser für es missliche Lage wieder herausgeführt werden? Wie könnte also im Sinne der Pfadtheorie ein Pfadbruch gelingen? Notwendig ist hierfür zunächst einmal eine Kenntnis über alternative, vorteilhaftere Preissysteme. Denn wenn den Bahnbetreibern solche gar nicht bewusst sind und sie sie nicht einzuschätzen vermögen, werden sie auch nicht auf die Idee kommen, Wege aus dem Lock-in zu suchen. Der Verfasser entwickelt deshalb unter Rückgriff auf verhaltenswissenschaftliche Ansätze der Preispolitik sowie auf der Basis von Daten eines europäischen Eisenbahn-Verkehrsunternehmens ein agentenbasierten Simulationsmodell, das er zur Durchführung von Experimenten verwendet, mittels derer die Auswirkungen innovativer Wege der Tarifgestaltung im Eisenbahnverkehr aufgezeigt werden können.

Fasst man die Ergebnisse der verschiedenen Simulationsstudien zusammen, so wird deutlich, dass die Preissystementscheidungen eines Bahnbetreibers einen erheblichen, messbaren Einfluss sowohl auf die eigenen Umsatz- und Belegungszahlen sowie auf die der Wettbewerber haben. Des Weiteren zeigen die Ergebnisse der Experimente auf, dass es die Eisenbahn-Verkehrsunternehmen vermeiden sollten, feste oder kaufvolumensabhängige Rabatte zu gewähren. Zudem sollten sie sehr genau das Pricing-Verhalten ihrer intramodalen Konkurrenten beobachten, da dieses unmittelbare Auswirkungen auf ihren eigenen ökonomischen Erfolg hat. Ebenso machen die Ergebnisse deutlich, dass ein mengenbasiertes Revenue Management prinzipiell helfen kann die Umsatzerlöse eines etablierten Bahnbetreibers zu erhöhen, auch wenn dieser Effekt nicht in allen untersuchten Fällen auftrat. Die Zuteilungsregeln für die Sitzplatzkontingente sollten eine ständige Anpassung an die Marktgegebenheiten erlauben. Würden die etablierten Anbieter also solche alternativen Wege der Entgelttarifierung wählen, stünden ihnen damit grundsätzlich Wege aus dem Lock-in ihrer bisherigen Tarifgestaltung offen.

Mit seinem Werk hat der Verfasser somit auf interessante und innovative Weise die Theorie der Pfadabhängigkeit mit der Entwicklung eines Simulationstools, das für die Zwecke eines Pfadbruchs genutzt werden kann, verknüpft. Der Verfasser kann dabei erstens wohlbegründet aufzeigen, dass sich in der Geschichte der Eisenbahntarifierung pfadabhängige Prozesse vollzogen haben, die zu einem persistenten Muster der Tarifgestaltung geführt haben. Damit leistet er einen wichtigen branchenbezogen Beitrag zur Theorie der Pfadabhängigkeit. Mit der eigenständigen und kreativen Ableitung eines agentenbasierten Simulationsmodells zur Bewertung alternativer Tarifoptionen liefert er zudem nicht nur Ansatzpunkte dafür, wie die Akteure in der Branche aus dem Lock-in, der sie offenbar in ihrer Preisgestaltung hemmt, wieder entfliehen können, sondern auch einen Beitrag zur Forschung im Operations Research.

Das entwickelte Modell kann als Instrument zur Preisforschung und zur Entscheidungsunterstützung bei der Weiterentwicklung der Preisgestaltung von Verkehrsunternehmen eingesetzt werden. Ich wünsche dem Werk deshalb, dass es in Wissenschaft und Praxis die ihm gebührende Aufmerksamkeit finden wird.

Prof. Dr. Dr. h. c. Michael Kleinaltenkamp

Danksagung

Ein Dissertationsprojekt selbständig entwickeln zu können ist ein großes Privileg. Ohne die Deutsche Forschungsgemeinschaft, die das Pfadkolleg als betriebswirtschaftliches Graduiertenkolleg an der Freien Universität Berlin über viele Jahre finanziert hat und ohne das Engagement von Prof. Georg Schreyögg und Prof. Jörg Sydow für die dritte Kohorte wäre die Realisierung dieser Dissertation nicht möglich gewesen.

Ich möchte an erster Stelle meinem Betreuerteam ganz herzlich danken: Prof. Michael Kleinaltenkamp hat von Anfang an mein Vorhaben unterstützt und in entscheidenden Momenten vorangebracht. Nur durch seine Initiative konnte ich an für mein Projekt wichtigen Schulungen und Konferenzen teilnehmen. Prof. Catherine Cleophas verdankt diese Arbeit eine analytische Schärfe und einen klaren Bezug zur betriebswirtschaftlichen Disziplin des Operations Research. Ihre Erfahrung mit Erlössimulationen in der Airline-Industrie und ihre praktische Unterstützung waren wesentlich bei meinen Bemühungen ein Partner-Verkehrsunternehmen für die Konzeption des Simulationsmodells zu gewinnen. Prof. Klaus G. Troitzsch hat beeindruckend bewiesen, dass er sich in die Probleme eines Doktoranden in jeder Phase einer Dissertation hineinversetzen kann. Seine umfassende Expertise im Bereich agentenbasierter Simulation muss hier nicht gesondert hervorgehoben werden. Aus dem Team des high performance computing Zentrums der Freien Universität möchte ich mich besonders bei Dr. Loris Bennett bedanken, der mich geduldig in die Unix-Programmierung eingewiesen hat.

Den Kollegiaten des Pfadkollegs danke ich für die vielen Stunden, in denen sie ihre Gedanken zum Konzept der Pfadabhängigkeit und dazugehörigen Forschungsprojekten mit mir geteilt haben. Genauso wie den Organisatoren der Arbeitstreffen der Forschergruppe der European Social Simulation Association danke auch den Professoren und Doktoranden des Marketing-Departments der Freien Universität Berlin für ihr Feedback bei diversen Kolloquien.

Bei meinen transportgeschichtlichen Recherchen haben mir die Teams des DB Museums in Nürnberg, des Deutschen Technikmuseums Berlin, der Archive des französischen Staatsbahnen SNCF und des britischen National Railway Museum wertvolle Hilfestellung geleistet. Besonders hervorheben möchte ich die Hinweise von Prof. Colin Divall von der University of York. Prof. Liudger Dienel von der Technischen Universität Berlin hat nicht nur das Pfadkolleg als Gast bei der Langen Nacht der Wissenschaften unterstützt, sondern auch durch die Mitorganisation der Transport, Traffic and Mobility-Konferenzen eine Plattform für Mobilitätsgeschichte geschaffen.

Inzwischen glaube ich zu wissen, was Prof. Sydow am Anfang meiner Zeit im Pfadkolleg damit meinte, dass eine Dissertation ein risikoreiches Unterfangen sei. Dass die Zeit der Dissertation trotzdem eine schöne war, verdanke ich meiner Freundin Katarína, meinen Eltern und meinem Bruder Robin. Sie haben immer darauf vertraut, dass der Weg einer Dissertation das Risiko auch wert ist.

Berlin, im Juli 2014

The price system is just one of those formations which man has learned to use (though he is still very far from having learned to make the best use of it) after he had stumbled upon it without understanding it.

Friedrich Hayek 1945 in "The Use of Knowledge in Society", p. 528

Contents

List of figures

List of tables

List of abbreviations

ABM	Agent-based model
BLS	Bern-Lötschberg-Simplon railway
BR	British Railways
DB	German Railways (Deutsche Bundesbahn/Deutsche Bahn)
DRG	German Railways (Deutsche Reichsbahn-Gesellschaft)
ČD	Czech Railways (České dráhy)
ČSD	Czechoslovak Railways (Československé dráhy)
CFR	Romanian Railways (Societatea nationala de transport feroviar)
CIT	International Rail Transport Committee (Comité international des transports ferroviaires)
CIV	Uniform Rules concerning the Contract for International Carriage of Passengers and Luggage by Rail (Règles uniformes concernant le contrat de transport international ferroviaire des voyageurs)
COTIF	Convention concerning International Carriage by Rail (Convention relative aux transports internationaux ferroviaires)
EU	European Union
L&M	Liverpool & Manchester Railway Company
MÁV	Hungarian State Railways (Magyar Államvasutok)
NSB	Norwegian Railways (Norske Statsbaner)
ÖBB	Austrian Federal Railways (Österreichische Bundesbahnen)
OR	Operations research
OECD	Organisation for Economic Co-operation and Development
OTIF	Intergovernmental Organisation for International Carriage by Rail

PSO	Public service obligations
RM	Revenue management
SBB	Swiss Federal Railways (Schweizerische Bundesbahnen)
SCIC	Special Conditions of International Carriage
SNCB	Beligian National Railways (Société nationale des chemins de fer belges)
SNCF	French National Railways (Société nationale des chemins de fer français)
TGV	High-speed train of the French National Railways SNCF (Train à grande vitesse)
TOC	Train operating company
UIC	International Union of Railways (Union internationale des chemins de fer)
UPC	Universal Product Code
VdEV	Association of German Railway Administrations (Verband deutscher Eisenbahnverwaltungen)
VöV	Swiss Association of Public Transport (Verband öffentlicher Verkehr)
ŽSSK	Slovak Railways (Železničná spoločnosť Slovensko)

1. Introduction

Pricing can certainly be considered as the most sensitive element of the marketing mix. In perishable asset markets, allocating the right price at the right time is key to amortise investments made for the inventory. However, pricing is far from being costless or simple, but rather enabled by a set of "resources, routines, and skills that might help or inhibit a firm in setting the right price" (Dutta et al. 2003: 616). At the same time, pricing as a phenomenon of emergence and complexity constitutes a field business scholars are increasingly interested in (cf. Ihrig & Troitzsch 2013: 99).

Combining insights from the marketing, management and operations research disciplines, this work investigates on the history of pricing in the passenger railway industry and seeks to develop a tool supporting contemporary railways in setting the fares for their passenger services. More precisely, I elaborate on two central questions: First, whether the historical development of European railway tariffing represents the outcome of a path-dependent process. Second, assuming that a path can be reconstructed, whether there is at least one tariff structure that would constitute a more revenue-efficient alternative to the path from the perspective of a train operator. For this purpose, I reconstruct the central features of passenger railway tariffing in Europe since the emergence of the industry and I propose an agent-based revenue simulation model calibrated with empirical data. The model is designed to capture the dynamics of price-setting by competing modes of transport, consumer buying behaviour, and market outcome.

The thesis at hand is structured in four central parts: In the first section to follow, there is an outline of central theoretical assumptions including path dependence theory and different perspectives on price in the history of economic thought. After the second section comprising the development of the research questions and the deduction of appropriate research methods, third, the historical development of railway fares since the beginning of the railway age is reconstructed. Fourth, a market simulation model is developed in order to perform artificial price experiments with the aim of identifying promising pricing options for a focal train operating company.

For passenger railways, pricing is defined as the process of setting fares and their respective terms of use. Throughout this work, the terms "tariff" and "fare" are considered as synonyms. Since the early days of railways, fare policy issues have been largely discussed among academics, managers and stakeholders. Despite the vast experience in the field of fare policy the European railway sector can draw on, competing modes of transport (i. e., air and road transportation) have significantly gained market share from the 1960s on. The central argument of the European Commission to engage in revitalising the railway in-

© Springer Fachmedien Wiesbaden GmbH, part of Springer Nature 2014
N. Kellermann, *Searching for a path out of distance fares*, Edition KWV,
https://doi.org/10.1007/978-3-658-23112-5_1

dustry in the 1990s was "dissatisfaction with the price and quality of rail transport" (European Commission 1996: 3). Furthermore, back in 1996, the Commission stated that "[r]ail is felt not to respond to market changes or customers' needs, as other modes do" (ibid). Apparently, liberalisation measures introduced to renew railways did not lead to the positive effects observed in the telecommunications and airline branches. Passenger railways' market share continued to stagnate or even to decline in many countries, recently forcing the Commission to communicate to the EU parliament that "[r]ail passenger services have not kept pace with evolving needs in terms of offer or quality" (European Commission 2013: 7). In a press release dated January 30th, 2013, the Commission writes about a "vicious cycle of decline" (European Commission 2013a: 4) of railways in many EU member states.

I argue that rigidified patterns of pricing among passenger railways are one of the reasons for this development. More often than not, railways have been (and in part are) reluctant to introduce innovative forms of pricing. An excessive continuation of static fares hindered railway managers to react to new market conditions. Even if they were aware of a possibly path-dependent pricing strategy, managers of railway undertakings cannot always easily assess the potential consequences of their decisions when it comes to practical issues in pricing. This is not only because of the multitude of actions and effects arising in a same period of time, but also because marketing theories on pricing have not yet been fully implemented in business applications. For instance, though the assumption of loss-averse individuals in behavioural pricing theory (cf. Kahneman & Tversky 1979; Thaler 1985) has become widely accepted in marketing science, it lacks to be sufficiently implemented in decision support tools. Irrational individual behaviour towards the price stimulus is not yet part of state-of-the-art revenue management models although Talluri & van Ryzin (2005: 665) predicted advances in this field. Even though there is strong support for the formation of reference prices out of memorised transactions (cf. Briesch et al. 1997), train operating companies mostly rely on punctual market research for exploring price acceptance. Cheap advance purchase fares (cf. Prescott 1975; Dana 1998) are at least theoretically beneficial, but there are railways which do not offer any of them. Gourvish's (1986, 2002) seminal work on the history of the British Railways provides strong evidence for the necessity of fares to adapt to the competitive situation on each route. Yet, actions drawing on this insight are partially impeded by the lack of classical quantity-based revenue management applications. Facing heterogeneity of demand (cf. Allenby et al. 1998) and price learning effects over time both among competitors and consumers, it may be difficult for marketing managers to assess the large-scale effects of manipulations inspired by the price theory they have in mind. In the context of passenger railway markets, even limited pilot applications of new fare strategies can constitute a risky field experiment.

Thus, I see research opportunity for systematically reconstructing railways' pricing efforts in the past, and, based on the insights derived from this review, for building tools that facilitate the analysis of different pricing options suggested by marketing concepts. As they can be used as environments for artificial price experiments, agent-based simulation models are particularly suitable for this purpose. They provide the laboratory conditions needed without neglecting organisational and individual patterns of learning and decision-making.

2. Theoretical background and literature review

This dissertation builds on two central theoretical streams: the theory of path dependence as well as economic theories on the emergence of price.

2.1. Theory of path dependence

The theory of path dependence is a widely used approach in the social sciences. Stating that "history matters", it aims at explaining phenomena of rigidity that could not be anticipated in advance and that have been triggered by critical events. Thus, path dependence is always related with a process in which the previous state of a system determines the following one. Despite their notion of "past-dependence" (Antonelli 1997), phenomena of path dependence are not commonplace in the economy, but somewhat of an exception. What specific elements are needed to make a process path-dependent is described below.

2.1.1. First developments

While early reflections on increasing returns and inertia in the economy can already be found in Serra (1982 [1613], see also Sumberg 1991) and Veblen (1915, see also Penz & Priddat 2009), research on phenomena of path dependence and lock-in primarily goes back to the pioneering work of David (1975; 1985) and Arthur (1988; 1989). With his theory on the diffusion of technical innovations, Rogers (1962) had paved the way for a better understanding of the adoption or non-adoption of new technologies. Also Dosi (1982), who broached the issue of trajectories of technological development, can be seen as one of the antecedents of the theory of path dependence. Already in 1984, Hannan & Freeman had put researchers' attention to phenomena of excessive stability they called "structural inertia". In contrast to earlier publications, inflexibility is demonstrated by Hannan & Freeman to be the result of an evolutionary process instead of constituting a precondition for it.

Building on his prior research on technical choice and economic development (David 1969, 1975), Paul David opened the debate on path dependence with his 1985 article "Clio and the Economics of QWERTY", in which he argues that the configuration of the letters we use on computer keyboards is shaped by mechanical restrictions in the typewriter era, and therefore constitutes an inferior standard in terms of typing speed compared to another keyboard configuration (the Dvorak-keyboard). Brian Arthur (1989) outlines a theoretical model of technology choice that incorporates increasing returns to adoption, i. e. benefits of a technology depending on the number of its users. Hence, the early work on path dependence is strongly associated with technology diffusion processes.

© Springer Fachmedien Wiesbaden GmbH, part of Springer Nature 2014
N. Kellermann, *Searching for a path out of distance fares*, Edition KWV,
https://doi.org/10.1007/978-3-658-23112-5_2

On these foundations, North (1990) amplified the concept of path dependence with institutional economics, allowing him to explain the different macroeconomic development of nations and continents. Criticising the use of the term path dependence with the ubiquitous meaning of "history matters", Mahoney (2000) extends the concept of path dependence to social processes and institutions, considering path dependence as "historical sequences in which contingent events set into motion institutional patterns or event chains that have deterministic properties" (ibid: 507). Mahoney (ibid: 508) seems to consider self-reinforcing sequences and increasing returns as synonyms: "With increasing returns, an institutional pattern [...] delivers increasing benefits with its continued adoption". While, following this definition, self-reinforcing sequences are a source of continuous reproduction of a given institutional pattern, Mahoney introduces a complementing view of reactive sequences that can, at certain conjunctures, lead to enduring consequences of a decision. Pierson (2000) employs the concept of path dependence to explain change resistance in political institutions. Arguing that "social adaptation to institutions drastically increases the cost of exit from existing arrangements" (ibid: 492), Pierson writes that early decisions (or "accidents", p. 485) may lock-in future options.

2.1.2. The nature of increasing returns

Though Page (2006: 89) argues that increasing returns are "neither necessary nor sufficient for historical path dependence", a central aspect of path dependence which distinguishes the concept from a simple notion of "history matters" is that it involves increasing returns or positive feedback effects (sometimes also named externalities). These effects are more generally referred to as self-reinforcing mechanisms. In his article on self-reinforcing mechanisms in economics, Arthur (1988: 10) names four possible "generic sources" of self-reinforcement:

- large setup or fixed costs
- learning effects
- coordination effects
- adaptive expectations[1]

Self-reinforcement due to large setup or fixed costs refers to the common notion of falling unit costs with increasing output quantity. Learning effects are considered to "improve products or lower their costs as their prevalence increases" (North 1990: 94). Arthur (1992) argues that economic agents generally learn through the adaptation to feedback received from their environment. In his seminal work "Competing technologies, increasing returns and lock-in by historical events", Arthur (1989: 116) addresses the benefits of learning by writing that "[m]odern, complex technologies often display increasing returns to adop-

---

[1] Arthur originally employs the term "self-reinforcing expectations".

tion in that the more they are adopted, the more experience is gained with them, and the more they are improved". Coordination effects imply "the benefits of rule-guided behavio[u]r" (Sydow et al. 2009: 699). That is, transaction costs of interacting individuals are reduced by adopting a specific institution (i. e., a standard). North (1990: 94) describes this as "advantages to cooperation with other economic agents taking similar action". The interactive construction of preferences has been an important issue in economic research (cf. Nerlove 1958). Therefore, as a fourth source of self-reinforcement, adaptive expectations capture the fact that individual preferences are not necessarily stable; they may vary in response to the expectations of others (cf. Sydow et al. 2009: 700). In other words, an "increased prevalence [of a technology or product] on the market enhances beliefs of further prevalence" (Arthur 1988: 10). Identifying adaptive expectations as one of the drivers of stability in the economy, Brian Arthur pictographically demonstrated the problem of interdependence between individual decisions and collective behaviour in his El Farol bar example (cf. Arthur 1994a: 408 f.). The decision of going to a bar depending on the decisions of others to do so is one of the classical examples for which there is no deductive solution because "any commonalty of expectations gets broken up: if all believe few will go, all will go" (Arthur 1994a: 409).

Direct network effects, or network externalities, describe the phenomenon of a good or service being more beneficial as the number of users of that good or service increases. Because they are triggered by a combination of the four sources of self-reinforcement listed above, network effects can be conceptualised as another source of increasing returns (cf. Liebowitz & Margolis 1994). The classical example for positive feedback derived from the number of users is a telephone network (cf. Katz & Shapiro 1985). Thus, generally, the size of a network can directly determine its utility, even though the size of the Network may only involve potential customers (cf. den Hartigh & Langerak 2001) and though these effects do not necessarily occur automatically (cf. Afuah 2013).

Brian Arthur explains the possible indirect lock-in of technological standards with their attraction of compatibility to existing and newly developed products. In his 1990 Scientific American article he writes: "Technological conventions or standards as well as particular technologies, tend to become locked-in by positive feedback [...]. Although a standard itself may not improve with [time], widespread adoption makes it advantageous for newcomers to a field – who must exchange information or products with those already working there – to fall in with the standard, be it the English language, a high-definition television system, a screw thread or a typewriter keyboard" (Arthur 1990: 99[2]).

Farrell & Saloner (1985) explain "excess inertia" of inferior technical standards with the existence of standardisation benefits both on the supply and

---

[2] Please note that this citation refers to the originally printed version in Scientific American, not the slightly differing draft available through Google Scholar.

demand side of markets, assuming this phenomenon to occur in cases of in-complete information. Yet, they do not assume absolute irreversibility as they present an outlook how inertia may be overcome. Concerning the ways consum-ers can benefit from standardisation, Farrell & Saloner distinguish between di-rect network effects and so-called "market-mediated effect[s]" (ibid: 70; see also Farrell & Klemperer 2007). Liebowitz & Margolis (1994: 137f.) criticise this view. They generalise the term of network effects by saying that it describes a situa-tion "in which the benefits of owning a product, or using a standard, or, in fact, taking any action, increase[] with the number of people doing the same thing" (Liebowitz & Margolis 2013: 128).

Transferred from technology adoption to a broader scope of decision making, *indirect network effects* thus refer to complementing goods or services that make a focused good or service increasingly useful (cf. Koch et al. 2009). Al-so technologically compatible platforms meet this notion of network benefits. In this field, Koski & Kretschmer (2005) conduct research on the effects of what they call "within-standards competition" and "between-standards competition" in the mobile phone industry. One of their findings is that between-standards competition leads to more severe price wars than within-standards competition. Also grounded in the mobile phone industry, Meyer (2012) and Meyer & Klein-altenkamp (2011) explicitly study indirect network effects arising in two-sided markets. In this type of market, consumers and suppliers interact through an intermediary technological platform.

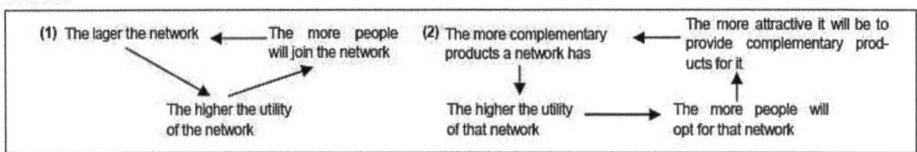

Figure 1: Direct and indirect network effects
Source: Koch et al. 2009: 69

For markets in general, Meyer (2012) consolidates the different views on positive feedback described above and augments it with a consumer perspective into a typology of self-reinforcing mechanisms. The central contribution of this systematisation of self-reinforcing mechanisms is its clear separation of learn-ing effects arising on the supply and the demand side of a market. Meyer (ibid: 30 ff.) considers four driving forces for technological lock-ins:

- Supply-side economies of scale
- Consumer learning effects
- Adaptive expectations
- Network effects

Supply-side economies of scale describe fixed cost degression, increasing purchasing power and learning curve effects arising for a firm that succeeds to increase its output volume. Thus, supply-side economies of scale include learning effects in production. Reversely, consumer learning effects refer to the benefits users gain from getting more experienced with a certain technology: "[o]ver time, consumers gain practice with the technology and learn to employ it in a more efficient way" (Meyer 2012: 31). While adaptive expectations are interpreted in the sense of Arthur outlined above, network effects subsume both direct and indirect ones.

2.1.3. Characteristics of and conditions for a path-dependent process

Apart from defining self-reinforcing mechanisms as drivers of a path-dependent process, this section aims at developing a more precise distinction of path dependence, specifically in what concerns constitutive features that make a given process a path-dependent one.

Definitions

Arthur (1989: 117) names two central properties of a path-dependent process: "inflexibility in that once an outcome (a dominant technology) begins to emerge it becomes progressively more 'locked in'; and non-ergodicity in that historical 'small events' are not averaged away and 'forgotten' by the dynamics - they may decide the outcome". Later, combining the insights of his previous work in a chapter of his 1994 textbook "Increasing Returns and Path Dependence in the Economy", Arthur defines path dependence as a special characteristic of increasing returns phenomena including the four following properties (cf. Arthur 1994: 28):

- Nonpredictability
- Nonergodicity
- Inflexibility
- Potential inefficiency

Nonpredictability refers to the fact that there is a no analytical solution to forecast the outcome of the process. However, though the outcome of the process is "predictably unpredictable", it is not completely open. The process is non-ergodic, which is to say there is "a multiplicity of potential 'solutions'" (Arthur 2006: 1559). For defining nonergodicity, Arthur (1994: 28) also mentions that "small events early on may decide the larger course of structural change. Furthermore, it is the property of a path-dependent process that "allocations gradually rigidify, or lock-in, in structure" (Arthur 1994: 28). Thus, the outcome is inflexible. Finally, because of the former characteristics, the selected solution, product or technology is not necessarily the most appropriate one – therefore, the outcome of a path-dependent process is potentially inefficient.

In his 2001 text "Path dependence, its critics, and the quest for 'historical economics'", Paul David defines path dependence mathematically as a special type of dynamic stochastic processes: "*Path dependence*, as I wish to use the term, refers to a dynamic property of allocative processes. It may be defined either with regard to the relationship between the process dynamics and the outcome(s) to which it converges, or the limiting probability distribution of the stochastic process under consideration" (ibid: 18, emphasis in the original). David then provides a positive and a negative definition of path dependence:

> "**A negative definition:** *Processes that are non-ergodic, and thus unable to shake free of their history, are said to yield path dependent outcomes.*"

> "**A positive definition:** *A path dependent stochastic process is one whose asymptotic distribution evolves as a consequence (function of) the process's own history*" (David 2001: 19, emphasis and bold in the original).

In his later work, David (e. g., 2007) gradually takes the perspective that path dependence "refers to a well-defined concept, not a theory"[3]. Adopting a critical viewpoint on the path dependence discourse and putting a strong emphasis on the inefficiency question, Liebowitz & Margolis (1995: 206 f.) develop a taxonomy of path dependence comprising three degrees. These degrees represent the "severity" of the outcome of a path-dependent process in terms of inefficiency:

> "There are three possible efficiency outcomes when a dynamic process exhibits sensitive dependence on initial conditions. [...]

> We will call instances in which sensitivity to starting points exists but has no implied inefficiency *first-degree path dependence*. Where information is imperfect, a second possibility arises. In this case, it is possible that efficient decisions may not always appear to be efficient in retrospect. Here the inferiority of a chosen path is unknowable at the time a choice was made, but it is later recogni[s]ed that some alternative path would have yielded greater wealth. In such a situation, which we will call *second-degree path dependence*, sensitive dependence on initial conditions leads to outcomes that are regrettable and costly to change. They are not, however, inefficient in any meaningful sense, given the assumed limitations on knowledge. Related to this second type of path dependence is *third-degree path dependence*. In third-degree path dependence, sensitive dependence on initial conditions leads to an outcome that is inefficient – but in this case the outcome is also remediable. That is, there exists or existed some feasible arrangement for recogni[s]ing and achieving a preferred outcome, but that outcome is not obtained (Liebowitz & Margolis 1995: 206 f., emphasis in the original).

---

[3] Cited from Paul David's lecture slights presented in the doctoral colloquium on path dependence, 14-15 May 2012 in Berlin.

Assuming that third-degree path dependence is the only form of path dependence which stands in conflict with neoclassical economics, Liebowitz & Margolis (1995: 207) conclude that "[i]n instances of third-degree path dependence, outcomes cannot be predicted even with a knowledge of both starting positions and the desirability of alternative outcomes. In a world where efficiency cannot successfully predict outcomes, some (most?) outcomes must be inefficient". They term this case "remediable inefficiency" (ibid: 224). However, though throughout their work, Liebowitz and Margolis do not claim that market failure due to increasing returns is impossible, they believe that those outcomes are "extremely uncommon" (Liebowitz & Margolis 2013: 129) in the economy.

The insight of potentially rigidified patterns of economic activities has been taken on by different academic disciplines, for instance by strategic management and organisation science (Leonard-Barton 1992; Holtmann 2008; Schreyögg et al. 2011).

In their work on organisational path dependence, Sydow et al. (2009) and Schreyögg & Sydow (2011) have advanced the understanding of path-dependent processes by building a phase model including the characteristic features of path dependence outlined by David and Arthur. Sydow et al. (2009: 696) define the phenomenon of path dependence on an organisational level "as a rigidified, potentially inefficient action pattern built up by the unintended consequences of former decisions and positive feedback processes". The phase model draws the development of a path from a situation of contingency, starting with which the scope of action gets gradually reduced by self-reinforcing mechanisms, finally leading to a lock-in situation. In its extreme form, the final phase of path dependence is characterised by excessive deterministic stability which can only be disrupted by exogenous shocks. According to Sydow et al. (ibid: 694), "alternative courses of action are no longer feasible" in a classical lock-in situation. Martin & Sunley (2006: 406) regard this as an "overly restrictive conception", proposing to focus on potential sources of change from within a path. Consequently, Sydow et al. (2009) propose a modified interpretation of lock-in in the context of organisational paths. They describe lock-in as "a preferred action pattern, which then gets deeply embedded in organi[s]ational practice and replicated" (ibid: 694).

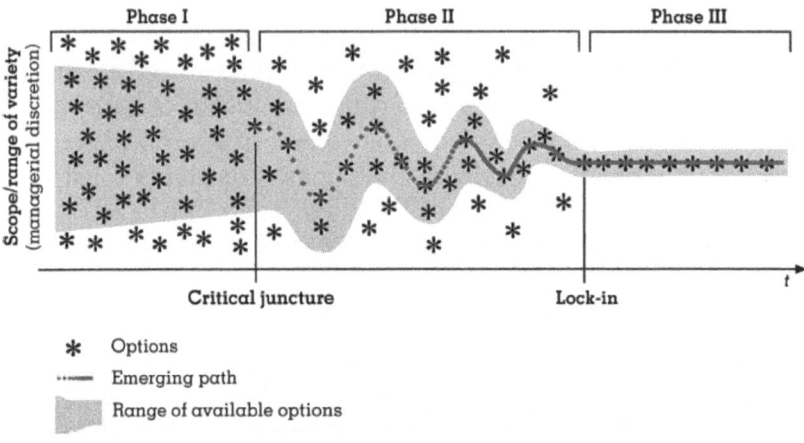

Figure 2: The constitution of an organisational path
Source: Sydow et al. 2009: 692

To sum up, path dependence has evolved from a concept of technological lock-in to a more general theory explaining the emergence of persisting states of inefficiency. It claims to be a new paradigm for economic theory and stands in contrast to neoclassical concepts of predefined equilibria. In Arthur's words: "With the acceptance of positive feedbacks, economists' theories are beginning to portray the economy not as simple but complex, not as deterministic, predictable and mechanistic, but instead as process-dependent, organic and always evolving" (Arthur 1990: 99). As this dissertation is oriented on an organisational (or in other words more business-related) perspective on path dependence, lock-in is regarded in this work as a remediable case of rigidified action according to the process model outlined by Sydow et al. (2009).

2.1.4. The struggle with empirical examples

The QWERTY debate

David's 1985 paper on the QWERTY keyboard as an example for an inefficient outcome of a path-dependent process has been fiercely criticised by Liebowitz & Margolis (1990), who clearly demonstrated that the inferiority argument of the QWERTY standard cannot be maintained. It has to be noted that the QWERTY story is a myth, however, an extensively cited one. Liebowitz & Margolis (2013) admit this, even though they perpetuate their criticism of what they call "Lock-in theory" (ibid: 151). Extending the debate on the keyboard letters, Hossain & Morgan (2009) run a student experiment in which they replicate the competition of typewriter platforms on a market. They find that "the market always manages to solve the QWERTY problem. In 60 iterations of dynamic platform competition, our subjects never got stuck on the inferior platform" (ibid: 435). Recently, the QWERTY discourse has been revitalised by the contribution of

Kay (2013), who runs search experiments in order to replicate the historical competition of typewriter standards. Kay (ibid: 1184) claims that "the success of QWERTY over Dvorak was no accident of history", but a merited victory for its superior compatibility. Drawing on this research, Vergne (2013: 3) argues that whether the QWERTY story is true or not, "[t]he biggest challenge with path dependence is not the theory itself but its empirical validation". Vergne supposes that it is the method of longitudinal case study research that impeded progress on the exploration of path-dependent phenomena:

> "Because suboptimality is not readily explained by conventional economics, many scholars believed that a research design based on the *ex post* identification of supposedly suboptimal outcomes would be well suited to provide empirical evidence of path dependence. Such a research design would distinguish more easily between neoclassical equilibrium and lock-in (as induced by path dependence). While this research strategy has some face value, it turned out to be a dead end. Despite an accumulation of historical case studies of so-called path-dependent trajectories over the past two decades, a significant portion of the scholarly community still does not 'buy' the path dependence story. Sure, we could blame the sceptics. But I'd rather blame the method" (Vergne 2013: 3).

Other empirical studies on path dependence

As stated above by Vergne, there were many attempts to find empirical evidence for path-dependent processes apart from the QWERTY case. In their so far latest publication they dedicated to the "troubled path of the Lock-in Movement", Liebowitz & Margolis write: "Arthur, David, their students and others were looking for empirical support in standards or technologies such as video recorders, railroad gauges, nuclear reactors, automobile propulsion, quadraphonic audio, and particularly QWERTY" (Liebowitz & Margolis 2013: 135). In fact, researchers around Paul David and Brian Arthur firstly chose network technologies to illustrate their perception of technologies being socially constructed, and therefore prone to phenomena of path dependence. Emphasising the long-lasting importance of seemingly small historical events, David & Bunn (1988) published an article on the standardisation process in electricity supply. They write:

> [Technical] systems such as the railroads, electric-light and power utilities, and telephone networks should be regarded as both society-shaping and 'socially constructed'. These technologies have been built up sequentially, through an evolutionary process in which the design and operation of constituent components were adapted to the specific technical, economic, and politico-legal circumstances in which new opportunities and problems were perceived. Those perceptions, usually, were formed on the basis of experience acquired through the operation of pre-existing sy[s]tems having some of the same or analogous functions as the ultimate standardi[s]ed technology (David & Bunn 1988: 166).

A frequently cited study on technological path dependence is the case of nuclear power reactors presented by Cowan (1990). Cowan argues that technically inferior light water reactors dominate the market due to the early choice of this technology by the United States Navy. Competing networks and proprietary standards are the field of Postrel (1990), who describes the development of the quadrophonic sound standard. The empirical example of the VHS video recording standard vs. Betamax outlined by Cusumano et al. (1992) and others continues to be largely discussed. In their research on network effects in the consumer electronics market, Dranove & Gandal (2003) find that the announcement of DivX temporarily hindered the diffusion of the DVD technology. With his dissertation, Kirsch (1996) contributes a study on the rivalry between electric and combustible propulsion in economic history. The area of economic innovation in the context of network effects has been of special interest for critique for Stan Liebowitz and Stephen Margolis (e. g., Liebowitz & Margolis 1994).

Another empirical study on path dependence was performed in the field of the U.S. beer market (cf. Barnes et al. 2004). Holtmann (2008) conducts research on business model rigidity in the case of the Bertelsmann book club. A recent study on path-dependent diffusion of airplane production technologies is presented by Greve & Seidel (2014). This list of publications is by no means a complete one, but tends to illustrate the many different empirical areas in which researchers tempted to track path dependence. Studies of path dependence specially related to the railway industry are outlined below.

2.1.5. Railways and path dependence

Phenomena in the railway sector as an illustration for path dependence have been extensively studied by economic historians under technological and institutional aspects. Adopting an institutional perspective on railways, Andersson-Skog (2009) provides an overview of studies linked with the railway sector and path dependence. While Scott (2001) emphasises initial technical developments as a source of path dependence in his work on the British "coal wagon problem", Andersson-Skog observes that "The railway sector is [] an industry where distinct development paths and regulatory styles have developed in different nations, regardless of the common technological base" (ibid: 70).

Dobbin (1994) describes the fundamentally different early development of railways and railway policy in the United States, Britain, and France by reconstructing the underlying path-dependent processes. One of the aspects of railway development he sheds light on is the pricing policy of railway companies, interests of consumers and governmental regulation in different periods of time. Already in the very beginning of the railway age, companies are confronted with a tendency of monopolisation (cf. ibid: 66 ff.), leading to calls for interventions and antitrust-measures. Building on his studies on standardisation in spatial networks, Puffert (2002; 2009) presents elaborated work on path dependence using the example of railway gauges and their (non-)standardisation in different regions all over the world. He employs simulation models to show the dynamics of conversion and non-conversion to standardised gauges in different geographical regions (cf. Puffert 2009: 255 ff.) and also links his findings to the problems of interoperability in the European single market (cf. ibid: 313 f.).

2.2. Searching for the value: the theoretical emergence of price

Since price-setting activities of one or more firms are the main focus of the dissertation at hand, a detailed review of the literature on the emergence of market prices is needed. This is even more necessary because explicit theoretical assumptions of how and when prices are set or changed are not always easily found in management literature. While operations research scholars basically tend to optimise a given setting or to solve a practical problem, theoretical problems of pricing are primarily addressed in marketing science, where pricing is conceptualised as the most prominent element of the marketing-mix (cf. e. g., Diller 2008: 21 ff.). Yet, a gap between theory on pricing and daily practice within firms is also identified in the marketing literature (cf. Simon & Fassnacht 2009: 10). Diller (2008) distinguishes two different basic theoretical approaches for pricing from a firm's perspective: "classical" and "behavioural". While classical models are oriented on microeconomics, behavioural models explicitly emphasise individual decision-making and psychological theories. Additionally, more pragmatic or – at first sight – apparently "theoryless" pricing approaches can be observed among practitioners.

The following sections are dedicated to shed light on the theoretical starting points of pricing, they include the different "classical" theories as well as behavioural aspects of price. Building on this theoretical review, pricing applications developed in OR and pricing strategies employed in business practice can be inspected on their implicit theoretical assumptions in chapters 2.3. and 2.4..

2.2.1. Pre-classical and classical economics

In his book "A Treatise of Taxes and Contributions" first published in 1662, William Petty develops a theory of value conceptualising price in three categories: (i) the *natural value* of a good[4] involving the means of subsistence necessary to produce it, (ii) the *accidental value* of a good formed by "contingent causes" influencing its natural value, and (iii) the *political price* of a good as a result of state interventions (cf. Kurz 2008b). Also Richard Cantillon argues in his book "Essai sur la nature du commerce en général", published in 1755, that the natural price of a good is determined by its production cost. Thus, every good has an inherent value. Cantillon explains deviations of market prices from the natural, inherent price with a reaction of price to changes in demand, but assumes the supply side reaction to lead back to the natural price (cf. Strohmaier 2008). The theory of value developed by the French physiocrate François Quesnay (e. g., in his Tableau Économique first published in 1758) comprises two general categories of value: the *valeur usuelle* (value-in-use) and the *valeur vénale* (value-in-exchange). However, Quesnay assumes that there is a *prix fondamental* which

---

[4] Note that among classical economists, at least Jean-Baptiste Say (2006 [1803]) made clear that a good can be either a material object or an immaterial one. Vargo & Lusch (2004) draw their service dominant logic on the interpretation of a good having been perceived as a tangible resource only.

includes all cost for raw materials, wages and deterioration of asset capital (cf. Eichert 2008; see also the influence on Vargo & Lusch 2004).

A scholar who personally knew Quesnay, Adam Smith, develops a theory on the component parts of price in his famous book "An Inquiry into the Nature and Causes of the Wealth of Nations" published in 1776. According to Smith, market prices depend on random and short-term influences. Through competition, they will align with the natural price of a good, which consists of the addition of three basic components: (i) wages of labour, (ii) profits of capital, and (iii) the rent of lands. Although institutional circumstances, e. g., monopolies, can keep market prices above natural prices on a longer timeframe, market prices can never permanently remain lower than natural prices (cf. Sturn 2008: 74 f.). In line with Smith, David Ricardo estimates that a natural price covers all production cost. For Ricardo, incorporated work in a product is the best approach to calculate its value-in-exchange. Again, sudden changes in demand can have a strong influence on market prices, but Ricardo presumes that those phenomena are random without any underlying law. Therefore, they are considered to be outside the scope of scientific investigation (cf. Ricardo 1817; Kurz 2008).

In contrast to most of his contemporaries, and especially to Ricardo, Thomas Malthus postulates in his "Principles of political economy" that the quantity of work necessary for producing a good is not consistent with its value-in-exchange. Opposing Smith's component theory of price, Malthus argues that exclusively demand and supply can be considered as determinants of market prices both on the short and on the long run (cf. Malthus 1820; Kalmbach 2008). Jean-Baptiste Say, who formulated the famous "loi des débouchés" in his 1803 "Traité d'Économie Politique", accepts the production cost approach but is also one of the first scholars to bring a utility perspective on price. For value, Say employs the terms *valeur réelle* and *valeur relative*. He defines the former as derived from production cost, while the latter involves the relation of prices amongst themselves. Say was the first scholar to explicitly introduce the term utility by writing that the production process is not simply a creation of material, but a creation of utility:

> "Cette faculté qu'ont certaines choses de pouvoir satisfaire aux divers besoins des hommes, qu'on me permette de la nommer utilité. [...] La production n'est point une création de matière, mais une création d'utilité" (Say 2006 [1803]: 80 f.).

As a scholar of the classical era of economic thought, Say assumes money to be limited to a simple representation of real assets. Thus, he assumes that economic agents would act without considering nominal prices, that is, they would not react to a proportional change of all prices.

John Stuart Mill, who is predominantly associated with utilitarianism, adopted a theory of value based on Quesnay's assumptions on value-in-use and value-in-exchange. Still, in Mill's 1848 "Principles of Political Economy", there is an objective value of a good including its production cost and an appropriate level of profit. However, following Mill, the price of a good is determined by its individually perceived utility or by the difficulty to achieve it. A good can only have a value-in-exchange if it generates utility *and* if its creation requires some kind of effort (cf. Aßländer & Nutzinger 2008).

Being the first political economist to define a demand function of the price, Antoine Augustin Cournot (1938 [1838]) describes price-setting in a monopoly and duopoly situation in his "Recherches sur les principes mathématiques de la théorie des richesses". In a monopoly or duopoly, the price of a product or service is the outcome of a quantity decision made by the supplier(s). Following Cournot, price formation can be retraced by static mathematical analysis (cf. Bofinger 2011: 122 ff.). For this, demand information is represented in a negatively inclined linear function assigning a certain demand quantity to a given price. In a monopoly situation according to Cournot, a firm will set a unique price for its product at the point where marginal revenue equals marginal cost (differing from the perfectly competitive situation in neoclassics, in which a firm simply accepts the market price and adopts quantity to it until price equals marginal cost). In a duopoly situation, Cournot considers a larger market-leading firm making an initial quantity decision according to the marginal revenue equal to marginal cost principle and a smaller follower.

2.2.2. Neoclassical economics

For representing the marginalist revolution as a new period of economic thinking, three names stand out: William Stanley Jevons, Léon Walras, and Alfred Marshall. However, the first scholar who conceptualised marginal utility was Hermann Heinrich Gossen with his 1854 book "Entwickelung der Gesetze des menschlichen Verkehrs, und der daraus fließenden Regeln für menschliches Handeln"[5]. Gossen positions himself in an ambivalent way towards the question whether the price of a good does incorporate prior work effectuated to produce it: he writes that an equal nominal price of a good represents the fact that it caused an equal amount of work to society (cf. Kurz 2008a: 196 f.). Nevertheless, Gossen (1854: 46 f., 87) states that from an individual point of view, there is no absolute value of a good – a good can become almost valueless for an individual in case of saturation while it will keep its value-in-exchange.

The movement towards a perception of price as a relative dimension becomes clear with William Stanley Jevons's "Theory of Political Economy" published in 1871. For Jevons, the value of a good is exclusively determined by its utility, not by its production cost. Additionally, Jevons doesn't only see utility as being relative to the utility of other goods, but also to be different between individuals and varying with the circumstances in which the good is supposed to be used. Jevons's *law of indifference* implies that a good will only have a single price in the condition of a perfect market excluding all sources of differentiation. Put the other way around, prices for the same kind of good will vary due to

---

[5] Walras acknowledged this in the fourth edition of his "Éléments" published in the year 1900.

incomplete information or personal, temporal, and spatial differences in the perception of its value (cf. van Suntum 2008). Jevons's paradox of value involves the phenomenon that goods with a high utility, e. g., water, are betimes valued less than goods with a low utility such as diamonds.

As mentioned above, Léon Walras was a founding scientist of marginalist, or neoclassical economics. Walrasian equilibrium price theory can certainly be considered as the central neoclassical paradigm, although it has also been discussed under the aspect of path dependence (cf. Bridel & Huck 2002; Jaffé 1967; Schwalbe 2008). As one of the very few scholars explaining how exactly a market price emerges, Walras (1988 [1874-1926]) supposes a mechanism of gradual price adaptation (*tâtonnement*) leading to a single general equilibrium. The concept of *tâtonnement* holds for simple commercial exchange but not for transactions involving a production process. A trial-and-error procedure to find the equilibrium price would lead to irreversible commitments in transformed materials and paid wages that would influence subsequent transactions. Walras's theory of *tâtonnement sur bons* presented in the 4th edition of his Éléments d'économie politique pure" (1900) is interpreted to solve the problem of possible path-dependent processes in case of out-of-equilibrium exchanges: The Walrasian auctioneer excludes any transaction before the equilibrium price has been determined (cf. Jaffé 1967: 13 f.; Schwalbe 2008: 255 f.). If this condition is not fulfilled, multiple equilibria differing from the theoretical equilibrium price are possible. The outcomes in such a situation strongly depend on the initial conditions, i. e. on the initial random price at the beginning of the process. Walras himself noted on this problem of path dependence:

> "[T]he tâtonnement of production represents a complication which did not exist in the case of exchange. [...] In the production process, there is a transformation of productive services into products. If specific prices for those services are called, and specific quantities of products are fabricated which do not correspond to the equilibrium price and equilibrium quantities, not only other prices need to be called, but also other quantities of products need to be fabricated. Considering this circumstance, in order to put into effect a rigorous tâtonnement in the realm of production as good as the one in the realm of exchange, it has to be supposed that entrepreneurs represent by *tickets* (*"bons"*) the consecutive quantities of *products*. These quantities are first determined randomly, and then increased or diminished in case there is an excess of the sales price on the production price, or inversely, until both prices are equal" (Walras 1988 [1874-1926]: 309, emphasis in the original, translated by N. K.).

The problem of irreversible production functions is also addressed by Newman (1960). Referring to the question how exactly the neoclassical equilibrium is reached, he writes:

> "We are left with a fairly clear picture of what industrial equilibrium means, but with little clue as to how such equilibria are attained, if indeed they ever are" (Newman 1960: 593).

In his "Principles of Economics", Marshall (1959 [1890]) develops a more detailed theory on prices including market dynamics in time. On a short term, price will strictly adopt on the quantity available on the market until all of this quantity is sold. Marshall calls this a *market price* representing temporary market equilibrium. A long-term normal price of a good emerges when the market price equals the bid price calculated out of variable production cost, while a mid-term market equilibrium emerges out of a market price equal to short-term production cost including fixed and variable cost. Hence, other than Jevons, Marshall reintroduces production cost as one of the determinants of monetary value. He illustrates this view with the metaphor of value being derived from the two blades of scissors: utility *and* real cost of production (cf. Caspari 2008).

2.2.3. New Austrian Economics

The term New Austrian Economics is most prominently associated with Friedrich Hayek and Ludwig von Mises. Building on the work of antecedent Austrian economists, namely on Carl Menger and Eugen von Böhm-Bawerk, Hayek, Mises and their adherents shared the common aim of finding adequate methods to investigate on social processes arising in the economy (cf. Ehret 2000: 94). Therefore, scholars in the thinking of New Austrian Economics have a – both temporal and methodological – bridging function between pure neoclassical and New Institutional Economics.

Kirzner (1994) provides a comprehensive three-volume-selection of the works published by authors he attributes to the paradigm of New Austrian Economics. Together with, for instance, Eugen von Böhm-Bawerk, he names Carl Menger as a representative of the "founding era" of the community. In his works on political economy, Menger (1871, 1883) conceptualises price as an unintended outcome of the interplay of individual intended behaviour. Menger considers his predecessors as driven by "essentialism" who failed to deliver a satisfying theory of price because they concentrated on the question how a good is generated. Instead, Menger suggests concentrating on consumers' behaviour of valuation and of purchasing of goods. Thus, according to Menger, there is no objective value of a good, and no exchange of value-equivalent goods. Individuals engage in an exchange process because they have different valuations for a given good (cf. Milford 2008). According to Menger, the value of a good emerges out of its capacity to cover a defined human requirement or need. This capacity is a necessary condition for value; it forms the relation between the individual and the good. As a sufficient condition for value to emerge, Menger states that the good has to be scarce to some extent because otherwise, no economic exchange would be needed to acquire it (cf. Ehret 2000: 106). In other words, a good is valuable because it can be used for covering human needs and because it can be exchanged for other (non-available) goods needed to cover other needs[6]. Kirzner writes on the Mengerian vision:

> "In the Ricardian view of the world, the economic phenomena which econom-
> ic theory can account for [...] are those rigidly determined, at least in the long
> run, by physical realities. [...] Wealth must, after all, be defined in terms of
> human needs and desires. The economic explanations must rely upon the be-
> haviour of 'economic men'" (Kirzner 1994, volume I, p. xiv).

Concerning prices, in essence, Menger states that market prices emerge in the borders of the market participants' reservation prices (cf. Milford 2008: 316); he also provides a taxonomy of determinants for the emergence of those prices. The reservation price on the supply side is simply considered as the lowest price on which the seller still would accept the transaction, while the highest price a buyer would still accept is the reservation price on the demand side[7]. Partial market equilibrium can be reached (but is not necessarily reached) through an iterative process of learning performed by all market participants seeking to improve their position. Price is also affected by the activity of *arbitrageurs* who uncover previously hidden price information (cf., e. g., Hayek 1945: 522). Consequently, money is limited to the role of a medium of exchange.

In the perspective of Austrian Economics, three central elements differ to pure neoclassics: (i) the importance of knowledge, (ii) the dimension of time, and (iii) the dimension of intersubjectivity (cf. Vaughn 1994: 112 ff.).

Concerning the knowledge dimension, instead of building economic analysis on the "imaginary *homo oeconomicus*" (Mises 1944 in Kirzner 1994, volume III, p. 120), Mises seeks to develop a more realistic individual economic agent he calls *homo agens*. The latter is characterised as "often weak, stupid, inconsiderate, and badly instructed" (ibid). A classical publication on this issue is Hayek's 1945 paper "The Use of Knowledge in Society", in which he conceptualises price as an efficient carrier of information helping individuals to continuously adopt their economic plans. However, the price system is only "[t]he first half of the solution" (Vaughn 1999: 133). In fact, for Hayek, there is a broader variety of knowledge including private and tacit knowledge (cf. Vaughn 1994: 135).

The time dimension in New Austrian Economics is probably best illustrated by von Böhm-Bawerk's notion of interest rates as the intertemporal price of money (cf. Allgœwer 2009: 48; Böhm-Bawerk 1889) In contrast to neoclassical economics, Austrian economists distinguish between "Newtonian time" – the space between fixed initial conditions and a predetermined outcome – and what they name real time, a sequence in which "the world changes as a consequence[] of human action and learning takes place" (Vaughn 1994: 135).

In the realm of intersubjectivity, social learning and expectations form an essential part of the New Austrian paradigm. Not only that the *homo agens*

---

[6] This theory of value solves Jevon's paradox of value (cf. chapter 2.2.2).
[7] The notion of reservation prices can be traced back to the "Deutsche Gebrauchswertschule" represended among others by Gottlieb Hufeland, Friedrich Julius von Soden, and Karl Heinrich Rau.

permanently re-evaluates her or his preferences (cf. Vaughn 1994: 90), she/he continuously adopts her or his economic plans to changing external conditions and to the plans of other individuals. In consequence, changing preferences and changes in agents' knowledge through time create a permanent instability opposed to neoclassical equilibrium theory. Hayek's response to the fundamental problem of instability arising with incomplete knowledge and changing preferences is that social rules and institutions take a coordinative function for the market process (cf. Vaughn 1999). However, in contrast to later conceptions of institutions – for instance, the one in North (1990) – these rules are more of a spontaneous character (cf. Vaughn 1994: 124 f.) than rather stable outcomes of a long-term historic process. "Austrian" institutions are shaped by the individuals' expectations, plans, and activities (cf. Ehret 2000: 99).

2.2.4. New Institutional Economics

Going back to the seminal work of Ronald H. Coase (1937) and later of Oliver E. Williamson (1985), New Institutional Economics have developed a set of widely discussed theories on economic exchange: Property Rights Theory, Agency Theory (sometimes also referred to as Principal-Agent-Theory), and Transaction Cost Economics.

All three approaches have in common that they define institutions as the framework in which economic exchange takes place. Making these institutions available and maintaining them involves cost. Therefore, different institutional settings can be compared with regard to their efficiency for providing the framework for exchange (cf. Ebers & Gotsch 2006: 248). Scholars in the paradigm of New Institutional Economics tend to perform the economic analysis of institutions with the help of instruments developed in neoclassical microeconomics. Though relying on the concepts of neoclassics, the three theoretical streams involve a number of differing assumptions which are presented in more detail below.

In the framework of Property Rights Theory, individuals are supposed to maximise their utility by using scarce resources available to them. The acquisition and the enforcement of property rights on a resource imply transaction cost. The more extensive any "attenuation" (Furubotn & Pejovic 1972: 1140) of property rights on a given resource is, the less it can contribute to the individual's utility. In addition to the neoclassical notion of utility maximisation, agents in the perspective of Property Rights Theory can have material objectives measurable in quantity as well as immaterial ones like self-fulfilment, prestige, power, or leisure (cf. Ebers & Gotsch 2006: 249).

The second New Institutional Economics theory, Agency Theory, conceptualises the economy as a nexus of contracts. It focuses on the institution of the contract determining the economic exchange between a constituent ("principal") and a contractor ("agent"). Contracts can be of written formal, or of informal character. Again, all agents are supposed to act as utility-maximisers. Though, this behaviour includes aspects of cheating, artifice and possible deliberate retention of performance (cf. Ebers & Gotsch 2006: 261). Additionally, the partners can have different degrees of risk-aversion. Taking the perspective of the principal, Agency Theory puts an emphasis on the contractual difficulties arising in situations of information asymmetry between principal and agent. In order to cope with this deviation from the idealised situation of a perfect neoclassical exchange, agency cost arises for both transaction partners (for different types of agency cost, see Ebers & Gotsch 2006: 262).

The most recent theory in the paradigm of New Institutional Economics, Transaction Cost Economics, focuses on the institutional arrangement in which economic exchange takes place – it provides an instrument to compare different arrangements with regard to the transaction cost they involve (cf. Ebers & Gotsch 2006: 277 ff.). Williamson (1985) introduces two central assumptions on economic agents: (i) bounded rationality, i. e., a limited capacity of individuals to gain, process and store information, and (ii) opportunism, defined as self-interest including the possible use of artifice, cheating and retention of information. For Williamson (ibid: 52 ff.), the amount of cost arising from a transaction is influenced by three factors: the asset specificity of the transaction, the extent of uncertainty connected to it, and the frequency of the transaction. Depending on these factors, either the institutional arrangement of the market, the institutional arrangement of hierarchy or hybrid forms of arrangements can turn out to be transaction-cost-optimal.

Compared to the neoclassical paradigm, firms in New Institutional Economics are not perceived as simple units of production, but as institutions that are formed through the contributions of individual agents. The statement that any form of economic exchange is connected with cost opens a new perspective on the emergence of organisations. Concerning the pricing policy of a firm, New Institutional Economics have inspired management research in the field of information economics. This approach bears the insight that determining and changing prices is associated with transaction cost: potential buyers face search cost for information and only possess a limited capacity to process (and to memorise) it. On the other hand, while being imperfect due to the assumptions listed above, the setting and change of prices cannot longer be assumed costless from a supplier point of view as it is conceptualised in the Walrasian model. Conversely, consumers following diverse objectives instead of being fully utility-maximising can be supposed to allow for a certain freedom of manoeuvre in the field of pricing. What is more, Agency theory puts the focus to the fact that there can be knowledge asymmetries in prices. While the principal may have an interest in a specific service, only the contractor hired for fulfilling this service (i. e., the agent), may know what specific resources are really necessary. Thus, this form of price non-transparency can be disadvantageous for the principal.

2.2.5. Behavioural pricing and reference price research

Behavioural pricing theorists do not consider strictly monotonic decreasing demand functions. According to the stimulus-organism-response model (cf. Hoyer & MacInnis 2007), they aim at understanding and explaining the complex individual processes triggered by price stimuli (cf. Simon & Fassnacht 2009: 145 ff.). Therefore, they develop hypothetic constructs relying on a variety of theories, many of them derived from psychology.

Behavioural models of pricing can be grouped into three categories: (i) activating processes, (ii) cognitive processes, and (iii) intentional processes (cf. Diller 2008: 94 ff.). Among the underlying theories, information economics as a part of New Institutional Economics are used for explaining consumers' price searching activities. However, behavioural pricing theorists assume that reaction to the price stimulus may not only be boundedly rational, but even irrational or quasi-rational. Most prominently in the field of cognitive processes, behavioural pricing theory employs insights from psychology. Based on Helson's (1964) adaptation-level theory, Monroe (1973) finds new insights on buyer's price perceptions and contributes a decisive part to a theory of reference prices. Monroe purposefully intends "to shake the belief" (ibid: 78) of the inverse price-demand relationship assumed in traditional economics. With their assimilation-contrast theory, Sherif et al. (1958) pave the way for understanding price threshold effects. Building on the range theory developed by Volkmann (1951), Parducci (1965) develops a range-frequency-theory of relative effects of price stimuli depending on their addressed subcategory of range and their frequency.

Kahneman & Tversky (1979; 1984) find evidence for irrational behaviour that stands in contrast to neoclassical assumptions on utility. With their Prospect Theory, they present an alternative utility theory which has initiated an extensive body of research in the field of pricing. In the framework of Prospect Theory, lower prices than expected by the individual are perceived as "gains", whereas higher ones are seen as "losses". Thus, not the nominal price is decisive for a buying reaction, but its distance to the average individually perceived price.

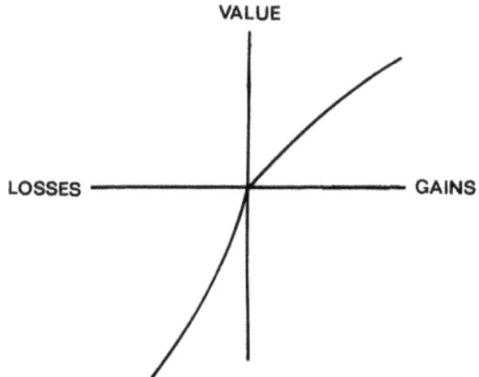

Figure 3: A theoretical value function of loss-averse individuals
Source: Kahneman & Tversky 1979: 279

Thaler (1980, 1985) further develops these insights to a theory on mental accounting. This way of accounting applies equally to organisations, households and individuals – it does not follow rational rules, but is deeply shaped by attributing gains and losses to different mental categories. Thaler argues that prior economic models fail predicting the behaviour of average consumers because they consider consumers as "robot-like experts" (Thaler 1980: 58). Instead, he supposes Prospect Theory to cope better with "a very complex and demanding" world (ibid: 59). For understanding consumer behaviour, Thaler (1985) basically introduces two central assumptions[8] violating conventional microeconomic principles: First, money is "supposed to have labels attached to it" (ibid: 200). This means that budgets may be accorded to different categories of products, making the fungibility assumption on money obsolete. Second, consumer behaviour can be altered by the temporal and topical context in which the decision is made (cf. ibid). For illustrating these phenomena, Thaler collected a number of short anecdotes on consumer behaviour that should not be left out from this dissertation:

---

[8] Thaler (1985) also elaborates on a more specific phenomenon that stands in contrast to conventional theory, which is consumer buying behaviour concerning gifts.

> "1. Mr. and Mrs. L and Mr. and Mrs. H went on a fishing trip in the northwest and caught some salmon. They packed the fish and sent it home on an airline, but the fish were lost in transit. They received $300 from the airline. The couples take the money, go out to dinner and spend $225. They had never spent that much at a restaurant before.
>
> 2. Mr. X is up $50 in a monthly poker game. He has a queen high flush and calls a $10 bet. Mr. Y owns 100 shares of IBM which went up 2 today and is even in the poker game. He has a king high flush but he folds. When X wins, Y thinks to himself, 'If I had been up $50 I would have called too.'
>
> 3. Mr. and Mrs. J have saved $15,000 toward their dream vacation home. They hope to buy the home in five years. The money earns 10% in a money market account. They just bought a new car for $11,000 which they financed with a three-year car loan at 15%.
>
> 4. Mr. S admires a $125 cashmere sweater at the department store. He declines to buy it, feeling that it is too extravagant. Later that month he receives the same sweater from his wife for a birthday present. He is very happy. Mr. and Mrs. S have only joint bank accounts (Thaler 1985: 199).

Also Kahneman et al. (1991) illustrate their findings on anomalies of consumer behaviour with anecdotes. Concerning the endowment effect causing people to "demand much more to give up an object than they would be willing to pay to acquire it" (ibid: 194), they provide the following narrative:

> "A wine-loving economist we know purchased some nice Bordeaux wines years ago at low prices. The wines have greatly appreciated in value, so that a bottle that cost only $10 when purchased would now fetch $200 at auction. This economist now drinks some of this wine occasionally, but would neither be willing to sell the wine at the auction price nor buy an additional bottle at that price" (Kahneman et al. 1991: 194).

Prospect Theory with its concept of a psychological reference point dividing a concave value function for gains and a convex one for losses has had a vast impact on subsequent research. It has been grounded and replicated in numerous experiments (cf. Kalwani et al. 1990; Kalwani & Yim 1992; Kalyanaram & Little 1994; Mazumdar et al. 2005) and further developed towards an economic theory (cf. Tversky & Kahneman 1991). The findings of Krishnamurti et al. (1992) also show consumers responding asymmetrically to gains and losses, but the direction of the asymmetry depends on the circumstance whether a good is already stocked out or not. Kalyanaram & Winer (1995) find that Prospect Theory is an adequate, generalisable way of modelling individual behaviour. In their 2005 book on airline revenue management, also Talluri & van Ryzin expect "behavio[u]ral theories of demand to influence RM practice more directly in the years ahead" (2005: 665). In further experiments, Ariely et al. (2003) show that observed demand curves do not necessarily result from stable preferences. Lambrecht & Skiera (2006) detect a flat-rate bias and a pay-per-use bias in consumer buying decisions. Relevant details from the contributions listed in this short overview are described below.

Prospect Theory & reference prices

For the practical use of Prospect Theory, a reference point representing the individual's expected price is needed. The formation of price expectations or "price beliefs" (Erickson & Johansson 1985) by prior experience can generally be captured in the reference price concept. The concept goes back to the seminal work of Helson (1964), Emery (1970) as well as Monroe (1973) and is largely employed in marketing science. Referring to Helson's work, Popescu & Wu (2007: 413) provide a concise definition of the grounds and nature related to reference prices: "The marketing literature provides compelling empirical evidence for the dependence of demand on past prices. [...] [C]ustomers respond to the current price of a product by comparing it to an internal standard that is formed based on past price exposures, called the *reference price*" (emphasis in the original).

Referring to Monroe (1973), Mazumdar et al. (2005: 84) define reference prices as "standards against which the purchase price of a product is judged". Using Universal Product Code (UPC) scanner data from supermarkets, Winer (1986) finds empirical support for using the reference price concept. He employs reference prices together with nominal prices for estimating the probability of purchase of a frequently bought consumer good and finds that incorporating both reference prices and nominal prices better explains consumer buying decisions. Kalwani et al. (1990) develop a model of reference price formation out of past prices with a price reaction function derived from price expectations and other influencing factors. Their findings of consumer buying behaviour in a situation of differing observed prices to the expected ones in coffee retailing are consistent with Kahneman's and Tversky's Prospect Theory. Kalwani & Yim (1992) pursue this research on reference prices by directly measuring consumers' price expectations in situations of promotional discounts occurring in different frequency and depth – they find strong evidence for the existence of reference points and loss aversion. Also grounded in retailing, Greenleaf (1995) attempts to find an optimal pricing strategy for firms over a defined time horizon by modelling the reference price effect of price promotions. Arguing that "there is now sufficient empirical evidence from the marketing literature to strongly support the reference price concept", Kalyanaram & Winer (1995: G161) derive empirical generalisations from reference price research comprising three central aspects:

> "First, there is ample evidence that consumers use reference prices in making brand choices. Second, the empirical results on reference pricing also support the generali[s]ation that consumers rely on past prices as part of the reference price formation process. Third, consistent with other research on loss aversion, consumers have been found to be more sensitive to 'losses', i. e. observed prices higher than reference prices, than 'gains' (Kalyanaram & Winer 1995: G161).

Briesch et al. (1997) provide a summary of different conceptualisations of reference prices in the marketing literature. The authors of the study find that a memory-based approach in modelling reference prices is the best way to accurately predict consumers' buying behaviour.

2.2.6. Comparison

Relying on the analysis of the theoretical perceptions on price outlined above, this section aims at exposing a brief overview on the central aspects of economic thinking in different periods and in distinct scientific communities. I admit that this comparison can only be an excessive simplification of the theoretical framework developed in the history of economics by different groups of scholars. Nevertheless, the following scheme attempts to provide a condensed summary of the central ideas of different economic theories.

In the classic era of economic thought, the natural price of a good was commonly perceived as the value of its production cost[9]. Deviance from natural prices was assumed contingent, temporal, due to a lack of competition, or forced by state intervention. Cost-based and pragmatic pricing strategies may be oriented on this classical pricing paradigm. Among neoclassical (or marginalist) authors, Walras and Marshall prominently broach the issue of pricing. They build on the fundamental thought of an intersection point fitting aggregated demand and aggregated supply derived from individual utility and conditions of production. Primarily because of its perfect rationality assumption, neoclassical equilibrium theory is considered too far away from real-world phenomena for being used in marketing science (cf. Kuß 2011: 183). Nevertheless, even pricing research in a business context relies widely on basic constructs embodied in microeconomic theory, e. g., using demand functions, differential pricing (cf. Simon & Fassnacht 2009: 263 ff.; Botimer & Belobaba 1999), and elasticities (cf. Diller 2008: 321). New Austrian Economics scholars have "an ambivalent attitude" (Vaughn 1999: 129) to equilibrium theory. They do not share the neoclassical assumption of economic agents to have perfect knowledge on all market parameters. Authors around Menger, Mises and Hayek put an emphasis on the social and temporal aspects of economic exchange. They challenge neoclassical economics but do not provide a throrough alternative to them; therefore New Austrian Economics form a bridging position to later advances in economic thinking. New Institutional Economics also affiliate to neoclassical theories but introduce the concepts of bounded rationality and opportunism. They state that any economic exchange causes cost. The extent of that cost depends on the institutional arrangement in which it takes place. Behavioural theories on price shed light on the psychological effects of price perception and price expectations. There is broad empirical evidence for loss aversion and reference price building among consumers. A central implication of behavioural pricing theory is that organisations are not just "quantity-adopters", but are actively involved in

---

[9] Except for Malthus, who didn't accept incorporated work as a measure for the value of a good.

the emergence of price levels and market outcomes through their price-setting activity. However, individual judgement of the price stimulus is subject to complex processes which cannot be predicted by conventional economic theory.

Era of economic thought Pricing aspect	Classical Economics	Neoclassical Economics	New Austrian Economics	New Institutional Economics	Behavioural Pricing
Source of the value of a good	Incorporated work	Utility (Marshall: utility & production cost)	Subjective judgements on value-in-use and value-in-exchange	Utility	Utility
Underlying concepts of markets	Self-regulating, automatically coordinated	Tending to a single equilibrium; highly hypothetical and idealised	Dynamic, tending to partial equilibria via learning and adaptation	Imperfect, shaped by institutions as "rules of the game"	Involving fragmented, heterogeneous demand
Rationality and behaviour of economic agents	Following their individual interest, subsistence-seeking, profit-seeking	Homo oeconomicus, utility-maximising, firms: profit-maximising	Homo agens, problem-solving, permanently adopting to new knowledge and others' preferences	Utility-maximising, but boundedly rational and opportunistic	Quasi-rational or irrational, loss-averse, influenced by cognition and emotion
Role of money in the economy	Exclusively being a veil of real-assets	Separate, influencing entity of the economy	Medium of exchange, interest as inter-temporal price of money	Separate, influencing entity of the economy regulated by institutions	Having labels attached to it; divided into mental budgets
Emergence of price	Natural price determined by incorporated work, betimes temporarily disturbed by irrational behaviour	Balance of demand and supply coordinated through the Walrasian auctioneer	Agreed between market participants based on their reservation prices, floating according to individual valuation and economic resources available	Rooting in neoclassical assumptions, coordinated through institutional framework	Implicitly through irrational buying behaviour of consumers

Table 1: A simplified comparison of perspectives on price in the history of economic thought

2.3. Theoretical status of revenue management approaches

This section is dedicated to provide a brief overview on the theoretical assumptions associated with revenue management practices. Revenue management, formerly called yield management, can certainly be seen as one of the most popular pricing practices in the last decades. Revenue management as a "new way to manage supply and demand" (Cross 1997: 3) through manipulation of product availability in time has spread to a variety of industries, being titled "one of the most successful application areas of operations research" (Talluri & van Ryzin 2005: xxv). Occasionally, revenue management is in the following abbreviated as RM.

From a RM perspective, the source of the value of a good is its near-term availability. The price of a good emerges out of the rational decision of a firm. This decision is iteratively derived from some sort of demand model and an optimisation procedure involving miscellaneous restrictions. In fact, technically, many revenue managers would not claim to set prices, but to optimise a given setting. However, the result of any RM activity is a specified price for a good or service. RM managers share an explicit micro-perspective with a partly neoclassical view on market outcomes.

The importance of managing tariff in the passenger transport industry has gained broader attention since the introduction of a computer reservations system at American Airlines in 1966 (cf. Smith et al. 1992; see also Copeland & McKenney 1988). In their annual report of 1987, representatives of American Airlines state that the purpose of RM is "to maximi[s]e passenger revenue by selling the right seats to the right customers at the right time" (American Airlines 1987 cited from Weatherford & Bodily 1992: 832). Also for airlines, Belobaba (2009: 73) defines revenue management as "the subsequent process of determining how many seats to make available at each fare level". More generally, Talluri & van Ryzin (2005) write that the innovation of revenue management consists in providing "technologically sophisticated, detailed, and intensely operational" (ibid: 4) methods of decision-making with the objective of increasing revenue. They point out that management decisions have to be taken on structural issues (e. g., posted prices vs. negotiations), on nominal price-setting, and on quantity questions (e. g., capacity allocation to defined segments). Thereby, they explicitly rely on a *tâtonnement*-like equilibrium theory, understanding the process of price formation as the result of "the forces of supply and demand" (ibid).

Chiang et al. (2007) present an extensive overview of research on revenue management, all being "concerned with creating and managing service packages to maximi[s]e revenue" (ibid: 98). Primarily dedicated for airlines, but reaching out to public transport in general, Belobaba (2009) lists three "economic principles" (ibid: 76) for determining prices: cost-based, demand-based (i. e. pure price discrimination), and service-based pricing (i. e. product differentiation). The cost-based approach is divided into two subgroups: marginal cost and average cost pricing. Belobaba excludes the option of marginal cost pricing because of airlines' short-term marginal cost of nearby zero, and for reasons of non-perfectly competitive markets. Thus, he neglects theories on monopoly pricing and monopolistic competition. Belobaba basically refers to microeconomics, re-introducing cost arguments into the "principle" of service-based pricing (ibid: 77 f.). Belobaba's demand-based principle of pricing refers to price discrimination theory first introduced by Arthur Cecil Pigou. A major contribution of this Keynesian economist is the concept of price discrimination by a monopolist from first to third degree introduced in his book "Economics of welfare" (cf. Pigou 1999 [1920]). Price discrimination according to Pigou can be considered as a further development of Cournot's monopoly theory (cf. Cournot 1938 [1838]), and as an extension to pure neoclassical equilibrium theory. It involves three discrete degrees:

> "[W]e may distinguish three degrees of discriminating power, which a mo-
> nopolist may conceivably wield. A first degree would involve the charge of a
> different price against all the different units of commodity, in such wise that
> the price exacted for each was equal to the demand price for it, and no con-
> sumers' surplus was left to the buyers. A second degree would obtain if a mo-
> nopolist were able to make n separate prices, in such wise that all units with a
> demand price greater than x were sold at a price x, all with a demand price less
> than x and greater than y at a price y, and so on. A third degree would obtain if
> the monopolist were able to distinguish among his customers n different
> groups, separated from one another more or less by some practicable mark,
> and could charge a separate monopoly price to the members of each group"
> (Pigou 1920: chapter XVII, §5, emphases in the original).

Note that any form of price discrimination presupposes the existence of some form of monopolistic power of the supplier. Since the contribution of Chamberlin (1962) on monopolistic competition, and notably with the contem-poraneous insights on imperfect markets, this situation can be understood in a broader context than just factual monopolies.

Degree of price differentiation	Description
1st	An individual price for each consumer, entirely eliminating the consumers' surplus
2nd	Self-segmentation of consumers into different categories of price
3rd	Segmentation of consumers by the monopolist into different categories of price

Table 2: Degrees of price discrimination by a monopolist
Source: derived from Pigou 1920; Simon & Fassnacht 2009: 263 ff.

Pigou's concept of price discrimination continues to have a large impact on scholars dealing with price theory and practice. In their taxonomy of perish-able asset revenue management approaches, Weatherford & Bodily (1992) de-scribe customer segmentation in revenue management as follows:

"The common mechanism used to segment customers in yield-management situations is the time of purchase; that is, the less price-sensitive customer generally waits until the last minute to make reservations. On the other hand, people who make their reservations early are generally more price sensitive; they are willing to trade away some flexibility for a reduced price. The discount customer is thus buying a product that is truly differentiated; it has less flexibility, thus it has less value" (Weatherford & Bodily 1992: 832).

Already Walras (1988 [1874-1926]) observes similar price-discriminating behaviour of merchants. Concerning the time of purchase he notes that book editors subsequently release cheaper editions of a specific book. Furthermore, chocolate manufacturers use different packaging for the same content, and theatres sell their seats in different price categories despite the fact that "les différents prix ne sont nullement proportionnels aux frais de production de ces places" (ibid: 667 f.).

Though, as described above, revenue management practices are frequently associated with price discrimination, especially with the seminal work of Pigou (1920), there is a broader theoretical foundation of this "mainstream business practice" (Talluri & van Ryzin 2005: xxv).

Hayek (1928) criticised the neoclassical view of a single equilibrium price when he stated that "even at certain times within a static economy, different conditions ensue and hence different prices are formed" (Hayek 1928 in Kirzner 1994, volume III, p. 163). Indeed, the spread of revenue management to a variety of industries may appear as an "anomaly of sorts" (Talluri & van Ryzin 2005: 333) because it stands in contrast to many aspects of neoclassical price theory. Prescott (1975) shows in his example of hotel rooms that the law of one price can even be broken in a perfectly competitive market if there is a supply-side price precommitment combined with demand uncertainty. Also in a context of demand uncertainty, but more in line with second degree price discrimination theory, Dana (1998) shows that price dispersion by advance-purchase discounts is economically efficient. This situation occurs if there are consumers with a relatively high certainty of demand but a low monetary valuation for the product as well as consumers with a high uncertainty of demand and a high valuation for the product. That setting is frequent in the passenger transportation industries. Consequently, Talluri & van Ryzin (2005: 345 f.) develop an example of Dana's insights in a simplified airline revenue management model.

In the field of peak-load pricing, Bergstrom & MacKie-Mason (1991) demonstrate that this form of pricing can lead to a higher capacity of the investigated good and lower prices than in a situation of uniform pricing. However, this outcome strongly depends on the preference structure of consumers and their distribution of preferences. Dana's 1999 research on peak-load pricing under uncertainty about the peak times concludes that peak pricing has a demand-shifting effect that reduces overall capacity cost. Price dispersion is theoretically possible because revenue managers can "[e]xploit[] the fact that lower-priced units stock out at the peak time before they stock out at the off-peak time" (Dana

1999: 456). In a situation of extremely inelastic demand for off-peak services, peak prices may even be lower than the off-peak ones (cf. Bailey & White 1974).

Partly, operations research scholars also incorporate behavioural aspects of price in their models. In the OR literature, Popescu & Wu (2007) and Nasiry & Popescu (2011) have significantly contributed to introducing behavioural pricing theory into revenue management by "providing very general nonlinear reference-dependent demand models that capture dynamics in the reference effect as the reference price shifts" (Popescu & Wu 2007: 424). Questions of discounts and consumer behaviour are frequently addressed in journals focused on the transportation industry. For instance, see Yeoman (2013; 2013a) in the Journal of Revenue and Pricing Management or Bonsall et al. (2007) in Transportation Research. From the contribution of von Massow & Hassini (2013), operations researchers get insights how to fine-tune prices within the price perception borders of consumers.

In sum, from a theoretical perspective, revenue management is more than just a sophisticated method of applying price differentiation. In fact, there is a broader theoretical foundation underlying this very common business practice including behavioural aspects of price. However, applying RM alone does neither automatically increase revenue, nor generate competitive advantage, nor does it suspend possible restrictions to a change of an organisation's price-setting activities. Desiraju & Shugan (1999) point out that a single price is more appropriate in case there is no correlation between time of purchase and maximal willingness to pay. Lancaster (2003) alludes to the fact that applying RM – or "reserving a portion of inventory for the higher-paying market segments when customers are available at a lower fare" (ibid: 159) – involves a financial risk. Pölt (2011) even predicts a "fall" of airline RM if it is applied traditionally in a context of more rigorous competition and increased price transparency. Reflecting on these limits, Cleophas & Frank (2011) list ten myths associated with revenue management. They conclude:

> "RM does, after all, maximi[s]e revenue in many cases – but not in all cases, and not regardless of other indicators. It may be more correct to claim: RM can be used to maximi[s]e revenue while observing constraints regarding further indicators" (Cleophas & Frank 2011: 27).

2.4. Pricing in business literature and practice

Pricing in business is at first instance associated with one of the elements of the marketing mix (cf. McCarthy 1960, for a critical review see van Waterschoot & van den Bulte 1992). Because of the immediate effect of a price measure, pricing is considered as the most sensitive variable of the 4P's. However, as Dutta et al. (2003) point out, the process of price-setting and changing in a business context involves cost and practical difficulties. Indeed, managers face the fact that prices are a complex issue comprising numerous parameters to be controlled (cf. Simon & Fassnacht 2009: 6). Pricing theorists frequently claim that managers have difficulty in transferring pricing concepts into business practice (cf. Simon & Fassnacht 2009: 10). Congruently with the observation made by many scholars throughout the history of economic thought, Scholl & Totzek (2011: 34 ff.) claim that it is a fundamental error of practitioners to assume pricing to be an entirely rational issue. Both on the supply and demand side, social aspects like price acceptance and perceptions of price play a major role.

The variety of theories in the field of price has led to different streams of adoption in businesses. One of the founding scholars of academic business research in Germany, Erich Gutenberg, noted that "the determination of the retail price does not generate less difficulty in business practice than it does in business theory" (Gutenberg 1958: 84, translated by N. K.). Gutenberg dedicates a large part of the sales volume of his seminal work "Grundlagen der Betriebswirtschaftslehre" to the issue of pricing (Gutenberg 1955, 1984). He systematically collects microeconomic insights on pricing, starting with price policy in monopolistic, oligopolistic and atomistic markets either on the demand and/or supply side. This leads him to elaborated mathematical calculations on optimal pricing in a given set of conditions and to game-theoretic reflections on competitor behaviour. Finally, Gutenberg broaches the issue of price discrimination and (silent) collective action among firms. In contrast to pure neoclassical theory, Gutenberg states that consumer behaviour, and thus, the effect of any pricing decision made by a firm, is uncertain and that any process of adaptation of price takes time (cf. Gutenberg 1984: 182). Gutenberg's central contribution to business theory is to clearly conceptualise pricing as a marketing instrument to be controlled by the firm. Published in advance to McCarthy (1960) in the early era of post-war business literature, this understanding of firms and markets can be considered as a base for reconnecting business research in the German-speaking area to the emerging academic discipline of marketing.

There has been large effort both in marketing literature and practice to systematise concepts on price that can be found. Similar to Rao (1984), who provides an early systematic overview of pricing concepts used in marketing involving some way of customer segmentation, Tellis (1986) attempts to build an overall synthesis of such pricing strategies. Despite the fact that some collective characteristics of consumers are part of Tellis's taxonomy, they are not exhaustive. Price managers may also face ambiguous objectives to follow and thus have difficulty in clearly identifying a pricing strategy for their organisation.

Taxonomy of Pricing Strategies

Characteristics of Consumers	Objective of Firm		
	Vary Prices Among Consumer Segments	Exploit Competitive Position	Balance Pricing Over Product Line
Some have high search costs	Random discounting	Price signaling	Image pricing
Some have low reservation price	Periodic discounting	Penetration pricing Experience curve pricing	Price bundling Premium pricing
All have special transaction costs	Second market discounting	Geographic pricing	Complementary pricing

Table 3: Towards a systematic view on price in marketing
Source: Tellis 1986: 148

More recently, the issue of dynamic pricing has been discussed both in academia and practice. Primarily dedicated for describing and developing business models, Osterwalder & Pigneur (2010) provide an overview on what they call pricing mechanisms. They draw a simple but illustrative comparison between static and dynamic approaches in pricing (for dynamic pricing, see also Bitran & Caldentey 2003). As the comparison appears rather self-explaining, it is merely cited below. Yet, beyond that typology, theoretical background knowledge is needed to decide whether to implement one or another of these strategies in a business application.

Fixed menu pricing		Dynamic pricing	
Predefined prices are based on static variables		Prices change based on market conditions	
List price	Fixed prices for individual products, services, or other Value Propositions	*Negotiation (bargaining)*	Price negotiated between two or more partners depending on negotiation power and/or negotiation skills
Product feature dependent	Price depends on the number or quality of Value Proposition features	*Yield management*	Price depends on inventory and time of purchase (normally used for perishable resources such as hotel rooms or airline seats)
Customer segment dependent	Price depends on the type and characteristic of a customer segment	*Real-time-market*	Price is established dynamically based on supply and demand
Volume dependent	Price as a function of the quantity purchased	*Auctions*	Price determined by outcome of competitive bidding

Table 4: Static and dynamic forms of pricing
Source: Osterwalder & Pigneur 2010: 33

Though the operations research discipline has largely increased manage-rial attention to the domain of price-setting, the most frequent strategy among practitioners is probably still the cost-plus pricing approach, in which price is simply calculated out of production cost and an additional profit margin (cf. Diller 2008: 42; Simon & Fassnacht 2009: 81). From a theoretical point of view, this way of pricing can be associated with the classical school of economic think-ing. One of the detriments of cost-based pricing is that it implies that price will rise in a situation of underutilised assets, because fixed cost is distributed to a smaller set of output. In their guidebook on the strategy and practice of pricing, Nagle & Holden (2002) criticise the important role of cost-plus pricing in busi-ness practice. They argue that cost-plus pricing could spread "because it carries an aura of financial prudence" (ibid: 2). For transport operators, this approach can lead to a spiral of price increase and drop of demand in which the last pas-senger would have to bear the entire fixed cost. Already in 1900, the Swedish economist Gustav Cassel describes that fatal cycle of price increases in a passen-ger railway example (cf. Cassel 1938 [1900]: 60). Additionally, it may appear that cost-plus prices will face a different consumer valuation on the market, either leading to a failure in selling the firm's products or excess demand in case con-sumers have a much higher valuation for the product than the cost-plus ap-proach suggests.

A more radical way of introducing consumer focus to pricing is the lifecy-cle approach. In this way of pricing, separate pricing elements of a good are summed up to an overall price of use of a product. This effective price of usage is perceived as the cost of purchasing and using a product – in other words, as the sum of all out-of-pocket payments made by consumers (cf. Diller 2008: 30 ff.). Thus, it represents a cost-based pricing approach developed strictly from the consumer perspective.

Besides simply reproducing the competitors' prices, another typical ap-proach in pricing followed by practitioners is the price/service scheme, in which quantity or other product features are manipulated together with nominal pric-es. As outlined by Diller (2008: 31), price does not only consist of a nominal amount of money, but always goes with a scope of services associated to that specific nominal price:

$$p = \frac{nominal\ price}{scope\ of\ services} \quad (1)$$

Generally, other than the cost-based approach, one can observe diverse combinations of elements of psychological pricing, price differentiation and dy-namic pricing among practitioners. The application of these approaches de-pends on the conditions in specific markets. Mostly, the buying reaction of con-sumers or effects of competitor pricing action are estimated in elasticity figures on a defined time horizon. This also implies that so far, the process of consumer reactions to price and the longer term effects of it are rarely perceived as an issue for practical price management. Therefore, those dynamics released by pricing decisions are much less implemented in business applications. Hence, when it comes to practical decisions of price-setting, firms face difficulty in assessing the long-term consequences of a pricing decision. This is not only because of the multitude of actions and effects arising in a same period of time, but also because some theories on price accepted in the marketing literature have not yet been fully transferred to practice.

3. Establishing the research framework

The theory of path dependence explaining the emergence of a persistent pricing pattern, behavioural theories of price add to conventional pricing concepts by reflecting the psychological aspects of consumer choice. Together, these theories form the theoretical core for empirical research in this dissertation. The theory of path dependence bears to potential to better understand price formation in a given economic sector and can be used together with complementary theories and concepts to explore options for strategic agency in the field of price-setting. This chapter is dedicated to develop an appropriate research agenda for investigating on path dependence and on effects of behavioural reaction to price in the empirical context of passenger railways.

Phenomena in the railway sector as an illustration for path dependence have been extensively studied under technological and institutional aspects (e. g., Scott 2001; Puffert 2009), but have not yet been employed to illustrate path dependence in an organisational context. Andersson-Skog (2009) recommends studies on path dependence in the railway sector as "an interesting case to explore in the pursuit of identifying different path-dependent processes and outcomes from several perspectives with different dynamics: technology, market and organi[s]ation and regulation and policy feedback" (ibid: 71). However, she observes that "[T]he concept of path dependence [...] is rarely used explicitly in railway studies, even if researchers frequently touch upon path-dependent issues" (ibid: 76). From the organisational point of view, there is special interest on the question *how* self-reinforcing mechanisms are set in place and how they interact. Further, developing path-breaking intervention strategies for organisations requires a detailed understanding of the actual drivers of the path (cf. Sydow et al. 2009: 705).

In their open agenda for research in complex adaptive systems, Miller & Page (2007) recommend research effort on the question how decentralised markets generally equilibrate. They ask: "Is there a coherent, plausible model that can help us understand the mechanism by which prices form in decentrali[s]ed markets?" (ibid: 243). The real-world process of price formation is obviously not the pure Walrasian one, nor can middle-range theories on individual price reaction entirely explain it. Particularly, other than the concept of path dependence, conventional pricing theory lacks to explain the emergence of a persistent suboptimal pricing pattern. What is more, inertia and potential inefficiency of pricing is a topic that has so far been avoided by many scholars. Dutta et al. (2002, 2003) describe pricing as a "strategic capability" rarely addressed by researchers "because [they] assume that the processes by which prices are set or changed are relatively costless or simple [...]" (2003: 616).

According to Garber (2012), improvements in pricing and sales are a central future issue in marketing. From a price theoretic point of view, there is in-

© Springer Fachmedien Wiesbaden GmbH, part of Springer Nature 2014
N. Kellermann, *Searching for a path out of distance fares*, Edition KWV,
https://doi.org/10.1007/978-3-658-23112-5_3

commensurability between behavioural pricing concepts and conventional microeconomics. Thus, there is a need for research which allows bridging (irrational) individual behaviour and aggregated market outcome. This gap can only be filled by conducting research with the help of agent-based computational models, that is, models incorporating individual rules of behaviour in order to produce an open market outcome. Referring to this problem, Brian Arthur writes:

> "Standard neoclassical economics asks what agents' actions, strategies, or expectations are in equilibrium with (consistent with) the outcome or pattern these behaviors aggregatively create. Agent-based computational economics enables us to ask a wider question: how agents' actions, strategies, or expectations might react to – might endogenously change with – the patterns they create. In other words, it enables us to examine how the economy behaves out of equilibrium, when it is not at a steady state" (Arthur 2006: 1552).

Despite a raising interest for using agent-based simulations in marketing research, the method is still in a state of "infancy" (Held et al. 2014: 5) compared to other methods of analysis employed in the field. Thus, using agent-based models in a marketing context helps to advance our understanding of the deeper structures and processes of market interaction from discrete exchange to interdependent relationships (cf. Buttriss & Wilkinson 2014). Cleophas (2012: 241) suggests to apply out-of-equilibrium modelling by explicitly representing intelligent and strategic customers who "form expectations about the development of prices and based on this may delay their buying decision". So far, the marketing literature on reference prices strongly relies on empirical data from the fast moving consumer goods industry (Winer 1986, 1989; Greenleaf 1995; Kalyanaram & Little 1994; Kalyanaram & Winer 1995; Briesch et al. 1997), but is much less grounded in the transport industry. It is an open question whether the insights on reference prices gained from consumer buying behaviour towards prices of coffee, peanut butter, detergent, sweetened and unsweetened drinks, and tissue can be easily replicated in the passenger transportation industry. Though there is a similarity in the purchase frequency, transport markets are unequal in the extent of competition and in the way that they involve the offer of a non-tangible good. Thus, they may show different dynamics.

In the discipline of operations research, current revenue simulation models in airline revenue management usually incorporate an exponentially smoothed price learning factor (or the anchoring of the price experience with the lowest price ever paid as proposed by Nasiry & Popescu 2011), but no explicit behavioural reaction to deviations from the reference price. In fact, Popescu & Wu (2007) and Nasiry & Popescu (2011) already combine behavioural pricing theory and revenue management. However, their research is more related to abstract mathematical ways of modelling demand than to RM applications empirically grounded in a specific industry context. In their outlook in a paper on dynamic pricing strategies with reference effects, Popescu & Wu (2007) propose to conduct further research related to a firm's uncertainty about consumers' price memory, and related to the "Lucas critique" (Lucas 1976: 24 f.) involving the endogenous change of model parameters in econometric simulations. As far as I can see it, there has been very limited effort to include these aspects into revenue management models so far. Therefore, I seek to contribute to behavioural RM by introducing a theoretically and empirically grounded simulation model that incorporates supply-side competition and more social interaction not only in the shape of transactions between suppliers and consumers, but also among consumers themselves.

Concerning the field of empirical research, revenue management in transport is still commonly associated with airlines. Though RM has spread to a variety of industries (cf. Chiang et al. 2007), airlines are the predominant example in Weatherford's and Bodily's 1992 taxonomy on perishable asset revenue management. In contrast to the airline industry, revenue management problems have rarely been studied on passenger train operating companies. The articles of Strasser (1996) and Kraft et al. (2000) in Transportation Quarterly are exclusively dedicated to freight railway operations. As Sato & Sawaki (2012: 549) put it: "There are very few papers in the area of railway passenger [revenue management]". From their survey on railway revenue management literature, Armstrong & Meissner (2010) conclude the recommendation that future "work [shall be] performed to bring passenger rail pricing to the same level that is currently seen in more mature areas of revenue management" (ibid: 19). Airline revenue management is definitely one of those more mature areas and closely linked to problems occurring in passenger rail transport. However, rail involves some fundamental differences compared to air transport. Even in the closest business area to airlines, which is of long-distance transport by rail, there are important differences. To list some points, there are very many open tickets valid for a large number of trains without the necessity of re-booking. The industry also has established railcards, commuter tickets and rail passes; there exist extensive arbitrage opportunities due to the complex possible routes and, last not least, there is generally no check-in procedure. What is more, with their paper on the ten myths of revenue management, Cleophas & Frank (2011) challenge the common assumption that RM increases revenue in all cases. Thus, research is needed to explore whether investments in developing RM applications are a promising path for railways.

Althogether, this work addresses three research gaps: First, exploring the history of railway pricing as a non-technical example for path dependence in the sector contributes to research on lock-in phenomena. Second, adopting reference price research and behavioural pricing theory for integrating it into an agent-based simulation model seems promising to substantially enrich marketing as well as operations research. Third, developing a state-of-the-art revenue management model for railways is conductive for extending airline-oriented revenue management research to a broader area of price-setting.

This dissertation considers price-setting as a possible subject to path dependence; it is aimed at reflecting the historical development of pricing in the European railway industry in a process of path dependence. The first part of the work focuses on the question whether a persistent pattern in passenger railways' pricing emerged in the interplay of single carriers and relevant institutions over time. Because inefficiency of the observed pattern cannot be simply assumed, it is the aim of the second part of the research to explore on realistic alternatives for train operators affected with an inert pricing strategy. As the inefficiency question requires detailed investigation on a firm's markets and resources, this analysis cannot be performed for the whole industry, but rather for a focal train operating company. Thus, research effort is dedicated to the question what pricing parameters or components would constitute a – ceteris paribus – superior or even optimal pricing strategy for a contemporary passenger train operator. Inferiority or superiority of a tariff structure are strictly defined in terms of revenue generated with it. The following research questions result:

1. *Does the historical development of European railway tariffing represent the outcome of a path-dependent process?*
2. *Is there a tariff structure that would constitute a more revenue-efficient alternative to an identified path from the perspective of a train operating company?*

For elaborating on these questions, I adopt a mixed methods approach. At first place, with the aim of exploring railway pricing in the past and understanding different pricing approaches, this dissertation provides a detailed longitudinal analysis of the nature of the historical development of railway tariffing. Referring to the discourse on the QWERTY case, Vergne (2013) strongly recommends a cross-sectional research design for identifying inefficient outcomes of a path instead of just adding another historical case study to the body of literature on path dependence (cf. chapter 2.1.4.). Laboratory experiments, counterfactual modelling and computer simulation are the central methodological options Vergne has in mind for objectively comparing different outcomes of increasing returns phenomena. In an earlier paper, Vergne & Durand (2010) advocate a set of methods other than case studies for research on path dependence:

> "[T]he development of controlled research designs like simulations, experiments, and causal modelling is the only way to potentially supply strong evidence of this specific form of history dependence" (Vergne & Durand 2010: 752).

Additionally, as outlined above, there is a need for research linking behavioural pricing theories to aggregated market outcome. For these reasons, after gathering an understanding of railway pricing through a longitudinal case study, a second methodological approach is employed. Behavioural price reactions on the demand side are experimentally observed in combination with supplier decisions by building an agent-based simulation model. That model incorporates insights gathered in the path reconstruction process and combines them with empirical data and behavioural pricing theory for performing artificial price experiments. Thus, the qualitative part and the experimental part are complementary – the modelling of a transport market builds on the understanding of the development of pricing options available. Because the development of the path is reconstructed with the help of qualitative methods, simulation experiments can focus the inefficiency assessment of the given setting compared to other possible outcomes of different tariff structures. Thus, experiments with the simulation model are performed to find more efficient or theoretically optimal pricing approaches for train operators.

To sum up, once an understanding of the historical process of path formation has been gained with the help of a qualitative longitudinal research design, I seek to precisely describe the nature of an efficient alternative to the path-dependent pricing approach. This is conducted by means of an empirically grounded revenue simulation model. Thus, building on the insights of the qualitative part, I investigate on the quantitative effects of selected path-breaking changes in the pricing structure of a transport operator. More details on the respective methods and their application in this thesis are provided in the beginning of the empirical research chapters. Meanwhile, identifying a theoretically efficient alternative to the lock-in situation doesn't mean that it can be easily reached. On the contrary, a path is defined to be resistant to any attempts to break it. Nevertheless, there are studies on path-breaking activities that focus on the self-reinforcing mechanisms underlying a path to be changed (cf. Karim & Mitchell 2000). Any pricing alternative that can be identified as a result of running the simulation model must be considered as a first step of a process of deviation from the path. Though some empirical cases can be outlined within the framework of the longitudinal design, an empirical investigation on successful *implementations* of path-breaking initiatives in the passenger transport industry is beyond the scope of this dissertation. This work concentrates on understanding the emergence of a persistent pricing pattern and on identifying at least one quantifiable, realistic efficient alternative. Thus, simulation in the present context doesn't mean to replicate the emergence of a path. Neither does it mean studying how to break a path, though it might deliver a first orientation to do so.

4. The path of railway tariffing

To argue that railway fare policy in Europe was (and in part still is) the outcome of a path-dependent process implies the necessity to decompose the emergence of that path from its very beginning. Thus, this part of the dissertation provides a reconstruction of the price-setting path in railway passenger transportation in Europe dedicated to shed light on that specific part of railway history. It is an in-depth longitudinal study of passenger rail pricing in Europe, including the interplay of institutional, industry and organisational level.

4.1. Path reconstruction

Reconstructing a social phenomenon means to collect all available information on it that is needed to explain and to understand it (cf. Gläser & Laudel 2010: 37). Case study research (cf. Yin 2009; Ragin 1987; Eisenhardt 1991, 1989) in this work is employed to gather longitudinal qualitative data from a number of different passenger train operating companies that are representative of the industry on a European level and on a certain timeframe.

Although a single case may be convincing if it is a "talking pig" (Siggelkow 2007: 20, emphasised in the original), and "railway tariffing" could be regarded as a single case; it represents the common points of individual price structures of different train operators over time (cf. Ragin & Becker 1992). It does therefore not represent a single case study in its pure sense, but a multiple case study involving different railways and their pricing and a single theoretical focus on path constitution. Consequently, criteria need to be developed for selecting organisations of which tariff structures are to be examined. In other words, sampling selection criteria are to be outlined as a first step of the path reconstruction study. This selection is also important to cover the timeframe of interest (cf. Pettigrew 1990).

Seawright & Gerring (2008) recommend selecting cases by theoretical sampling if a specific phenomenon shall be illustrated in its extreme or typical characteristics. They systematise seven selection methods: typical, diverse, extreme, deviant, influential, most similar und most different. The non-stochastic, systematic case selection is motivated by the danger that just pragmatic selection (based on criteria of field access, complexity or time) may generate "highly misleading results" (ibid: 295). Seawright & Gerring (ibid: 295 f.) assume theoretical sampling case studies to allow a certain generalisation on the population beyond the selected cases. For Eisenhardt (1989) there is no preliminarily fixed number of cases that should be selected. However, "[...] a number between 4 and 10 cases usually works well" (ibid: 545).

© Springer Fachmedien Wiesbaden GmbH, part of Springer Nature 2014
N. Kellermann, *Searching for a path out of distance fares*, Edition KWV,
https://doi.org/10.1007/978-3-658-23112-5_4

In the present work, representative – or typical – features of railway tariff history are collected from organisations selected according to the following criteria: (i) temporal covering for a period of railway history, (ii) balanced relevance for that period of railway history (thus, including non-legacy carriers); (iii) relative share of (or impact on) the European passenger rail market; and (iv) geographical covering (thus, accounting for the importance of transit traffic). Consequently, case study research will concentrate on the most important economic areas for passenger railway transport. For the beginning of the railway age, this implies cases from Great Britain. For the following periods of railway history, France and Germany stand out. If the analysed data contains references to railways out of the focused markets, they are included as shadow-cases.

For coupling theory and process data, Langley (1999) recommends seven generic strategies to make sense of the information gathered. One of them is the narrative strategy, which is "the construction of a detailed story from the raw data" (ibid: 695). Among the remaining options, "temporal bracketing" can be used for structuring the described events. This strategy "permits the constitution of comparative units of analysis for the exploration and replication of theoretical ideas" (ibid: 703). Together with the narrative strategy, this work focuses on finding evidence for characteristic phases of a path according to the theoretical proposition of a path-dependent process outlined by Sydow et al. (2009). Temporal stages of path formation, constitutive features, and indicators are outlined according to the *path constitution analysis* method introduced by Sydow et al. (2012).

Concerning the nature of the material to be used for a qualitative study, Yin (1981: 58) makes clear that a "case study does not imply the use of a particular type of evidence. [...] The evidence may come from fieldwork, archival records, verbal reports, observations, or any combination of these." Applying this broad definition of data sources to the research questions of this work means to define appropriate sources of evidence that will provide information on the empirical price-setting of railway undertakings ("cases"). This information is needed to underlay the path of railway tariffing in its different stages. Additionally, possible options of price-setting discussed in academia and among practitioners have to be examined. In that sense, sources of data to be considered for the path constitution analysis comprise the following elements: academic publications on railway fares, publications on fares made by authors in the specific context of their time (contemporary published documents), historic compendia on the industry as well as on single train operators, and fares-related articles in railway periodicals. Furthermore, advertisement material on railway fares, and railway tickets as artifacts of a certain fare policy are reviewed. Finally, interviews with professionals in the field of transport pricing as well internal documents of train operators and publications made by railway institutions are considered as relevant sources of data for the qualitative part of the research.

Source
Academic tariff discourse
Contemporary published documents
Railway history publications
Publications on single TOC (incl. anniversary editions)
Articles in railway periodicals
Railway advertisement (incl. posters)
Artefacts, rail tickets
Interviews
Internal documents of train operators
Publications by railway institutions & transport associations

Table 5: Sources of data for the qualitative research

Constitutive features of a path are defined by Sydow et al. (2009: 698) and Sydow et al. (2012: 5). In its beginning stage, a future path is simply one of many different options, none of them being predetermined to become the dominant one. Therefore, early options of pricing in the railway industry need to be explored. As publications made directly from pioneer railways are hardly available, the academic tariff discourse is a valuable source of information for this purpose. Besides early ticket artefacts, works on railway history and railway-related secondary literature such as Dobbin (1994), shed light on the early stage of the path. Furthermore, crucial events that triggered the development of the presumed path need to be identified; this is performed through an analysis of relevant railway literature including industry magazines and anniversary publications that report on the pricing behaviour of different firms. Self-reinforcing mechanisms are the central feature that distinguishes path-dependent processes from others. For this reason, the different aspects of self-reinforcement outlined in chapter 2.1.2. are used as a predefined coding scheme for gathering evidence for them out of the raw data. To demonstrate the lock-in, persistence of a specific pricing pattern has to be described. This is mostly performed through illustrative artefacts and path-breaking initiatives documented in railway archives.

In sum, the research agenda for the historic reconstruction involves a theoretical sampling of train operating companies and is oriented on identifying constitutive features of a path. It assigns relevant sources of data to the different phases of path formation according to the following scheme:

Constitutive feature of a path (cf. Sydow et al. 2009: 698 ff.; Sydow et al. 2012: 5)	Research focus	Sources of data
Non-ergodicity	Contingency & early range of railway tariff implementations	Rail pricing discourse in academia (e. g., James 1891; Cassel 1938 [1900]; Locklin 1933)
		Railway historic compendia (e. g., Ziegler 1996; Gall/Pohl (ed.) 1999)
		Analysis of ticket artefacts (e. g., in museums)
		Secondary literature analysis (e. g., Dobbin 1994; Sarter 1927)
Triggering event	Critical decisions, accidents, etc.	Railway historic literature
		Industry magazines & reports
		TOC anniversary publications
		Archival document analysis (advertising)
		Pricing expert interviews
Self-reinforcing mechanisms	Economies of scale	Archival document analysis (advertising)
	Coordination effects	Transport statistics
	Complementarity effects	Review of institutions and their impacts
	Learning effects	Pricing expert interviews
	Adaptive expectation effects	
Lock-in / Persistence	Inertia of specific tariff structures	Failed tariff reforms
		Ticket artefacts
		Documentation on European Regulation
		Pricing expert interviews
		Documents of railway institutions

Table 6: Research agenda for the historic reconstruction

4.1.1. Historic timeframe

As the railway industry emerged in the beginning of the 19th century, this longitudinal study takes its natural starting point with the inauguration of the first passenger railway lines. Those lines were first built in the United Kingdom, where the Stockton and Darlington Railway "was the world's first steam-powered public passenger–carrying railway, [...] quickly followed by the world's first inter-urban trunk railway – the Liverpool and Manchester" (Casson 2009: chapter 1, p. 2). The inauguration of the Liverpool and Manchester Railway on 16 September 1830, which "proved to be one of the most significant developments in transportation history" (Donaghy 1972: 7), appears most suitable as an initial point in time because the line soon became a role model for all subsequent railway projects in the world. Though, indeed, choices of fare-setting were shaped by the previously existing means of transport as stagecoaches and riverboats[10], railway technology offered a completely new way of transportation in terms of speed, capacity and comfort (cf. Schivelbusch 2011 [1977]: 35). Compared to the stagecoaches, there was also a considerable opportunity for transport cost reduction, as a contemporary author observed:

> "The conveyance by waggons, caravans, and coaches, must ever prove expensive under the present system, even in the most favourable times, arising from the great prices paid by the proprietors for horses, the precarious existence of these animals employed in coaches and post-chaises, and the intolerable expense of their food" (Gray 1825: 15).

The year 1830 is also preferred as a natural starting point because any point in time before the beginning of the railway age would lead to an infinite regress problem back to the first commercial passenger transportation offer made in history. As the phase model of path dependence (cf. chapter 2.1.3) already considers a narrowed range of options in the contingency phase, the "history matters" restriction by former means of transport is consistent with the theoretical model used in this part of the study. The end point of the reconstruction is marked with the lock-in stage, or the evidence of persistence in time.

4.1.2. Data overview

Following a case study approach, I collected data from multiple sources (cf. Yin 1981; 2009) including archival documents and non-text sources such as commercial railway posters and ticket specimen to enrich qualitative data collection (cf. Jarzabkowski 2008). To gain a background understanding of the field, I conducted a limited number of interviews. Research also included quantitative elements like passenger transport statistics and organisations' price level and performance data. In order to deal with the relatively large timeframe under in-

---

[10] The German railway theorist Emil Rank writes: "The foundations of the calculation of fares on the first railways were in part constituted by the fares claimed on roads, rivers, channels etc. [...]" (Rank 1895: 272, translated by N. K.).

vestigation, I relied on railway anniversary publications to identify periods of change or of turning points in the industry (e. g., inauguration of first high-speed lines) which I then investigated in more detail. Publications on marketing and advertisement history of railways were another valuable source of information (e. g., Ebenfeld 2008; Favre 2011; Walz 1971; Gourvish 2002, 1986). A part of the data was gathered in the archives of the French national railways (SNCF) in Le Mans, in the British National Railway Museum in York, in the DB Museum in Nuremberg as well as in the German Museum of Technology in Berlin. As this study focuses on the commercial policy of railways, no data was collected on war tariffs.

Building on an extensive review of the material available, and according to the case selection criteria drawn from chapter 4.1., the following data collected from railway organisations, relevant institutions and stakeholders is analysed in detail: There are twelve academic publications on railway fares, seven contemporary publications of authors commenting on the railway policy of their time as well as seven books on railway history evaluated. Publications exclusively written by or for specific railway undertakings and anniversary editions account for six items in the qualitative sources database. 22 articles in railway periodicals and 23 graphics of railway advertising have been collected, many of the latter being posters. There are eighteen railway ticket artefacts. Three interviews have been conducted for a background understanding of the industry. Four dossiers of internal documents of train operators were acquired through archival research and submitted to a detailed analysis. Finally, seven publications by railway institutions including transport associations are regarded more closely.

Source	Items/Folders
Academic tariff discourse	12
Contemporary published documents	7
Railway history publications	7
Publications on single TOCs (incl. anniversary editions)	6
Articles in railway periodicals	22
Railway advertisement (incl. posters)	23
Artefacts, rail tickets	18
Interviews	3
Internal documents of train operators	4
Publications by railway institutions & transport associations	7

Table 7: List of qualitative data collected

4.1.3. Data analysis

Methodologically, the path of passenger rail pricing is explored within the structure of the phase model of path dependence elaborated by Sydow et al. (2009). Characteristic phases, constitutive features, and indicators are described according to the path constitution analysis method outlined by Sydow et al. (2012). Case study work is limited to the extent that constitutive features and indicators of the path (cf. ibid: 4 ff.) can be identified.

All collected information on the process of path creation is stored in a MAXQDA database for being arrayed, coded and analysed. MAXQDA is an academic tool for qualitative data analysis (www.maxqda.com). The coding scheme is determined by the theoretical framework involving three stages of a path-dependent process and the different forms of self-reinforcement outlined in the theory sections above. In addition to traditional coding based on texts, I coded pictures and leaflets on the purpose or message their carry. The main purpose of using MAXQDA is to organise data out of the different sources following the criteria of temporality, phases of path formation and possible positive feedback mechanisms. Moreover, organising the qualitative sources in a single database made the full scope of railway fares and managerial action transparent.

4.2. Phases of path formation

Any path-dependent process begins within a situation of contingency. Sydow et al. (2009: 692) describe this as "an open situation with no significantly restricted scope of action". Triggered by a "critical event" (ibid: 696), mechanisms are put in place, constituting stabilising factors of a more and more irreversible process. At the end, a lock-in emerges, meaning for the agents in the affected area that their scope of action gets limited in a way that their agency can just reproduce the status quo (cf. Dobusch 2008: 16).

4.2.1. From openness to persistence: fares in railway history

This chapter focuses on passenger fares in different periods of railway history. The chronological division is oriented on the work of Ziegler (1996) and Hanstein (2011). It reflects railway history as interplay of private enterprise and state intervention. Though the development described in the following did clearly not occur in parallel in all European countries, and did not affect all train operating companies in those countries at the same time, it reveals a certain isomorphic tendency of the railway sector that allows differentiating between three essential periods of railway history.

First experiments (1830 - approx. 1880)

Before the first railways were constructed, land transportation mainly re-lied on stagecoaches and navigation on rivers. According to Paul David[11], there were – at least in Britain – already existing practices, rules and regulations other than simple bargaining for those means of transport (see also chapter 4.1.1. for the question of timeframe). I assume a certain shadow of the past, or an influ-ence of the previous ways of pricing and ticketing in transport. However, I see the revolutionary technical innovation of railways as an organisational turning point (cf. Chandler 1977) that permitted an entirely new approach for setting passenger transport fares.

When the first railways were set up, it was undetermined how the pre-dominantly private enterprises should set their fares. Railway companies had no comparable predecessors in their market and faced a situation of openness in their fares policy. This came along with the fact that first railway lines were lo-cated in distinct geographical areas, i. e., independent from other railway lines or networks, and mostly operated by one single carrier (cf. Schiefelbusch & Ziener 2013: 221). The first railway system in the world emerged in Britain. In 1826, a company that should entail the breakthrough of the new means of transport received a concession by the British Parliament: the Liverpool & Man-chester Railway Company (L&M). According to Dobbin (1994: 198), the Railway Act dated May 5th, 1826 "reserved the company's right to charge whatever it pleased to passengers [...]". In contrast to that statement, Donaghy (1972: 70) cites the same act[12] authorising the L&M to charge what one would call a zone tariff today: The L&M was authorised to charge a fixed fare up to 10, 20 or more miles of distance. However it was, the first years of operation showed a fluctuation of prices due to demand uncertainty and to a lack of any operational experience. From the fares list published by the L&M in 1832, it can be seen that the L&M did not implement the zone fares it was initially authorised to, and in part, the company set different fares for the same travel segments for opposite directions. It additionally implemented an omnibus service for assuring non-rail feeders to the stations (cf. Donaghy 1972: 70 ff.), thus, it offered an intermodal connectivity that has only recently been re-invented. In contrast to the standard fares of rail-ways about a hundred years later, the first tickets of the L&M didn't comprise a free choice of train:

> "The railway ticket came into use on the L & M shortly after the line was opened. During the first months, the passenger had to go through a very com-plicated process to obtain a seat on a railway coach. Passengers were required to make application twenty-four hours before train time, giving their name, address, place of birth, age, occupation, and reason for travelling. They then had to travel on the train named on the ticket" (Donaghy 1972: 111).

---

[11] Personal communication at the doctoral colloquium on path dependence, 14-15 May 2012 in Berlin
[12] George IV, *c.* xlix, 5 May 1826

Given that railways were extremely superior in terms of transport capacity, speed and betimes in comfort, the relatively high fares of ships and coaches were not more than a clue for pricing decisions – the high demand potential allowed experiments in high and low price segments and new ways of product differentiation. Namely, it was not clear how demand would react in the context of the differing transport characteristics of the new technology. Though there are not many books from the beginning of the railway age available, in the early literature, proposals for seasonal pricing can be found as well as warnings of too low price-setting with the aim of attaining new demand. Early railway managers were also aware of a possible excess demand that could be limited by appropriate price-setting. In his 1840 book on railway fares, the Prussian railway pioneer August Leopold Crelle reflects on prices and profits, willingness to pay of different customer segments, the effects of social tariffs, the competitive situation of rail and on price elasticities in passenger transport compared to goods transport. Indeed, Crelle refers to revenue per mile, but sees this figure as a resulting variable from price-setting. Incidentally, he has difficulty in calculating that average as the first railway line in Germany opened in 1835 was shorter than one Prussian mile. Crelle strongly recommends setting prices of a line according to the competitive situation, especially emphasising the value of travel time and comfort. Coherently with Crelle's reasoning, the Prussian law on railway undertakings of 1838 let pricing under the sole discretion of the firms (cf. Speck 2011: 45). The German railway pioneer Friedrich List best illustrates the open situation for finding ways of pricing passenger services. He suggests to raise prices in peak times and to adapt prices to observed demand. To keep the original character of the sources, the citations are not translated:

> "Theils um allzugroßen Andrang abzuhalten; theils der Revenu halber wird während dieser Zeit [of the Leipzig trade fair] das Fahr-Geld [in covered carriages with windows from 1½] auf 2 Thlr. und [in uncovered seats from ¾ to] 1 Thlr. zu stellen seyn" (List 1833: 35).

> "Sollte übrigens die Erwartung der Unternehmer in Ansehung der Vermehrung der Passagiere [from 30 journeys without a railway to 60 journeys daily] hier nicht in Erfüllung gehen, so kann man das oben angesetzte Fahrgeld verdoppeln und die Fahrt auf der Eisenbahn wird immer noch wohlfeiler seyn, als jede andere Art zu reisen" (ibid).

In his book on the British Railway Clearing House, Bagwell (1968) describes the variety of fares in the early days of railways in Britain. Though it is an interpretation that the underlying tariff structures were not exclusively distance-based, Bagwell's notice is a strong indicator for a widely open scope of fare policy among the different pioneer railway operators:

> "The existence of almost as many kinds of railway tickets as there were different railway companies and the adoption of different rules for collecting tickets from passengers was bound to lead to misunderstandings" (Bagwell 1968: 30).

In 1851, a pooling agreement between companies serving London-Edinburgh via an Eastern and a Western route arranged by the Railway Clearing House came into force (cf. Bagwell 1968: 251). The pooling included that "[a]ll rates and fares between the same points were to be the same by whichever route passengers or goods travelled" (ibid). That so-called Octuple Agreement is an early example of a clearly non distance-based way of pricing that resembles to the modern origin-destination approach.

In contrast to the United Kingdom, where the "railway system was constructed entirely by private enterprise" (Casson 2009: chapter 1, p. 2), the private organisation of railways was doubted in France shortly after the first companies were founded (cf. Dobbin 1994: 95 ff.; for details on the political debates of the 1820s and 1830s, see Adam 1972: 66 f., 89 f.). From the very beginning of the railway age, the French state claimed the right of regulating prices (cf. Dobbin 1994: 153). In the first more precise regulatory guidelines, fixed kilometric rates were introduced for passenger transport. In the 1857 ministerial *cahiers des charges*, all tariffs in private passenger rail transport were harmonised on the base of distance (cf. ibid: 142ff.). This form of pricing was due to the regulatory aim of standardisation: "The rate-making formula that evolved became more complex over time but it was based on the principles of uniformity and coherence [...]" (ibid: 144). Nevertheless, train operating companies in France kept the right of initiative in pricing until 1907 and therefore a relevant range of agency in tariff purposes (cf. Favin-Lévêque 2009: 18). This is supported by the work of Wolkowitsch (2004) on secondary railway lines in France: other than the regulated *tarifs généraux*, operators could apply so-called *tarifs spéciaux* for increasing their local traffic and *tarifs communs* for through-traffic with their neighbours. It took until 1883 before the main line operators ("grands réseaux") agreed coherent and simplified tariffs among each other with the French Ministry of Public Works (cf. Wolkowitsch 2004: 422 f.).

Even though the British Railway Clearing House only set up official distance tables for clearing generated revenue (cf. Bagwell 1968: 51), there was a base for calculating fares drawing on the *Clearing House Book of Distance Tables* first published in 1853. The regulatory measures in France as well as the agreements made in Britain show that purely distance-based fares were among the real options railways could choose for pricing their services and that this option could even spread early through state intervention.

However, there is a body of academic literature on railway fares showing that distance-based pricing was not the unique, predetermined pricing option for railways, and still far from being taken for granted. The German railway theorist Franz Perrot was certainly one of the most radical opponents to distance-based pricing both in passenger and in freight transportation. He argues that tariffication in accordance to weight and distance is a completely wrong approach because variable costs and covered distance do not increase proportionally. Instead, he proposes a single tariff for every class he calls "Penny Porto" an-

alogue to the fees in British postal service (cf. Perrot 1870: 70 ff.). The Penny Porto is also mentioned in Bagwell (1968: 90 ff.) and in Galt (1865: xviii). The American researcher Edmund James (1891) provides a precise review of the academic
railway tariff discourse of his time, indicating that all contributions to that discourse have in common the search for a "system of tarification which would
eliminate as far as possible the element of distance" (ibid: 170 f.). As alternatives,
James refers among others to Perrot's Penny Porto and to the introduction of
zone tariffs realised by the Hungarian State Railways (MÁV)[13]. Zone fares as at
least not purely distance-based fare offers were in fact introduced in the kingdom of Hungary in the 1870s. Another critique on distance pricing was published by a British anonymous author ("M. A.") in 1865. Her or his pamphlet
which can be found in the British National railway museum in York involves the
proposal for a new long-distance line in Britain – the Imperial Railway – that
promises to provide cheaper fares for journeys between London and Scotland:

> "The truth is, that under the existing system the whole profit of all the rail-
> ways that reach the metropolis is derived exclusively from passengers who
> travel long distances upon them [...] (A. 1865: 10)."

> "One of the distinctive features of the Imperial Railway will be the unusual
> lowness of its fares, and the adoption of an unvarying but remunerative charge
> for long distances irrespective of the actual mileage. [...] [I]n no case will a
> higher fare be charged than - first class 20s., and second class, 15s" (ibid: 7).

Furthermore, the anonymous author argues that passengers would in fact
pay cross-subsidies for cheaper forwarding of rail freight:

> "Yet it is certain that five passengers with their luggage could be carried any-
> where for less money than a ton of coals. Why, then, should a third-class pas-
> senger, crammed into a wretched coop with fifty other persons, be forced to
> pay as much per mile as if he were four tons of coal? And why should a gen-
> tleman of moderate weight and dimensions, occupying the twentieth part of a
> first-class carriage, be charged as much for being carried on a railway as if he
> were ten tons of coal and filled two whole waggons?" (ibid: 10 f.).

In his book primarily devoted to fare collection in urban and regional
public transport, Bett (1945) argues that there is at least one fundamentally different option to distance pricing: "In fixing equitable fare tariffs there are really
two alternative principles which can be adopted; either (a) to charge according to
distance travelled, in effect making the mile [...] the unit charged for; or (b) to
charge at a fixed rate per ride, making the individual ride, irrespective of distance, the unit" (ibid: 39). The latter can be justified because "it may be said that
the passenger is not interested in distance as such and considers chiefly his de-
sire to be taken 'where he wants to go'" (ibid). In the notes to the list of rates
supplied by the North-Eastern Railway to the Royal Commission on Railways in
1867, the company reports that its charges are not determined solely according
to distance, but "[w]ithin the limits of the company's legal powers they are de-

---

[13] Though being part of the Austro-Hungarian Empire, the kingdom of Hungary ran an independent
state railway on its territory.

termined by the consideration, in the special circumstances of each case, of what will fairly remunerate the company for their current and capital expenditure, and of what the traffic is able to bear" (quoted in Hawke 1969: 80[14]).

The examples and literature listed above show a variety of tariffs in the early days of the European railway sector that refutes the assumption postulated by Deutsche Bundesbahn's former chairman Heinz Dürr, saying that "since the beginning of the railway age, fares were calculated according to the formula 'kilometre multiplied by passenger'" (Dürr 1992: 74, translated by N. K.). In fact, first train operating companies created simple relation prices because they initially only offered point-to-point connections without feeders and junctions. Partly shaped by antecedent structures of transport pricing, they experimented with different comfort classes and tested customers' willingness to pay (cf. Hawke 1969: 92). Along with the enlargement of their networks, companies faced the challenge of establishing internally consistent and externally compatible tariff structures. Hawke (ibid: 87) summarises the early railway pricing as follows: "The pricing policy of the railways was not adopted by a conscious decision, but grew with the development of the railway system". In other words, it was open whether any standard would emerge and if this would happen, it was ambiguous if pricing should be based on origins and destinations, flat-rates, zones, or proportionally on distance.

Mixed system of private and state railways (approx. 1880 – first half of the 20th century)

While the first railway lines were mostly set up by private enterprise, already in the end of the 19th century, European governments began to nationalise parts of the railway networks on their territory. Besides military motivations for state control on railways, there was also an economic one: The more European economies became interlinked, the more problematic seemed the variety of lines, tariffs and administrations of the railways (cf. Gall 1999: 29). In his book on the sociology of rail travel, Schivelbusch (2011 [1977]) writes about a "chaos" (ibid: 30) of isolated railway lines. Starting in the 1870s, more and more railways in Germany became state-owned, launching a development that clearly led to the establishment of state railways (cf. Gall 1999: 30). Nationalisation was in part aimed to integrate the different and uncontrolledly grown rail tariffs into a harmonised system (cf. ibid: 59, 61). Alberty (1911) justifies the nationalisation of the Prussian railways with the problematic diversity of fares:

> "Zu weiteren Bedenken gegen die herrschende Zersplitterung und Konkurrenz im Eisenbahnwesen gab die Mannigfaltigkeit, Unstetigkeit und Ungleichmäßigkeit der Tarife Veranlassung" (Alberty 1911: 161).

Until the process of nationalisation came to an end with the formation of state railways, private and public companies co-existed. This period is character-

---

[14] The notes may refer to freight transport only.

ised by a maturation and amalgamation of the industry, but also by a more and more sophisticated regulatory framework. As mentioned above, the French Ministry of Public Works agreed on common fare standards with the large railways in 1883. Even in Britain, where nationalisation did not occur before 1947, the 1921 Railways Act established a railway rates tribunal as a further regulatory authority: "The tribunal was to consider whether rates were reasonable and the best available means to raise revenue" (Lodge 2002: 43). British Rail didn't regain full (legal) freedom of pricing before 1962, when the jurisdiction of the tribunal was limited to the London area under the 1962 Transport Act (cf. Gourvish 1986: 472 f.).

Nevertheless, as the industry matured, railways continuously revised their fare structures with the aim of increasing revenue. They used the degrees of freedom left to them. The focus of the time (also observed by economists) was price differentiation or price discrimination (cf. chapter 2.3.). In his seminal work *Economics of welfare*, Pigou (1999 [1920]) terms price differentiation practices of railways ranging from speed and comfort of the trains up to the social status and the area of residence of passengers. Railways did not yet entirely opt for distance pricing, but kept on searching for an optimal fare structure, even if it happened that differential fares sometimes failed to fulfil their objectives:

> "Differential charging also resulted in rates that bore no relation to distance. Unequal rates for equal distances, equal rates for unequal distances, such as result from 'group' or 'blanket' rates, the practice of reducing the rate per mile as distance increases more than can be justified by the lower per-mile cost, the extreme case of charging a larger aggregate sum for shorter than for longer distances over the same line and in the same direction were all phenomena which grew up as a result of charging according to the conditions of demand. Rebating and other forms of personal discrimination resulted from the same policy" (Locklin 1933: 169).

> "The real difficulty lies in the choice, limited, as it is, by practical conditions, which a railway company has to make between various possible systems of minor markets. The search for the most advantageous system – from the company's point of view – has evolved, in practice, elaborate schemes of classification both for passenger traffic and for goods traffic" (Pigou 1999 [1920]: 302).

> "Railways, however, at least in the matter of passenger transport, […] provide a service which must be produced at the time that it is supplied. Consequently, the cost of service principle would seem to warrant higher fares for travel at busy seasons and at busy hours of the day than are charged at other times. Differential charges of this character are not […] exactly adjusted. It so happens that […] it is just for the most crowded parts of the day and week that the cheapest tickets (workmen's tickets and week-end tickets) are issued" (Pigou 1999 [1920]: 295).

The Swedish economist Gustav Cassel advocated for a clear business perspective for the set-up of passenger fares (Cassel 1938 [1900]). Being opposed to a cost-based calculation of price, he also recommended price differentiation for railways. Anyhow, he complains that some elements of price differentiation were randomly conceded to stakeholder requests:

> „Leider sind [the current tariffs] aber nicht aus einem einheitlichen, bewuss-
> ten Plane hervorgegangen, sondern stellen sich grösstentheils als nothge-
> drungenes Nachgeben den lautesten Forderungen des Publikums gegenüber
> dar. Diesen Charakter zufälligen Nachgebens tragen z. B. die Rückfahrkarten,
> die Rundreisekarten; sodann auch die zeitlichen Ausnahmetarife: die Som-
> mer- und Sonntagsfahrkarten; ferner die räumlichen: die Vororttarife und die
> Tarife, die dem Fernverkehr einen Rabatt gewähren, die Staffeltarife" (Cassel
> 1938 [1900]: 53).

Though there was a strong pressure from public authorities to set up coherent fare schemes, railways kept a certain degree of freedom in their pricing
policy (cf. Sarter 1927: 39 f.). Also flat-rate pricing primarily dedicated for leisure
travel continued to be a real option. A practical example of a somewhat alternative fare of the time is described in a recent historic publication by Schiefelbusch & Ziener (2013). The authors present the story of the "rover ticket" issued
by members of the Verband deutscher Eisenbahnverwaltungen (VdEV) for many
European destinations available from 1883/1884 on. Seeking to "avoid risky fare
experiments" (ibid: 228), participating railways agreed to mutually accept ticket
booklets for encouraging long-distance leisure travel. The booklets for round-
trips were subject to a coupon-lifting fare collection with the VdEV as a clearing
authority. Since the price for this booklet was calculated on a discounted kilometric basis, the offer can be interpreted to be in line with the kilometric fare
approach. However, shortly after the initial offer in 1883/1884, elements of flexibility allowing passengers to freely determine the route they wanted to travel
were introduced. This new degree of flexibility stood in contrast with a purely
kilometric fare calculation, it rather represented another early form of origin-
destination pricing. The tickets were discounted for leisure purposes and combined with restrictions as fencing criteria. What is more, coupons comprised
non-rail travel as they integrated steamboat and even carriage segments. Thus,
they represented a bundle of transport services weakening the importance of the
distance travelled in favour of a flat-rate transport arrangement commonly seen
in packaged holiday offers of our days. According to Schiefelbusch & Ziener
(ibid: 255), there was a considerable economic weight of the flat-rate offer, as it
accounted for more than 55 million Mark of revenue in 1905. Nevertheless, the
"rover-ticket" was withdrawn from the market at the beginning of World War I.
In the realm of flat-rate offers, Switzerland represents and outlying case: An explicitly non-kilometric offer was introduced in 1898 by a number of Swiss railway operators, which were by then in their last years of private organisation.
Since 1898, with a short interruption in 1918, there has been a flat-rate subscription offer in Switzerland (cf. VöV undated).

However, over the years, even in a country where state intervention was
very limited, charging passengers according to mile or kilometre travelled became more and more self-evident: "[T]he charge for an ordinary third-class ticket in this country [the United Kingdom, N. K.] is commonly 1d. per mile, based
on the shortest route between the stations in question" (Knoop 1923 [1913]: 227).
But still, "exceptional fares" (cf. Laundy 1949: 7) as an instrument to fill off-peak

capacity existed. This is also reported by Sarter (1927: 45) in his observations on the issue of "lack days" in British transport. What is more, theorists tried to examine *how* the element of distance should be taken into account, but did not consider it as the natural way of pricing. Consequently, Knoop (ibid: 227 ff.) lists other forms of pricing across Europe and the United States such as zone tariffs or uniform fares "regardless of the distance" (p. 227). Altogether, pure distance pricing was not yet established as a universal standard, as target group offers were common practice both among state-owned railways and private ones.

State railways (first half of the 20ᵗʰ century – 1990s)

In Switzerland, a referendum on the nationalisation of the large private railways held in 1898 led to the foundation of the Swiss Federal Railways in 1901 (cf. Arx 2001). By 1920, the railway nationalisation process in Germany was completed with the foundation of the Deutsche Reichsbahn-Gesellschaft. In other European countries, a similar process leading to the nationalisation of railways occurred. In France, regulated territorial monopolies were kept in place in the first instance, but were consolidated in 1938 into the SNCF, initially controlled by the French state holding 51% of the stock[15]. The United Kingdom initially favoured state regulation with the aim of vivid competition instead of nationalisation (cf. Ziegler 1996: 537). The "monopolistic tendency" (Dobbin 1994: 199) in the British railway industry was attempted to be limited by merger control. However, there was a consolidation on four major train operating companies ("big four") until 1923. According to the Railway Act of 1947, those companies were nationalised founding the British Railways (BR). Sweden followed as one of the last countries in Europe in 1952 with nationalising its private railways (cf. Andersson-Skog 2009: 80). With very few exceptions, regional private railway companies had been nationalised until approximately 1950. State railways evolved as uniformly administrated monopolies in the limits of the national territory.

Static, purely kilometric fares combined with fixed discount rates come along with the emergence of the state railways. As soon as European national states had established their respective railway organisations, pricing each passenger individually according to the travelled distance became unquestioned and a stable feature for many decades. Notably, the radical political changes to a planned economy in Central-Eastern European national states did not affect the structure of passenger fare schemes. There is no more debate on railway pricing among academics or practitioners retraceable until the early 1970s. If rates per mile or kilometre were criticised, it was in the purpose to add different sorts of supplements to the existing structure:

---

[15] The French state acquired the rest of the stock until 1982 and transformed the public limited company into the special status of an ÉPIC (Établissement public à caractère industriel et commercial). Cf. Favin-Lévêque 2009: 30.

"The railways [...] for many years have adopted flat rates per mile for passenger fares, regardless of whether the service is provided by the fastest trains with the most up-to-date rolling stock or by the slowest trains with out-of-date rolling stock [...]" (Laundy 1949: 3).

Despite marketing effort for stimulating business and tourist travel (cf. Ebenfeld 2008), annual reports of Deutsche Reichsbahn-Gesellschaft show an outstanding importance of ordinary tickets for the company's revenue. The 1934 passenger fares brochure of Deutsche Reichsbahn-Gesellschaft simply contains a table of distance fares per kilometre in each of the three classes (cf. Deutsche Reichsbahn-Gesellschaft 1934), so does the 1955 brochure of Deutsche Bundesbahn (cf. Deutsche Bundesbahn 1955). There is continuity to the Deutsche Bundesbahn fares brochure of 1987 which advertises special flat-rates, but keeps an ordinary purely kilometric rate of 20 Pfennig in 2nd class and 30 Pfennig in 1st class (cf. Deutsche Bundesbahn 1987). The ratio of 1.5 between 1st class and 2nd class prices was considered as equally natural as the kilometric fare itself. Also British Rail's passenger fares manuals of 1967/68 exclusively contain distances between stations. Thus, even if selective pricing was introduced by the BR later in 1968, calculating fares rigidly based on the distance requested was not limited to continental Europe (cf. Gourvish 1986: 471).

Continental ticket artefacts generally involved a reserved space for indicating distance. Distance fares generally comprised an extensive flexibility of use: free choice of train (only supplements for higher quality trains), stopover permitted, and a validity period ranging from several days to two months. The long validity mostly, but not exclusively, applied for international tickets. For international travel by rail, these features were institutionalised in the general conditions of carriage administered by the International Rail Transport Committee (cf. CIT 2013; 2013a). Moreover, there was no incentive for advance purchase, so that tickets were usually bought shortly before departure.

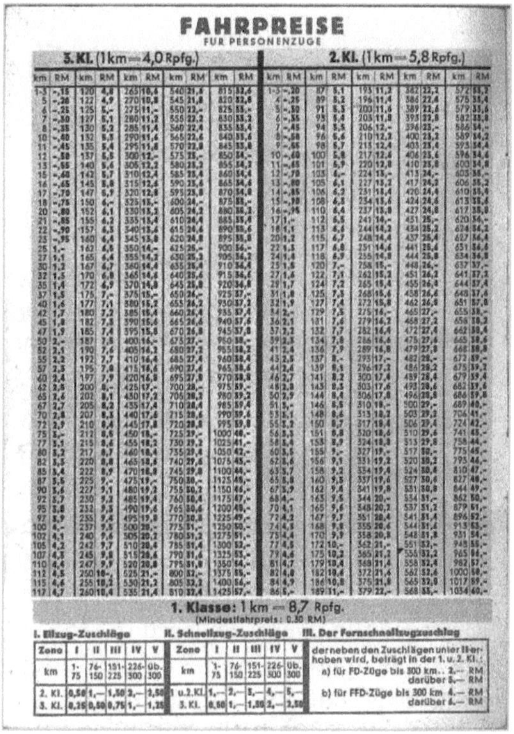

Figure 4: The backbone of DRG's pricing: a static rate per kilometre
Source: Deutsche Reichsbahn-Gesellschaft 1934

Figure 5: 74km of full fare rail travel. A conductor's copy of a 1959 Austrian Federal Railways ticket
Source: original

Figure 6: Two month validity for travel with the Austrian Federal Railways in 1991
Source: Collection of Bernd Kittendorf, available on bkcv-bahnbilder.de

A railway-specific phenomenon is the occurrence of discount cards, or railcards. Discounts were, and in part still are, applied to the fare derived from the kilometric or mileage rate. Percentaged discounts already had increasingly spread with price discrimination approaches. Those discounts were bundled in railcards available to everybody. Almost certainly, the first European 50% discount card was offered in 1891 by a number of – then private – Swiss railways under the name of *Halbtaxabonnement*. Replaced in 1898 by a flat-rate subscription, the half-price railcard reappeared in 1918 (cf. VöV 2007: 5 f.); it continues to be offered in our days. Slowly, railcards spread to other state railways, such as the SNCF and the Belgian national railways (SNCB) (see figures 7 and 8). A 1945 document from SNCF's archives shows that the half-price card existed in the time between the World Wars and afterwards[16]. Deutsche Bundesbahn and Deutsche Reichsbahn adapted very late by introducing their BahnCard in 1992 (cf. Klein 1993). After the fall of the Iron Curtain, railcards spread to middle-eastern European State railways (e. g., ČD/Czech Railways, MÁV/Hungarian State Railways, CFR/Romanian Railways). Railcards can be found in most European countries today, though their scope of discounts and availability has been reduced in the last years.

---

[16] Les archives SNCF, dossier 252LM11. Letter of the *Service commercial* dated 9 February 1945 answering a proposition to abrogate the half-price card.

Figure 7: Advertising the Belgian national railways' railcard in 1967
Source: Archives SNCF, Le Mans (item VDR1141)

Figure 8: SNCF's 50% reduction card in a railway poster from 1974
Source: Favre 2011: 182

Despite the introduction of discount railcards, even peripheral changes in the state railway's pricing policy did not occur before the late 1960s onwards, when besides pressure from individual transport by car, passenger air transport grew considerably. From that time on, state railways started to overcome their "marketing myopia" (Levitt 1960): they introduced a number of lump-sum fees and special fares. An illustrative example for this is UIC's 50th anniversary offer "InterRail" launched in 1972 (cf. Eurail Group 2012). For a detailed review of such offers in Germany and Britain see Bartelsheim (2008) and Feldbaum (2008). The new offers successfully stimulated demand but failed to produce the intended effects on the long run (see a discussion on fare efficiency in chapter 4.3.).

In a standard railway periodical of his time, Strobel (1977) calls a senior citizen offer introduced by Deutsche Bundesbahn established in 1968 an "uncharted area of fare policy" (p. 31, translated by N. K.). Though he pretends to follow a strategy moving beyond the uniform, static fares with fixed percentaged reductions (cf. ibid: 30 f.), there is no significant change to the status quo. More sophisticated forms of price discrimination were not introduced by DB before 1981 (cf. Krüger & Rößler 1989 [1981]). More generally, Deutsche Bundesbahn and other state railways didn't engage in fundamental changes of their fares. They concentrated on infrastructure development, product innovations and improvements in schedule by improving frequency and intervals, and by offering direct connections. For instance, TEE (Trans Europ Express) trains were introduced in 1957 to offer a rail alternative to business travellers who had started switching to airlines (cf. SNCF 2013a). On the national level, British Rail and Deutsche Bundesbahn introduced their InterCity product as a response to airline competition.

In international rail transport, tariff standards with common conditions were agreed (CIV, TCV/SCIC)[17] in order to allow through-ticketing for the entire journey. Along all these developments, the fundamental pattern of pricing in passenger rail transport remained unchanged. International fares represented an addition of the (kilometric) national ones and reductions were usually applied to a base fare compiled with the traditional method. Under the pressure of budget control and later of long-distance bus service liberalisation, the British Railways conducted market tests with off-peak fares from the end of the 1960s on (cf. Gourvish 2002). The British Railways' selective prices manual for sales personnel of 1974 shows a number of reduced fare tickets with rather complicated validity restrictions. This stands in contrast to the one of 1967/1968, which exclusively lists distances between routes (cf. British Railways Board 1967/1968; 1974: 682 ff.). Also other state railways began to reflect the necessity of a radical reform in their tariff systems. SNCF was among the first state railways to rethink its pricing policy when it came to the construction of a high-speed line between Paris and Lyon (cf. e. g., Meunier 2001; Faugère 2010). The new line was planned and realised to be 87 km shorter than the old line. Following the logic of standard fare calculation, this would have meant a reduction of the fare despite major investments for accelerating speed. Similar problems had occurred before with the construction of railway tunnels: those could be solved with introducing artificial tariff kilometres. But in the case of the high-speed line, a Transport Ministry official saw himself obliged to note:

> "Il peut paraître, a priori, normal que le prix d'un voyage entre Paris et Lyon sur la ligne nouvelle (425 km) ne soit pas inférieur au prix demandé actuellement sur cette même relation (512 km)"[18].

Archival documents show that research on alternative, more appropriate ways of pricing were conducted in the SNCF from 1968 to 1971. In a letter to the research department in charge with the commercial pricing study, SNCF's vice director general explicitly asks for going beyond kilometric pricing:

> "Le tarif [TGV] doit être établi indépendamment de toute notion de prix de revient des sièges kilométriques [...]."[19]

---

[17] See chapter 4.2.2. for details on these fares.

[18] Letter of Land transport directorate in the Transport Ministry to the director general of SNCF dated 9 January 1979 (Archives historiques SNCF, dossiers 20LM0554, 20LM0925)

[19] Archives historiques SNCF, dossier 26LM0465, letter of the vice director general Monsieur Hutter to the head of Service de la Recherche dated 12 June 1968. The vice director general also put in question the ratio of 1st class fares to 2nd class fares of 1.5.

The study group observed differential pricing of energy suppliers, airlines and British Rail's intercity product and elaborated on a "modèle prix-temps"[20] for SNCF's pricing. Despite those efforts, the introduction of the French high-speed train TGV in 1981 did not mean a radical change in fare policy (cf. interview with SNCF's directeur commercial voyageurs in Chlastacz 1981). Though subscription rebates were limited, the innovative ideas developed by the study group on prices were only applied in the fare supplements (TGV passengers had to buy a compulsory reservation including a supplement varying with the point in time of their trip). Concerning the base fare, there was no deviation from the standard distance approach. Nevertheless, the introduction of high-speed products may be seen as an initial point of path-breaking activities, as SNCF endeavoured a radical change in 1993 when it introduced its airline-oriented pricing system SOCRATE (cf. Costet 1992; Bromberger 1993; see also a critical analysis in Mitev 1996). The new pricing regime of 1993 is considered by Decreton (1995) as a fundamental breakthrough to non-distance fares:

> "De même, à la SNCF, l'abandon d'un «dogme» aussi fondamental que le tarif kilométrique marque le passage à des prix établis en fonction de la concurrence" (Decreton 1995: 642).

When the Spanish National Railways initially operated their high-speed line between Madrid and Seville, they introduced a fare structure derived from the TGV (cf. Paukner 1992). In end 1991, Deutsche Bundesbahn introduced its high-speed network with a relation-based pricing approach (cf. Becker 1992). Besides high-speed transport by rail, fare calculation for the remaining products continued to rely on distance. The influence of distance on the price was gradually limited by introducing a hypothetic tariff distance and a maximum price, later by applying a declining increase of price with distance. The latter approach has been implemented by the SNCF in the formula

$$P = a + bd \quad (2)$$

The price of travel (P) is calculated with the help of different constants (a) and different kilometric rates (b) depending on the total distance (d) the customer wishes to travel. That general approach for calculating the fares can at least be traced back to a 1983 synopsis written by SNCF's directeur commercial voyageurs[21].

---

[20] Archives historiques SNCF, dossier 26LM0465
[21] Archives historiques SNCF, dossier 20LM925, Exposé de M. Weber, Directeur Commercial Voyageurs, relatif à la politique commerciale voyageurs à la S.N.C.F., dated 21 September 1983

1.1. Prix de base général

1.1.1.Paramètres de calcul du prix de base général au 24 janvier 2013

Le prix de base seconde classe (pour les trajets dans certains trains autres que TGV) est calculé selon la formule : $P = a + bd$.

P étant le prix, a une constante, b le prix kilométrique et d la distance tarifaire.

Le prix plein tarif d'un billet pour un trajet effectué en 1ère classe est déterminé à partir du prix calculé en 2ème classe auquel est appliqué le coefficient de majoration de 1,5. Le montant obtenu est arrondi au décime d'euro supérieur.

Distance (d)		Constance (a)		Prix kilométrique (b)	
de	à	1ère classe	2ème classe	1ère classe	2ème classe
1	16 km	1,1066	0,7377	0,2765	0,1843
17	32 km	0,3561	0,2374	0,3080	0,2053
33	64 km	2,9447	1,9631	0,2273	0,1515
65	109 km	4,1088	2,7392	0,2117	0,1411
110	149 km	5,8115	3,8743	0,2027	0,1351
150	199 km	11,5013	7,6675	0,1697	0,1131
200	300 km	11,0328	7,3552	0,1719	0,1146
301	499 km	19,4147	12,9431	0,1466	0,0977
500	799 km	26,2317	17,4878	0,1311	0,0874
800	999 km	45,7997	30,5331	0,1074	0,0716

Figure 9: General price calculation for non-TGV long-distance trains of the SNCF
Source: SNCF 2013: volume 6, p. 5

Compared to the feeder bus service provided by the Liverpool and Manchester railway in 1830, or the steamboat coupons provided by the VdEV in 1883, there was very limited attempt of the state railways' pricing departments to provide seamless mobility across different modes of transport. The standard railway tariff simply did not comprise any non-rail service. The multimodal pricing approach was exclusively adopted by transport associations which spread in the European urban agglomerations from the late 1960s on. These associations offered fares for transport *in space* instead of distance fares on a line. Only in Switzerland, transport operators of different modes of transport have been cooperating more intensely. As stated above, with a short interruption in 1918, there had been a flat-rate subscription offer of the legal predecessors of the Swiss Federal Railways and partner operators – the Generalabonnement/Abonnement général – since 1898. But only since this offer included urban transport by bus and tramway in 24 major cities by 1990, it significantly gained popularity and came out of its marginal position it had in the 1980s (cf. VöV 2007: 10; VöV undated: 1). This means that the flat-rate offer was a rail-only (in parts rail and regional bus) one for nearly a hundred years before it was found that multimodality is an appropriate instrument for gaining new customers.

This chapter was dedicated to provide a brief outline on passenger fares across the periods of railway history. It collected facts that illustrate the emergence and the persistence of basic elements of the standard railway tariff in Europe, including the following features:

- Distance-based fare
- 1 passenger = 1 price
- Flexibility of use
- Railcards
- Monomodality (use of rail only)

The table stated below assigns the different epochs of railway history described above to the characteristic stages of path constitution (cf. Sydow et al. 2009: 692). After a period of openness of fare regimes among predominantly small and loosely interconnected railways, there is a process of harmonisation and deregulation leading to the development of the standard railway tariff. This type of fare is standardised on the distance travelled by each individual passenger. Hence, from an almost complete contingency in the early days of the railway industry, there was a steady process in which distance fares became the predominant pattern among railway operators ending in a lock-in situation. In the following chapters, there will be a discussion what mechanisms may have caused this development and whether the time after railway liberalisation in the 1990s constitutes a phase of continuous development along the path, dissolution of the path or even in some cases a breaking of the path.

Epoch	Approximate timeframe	Scope of fares	Stage in path constitution
Private railways	1830-1880	First experiments, various approaches	Contingency
Between market and state control	1880- first half of 20th century	Harmonisation and regulation	Closing
State railways	first half of 20th century- 1990s	Standardisation ("standard railway tariff")	Lock-in / rigidity Path-breaking initiatives

Table 8: Stages of path constitution and history of European railways

4.2.2. Narrowing the scope of action: self-reinforcement to distance fares

It has been so far documented that from a period of almost free and uncoordinated fare setting by many independent train operating companies, a stable pattern of price-setting according to the mile or kilometre travelled occurred in all European countries in the beginning of the 20th century – the standard railway tariff. It has also been shown that this development was not exclusively driven by regulation, but that many companies deliberately adopted the standard. This stands in stark contrast to the many different technical standards that have emerged before and during the state railway period. Europe has different conventions on driving left or right on a railroad, four major railway gauges[22], different clearance boundaries for rolling stock, various electricity supply systems and traffic control systems. What explains the common point in fare policy? Why was it – at first instance – economically reasonable to adopt distance fares?

From the perspective of path dependence theory, one out of several possible options gains momentum if it is triggered by self-reinforcing mechanisms. Those self-reinforcing mechanisms stand in the centre of the development of a path-dependent process – they also have to be traceable as "producers"[23] of path dependence in the case of railway tariffing. Stabilising and reproducing a path, they need to be effective for a longer period of time. Derived from the literature on increasing returns in the economy, Sydow et al. (2009: 698 ff.) describe four typical self-reinforcing mechanisms constructing an organisational path: coordination effects, complementary effects, learning effects and adaptive expectation effects. As this list excludes the rather simple notion of economies of scale, the analysis on self-reinforcing mechanisms in the case of railway fares begins with a short reflection on the role of scale effects in the industry (for more theoretical details on self-reinforcing mechanisms see also chapter 2.1.2.).

Economies of scale

Considering rail as a transport system with high initial investments and structural capacity reserves in the sense of increasing returns to adoption (cf. Arthur 1989), every additional user attained to the system generates lower average cost per unit (i. e. cost per passenger kilometre). Because economies of scale are usually considered in the production technology of a firm involving its output volume, Puffert (2009: 248) characterises this situation as "increasing returns [...] on the demand side of a market". Depending on the intensity of competition, more users on a fixed scheduled output of transport offers would theoretically either lead to increasing margins or even more users due to lower average prices until the full capacity is utilised. On the same dimension, decreasing returns are possible, leading to lower income and a continuously higher demand for (public) subsidies. This work focuses this thought on price-setting, searching for evidence of mechanisms that directly or indirectly generate additional traffic and/or additional revenue for train operating companies. In this view, economies of scale effects can be considered as intermediate effects. They root in one or more of the four self-reinforcing mechanisms listed below.

---

[22] 1435mm, 1668mm in Spain and Portugal except most parts of the Spanish high-speed network, 1600mm in Ireland and 1524mm in Finland and the former Soviet countries

[23] Pajunen (2008: 1451 ff.) differentiates between four characteristics of organizational mechanisms. One characteristic of a mechanism is named its "productive activity".

Coordination effects

Coordination effects render interaction between individuals respectively organisations easier, the larger the number of them who follow a form of "rule guided behavio[u]r" (Sydow et al. 2009: 699) is. From the supplier perspective, adopting a joint rule of tariffing (which was calculating the fare base on the kilometre or mile travelled), allowed for easily pricing any transport demand on and beyond the own network. In that sense, the term of direct network effects (Koch et al. 2009) largely corresponds to the notion of coordination effects.

In a situation of dispersed tariff structures of the many different railways in the early times of the industry, coordinating schedules and fares among different providers enabled successively more travellers to find an acceptable offer for their mobility need. Rail transport became increasingly attractive as the attainable network size grew. Thus, through-tariffing based on any standard would create additional (previously suppressed) demand given that there were capacity and cost constraints for stagecoaches. When railways developed from islands to – at first instance – regional networks, any standard that allowed internal or external through-tariffing between the lines and feeders was beneficial because there was an enormous potential for growth. Bagwell (1968) shows many details of technical and non-technical standardisation efforts in the United Kingdom, including fares. He illustrates how fares could be an obstacle to the growth of traffic (ibid: 27 ff.) and how through-booking was welcomed by passengers (ibid: 39 f.). He clearly shows the self-reinforcing process of attracting new member operators for through-tariffing and increasing passenger receipts (ibid: 60). It is the cooperation between companies with the aim of attracting more traffic that explains the slow convergence of pricing schemes of the railways:

> "With the development of inter-company co-operation fostered by meetings held at the Clearing House [...] the behaviour described above can be regarded as the pricing policy of railways in England and Wales before 1881. There were some exceptions [...], but most companies behaved similarly in the formation of their prices" (Hawke 1969: 89).

Also on the international level, initially, the networks of European railways were mostly dispersed despite the first international long-distance line in Europe opened in 1843 between Antwerp and Cologne. Before these networks became interconnected, there was no need to align business conditions among the operator firms for encouraging through-traffic. Though the standardisation process of international passenger fares only spread on a very long timeframe, it resulted in a practical use of distance fares:

Railways did not start to cooperate internationally in scheduling their trains before 1872 (cf. Schnell & Paganetti 1989 [1986]) and merely engaged in exchanging technical information through the International Railway Congress Association by 1885 (cf. Funk 1992: 1344). It took another eight years before the first International Convention concerning the Carriage of Goods by Rail entered into force in 1893 (cf. CIT 2013). This convention created an "administrative union" with a permanent secretariat. Administrative unions of the time were "institutionali[s]ed continuations of international diplomatic conferences" (OTIF 2013: 1), the most important being the world Postal Union. Thus, they represented the most elementary point of a path creation process in the area of socio-technical business conditions for transporting passengers and goods. Nevertheless, passenger transportation continued to be left behind from any common rules before the basic foundations of the administrative union gained momentum. The Genoa Conference of 1922 was a pioneering initiative for intensifying the cooperation between railways: it was the trigger for the foundation of the International Union of Railways (UIC) late in the same year (cf. Fink 1984). It took until 1928, when finally the existing goods carriage agreement was extended to the passenger branch with the entering into force of the Convention on the International Carriage of Passengers and Luggage by Rail (cf. CIT 2013).

The International Rail Transport Committee (CIT) which had been independently created by railways in 1902 in order to coordinate the details of the goods agreements was now put in charge for elaborating a detailed framework of international passenger transport by rail. The committee helped railways to apply the convention and augmented and explained the legal texts in the Uniform Rules concerning the Contract for International Carriage of Passengers and Luggage by rail (CIV). These juridical rules comprise basic elements of a transport contract with different carriers, they provide that "international tariffs shall contain all the special conditions applicable to carriage, in particular the information necessary for calculating fares" (OTIF 1980a: 2, see also OTIF 1980). A central element was the form and content of tickets, defining the minimal indication of departure and destination, route, class, fare and validity for all participating companies. Beyond the legal framework, the UIC arranged commercial activities such as the clearing of revenue between carriers in the Central Compensation Bureau. The relations between the International Rail Transport Committee and the UIC were not always free of tensions (cf. Bertherin & Leimgruber 2002). The conflict between the two industry associations was solved by separating technical and commercial co-ordination to be made by the UIC and the legal framework to be administered by the CIT. The TCV (Tarif commun international pour le transport des voyageurs), a common codex on international tariffing, was fully compatible with the rules of UIC and CIT. It has been applied by state railways since 1959 (cf. leaflets 106 and 130 in UIC 2006, 2008). Although the state railways' common international tariff was theoretically open for any form of fare strategy, practically, for decades, it was used as an agreement for the simple addition of distance kilometres of participating carriers. Today, the TCV is referred to as SCIC (Special Conditions of International Carriage). It is somewhat of a surprise that commercial agreements on international ticketing such as the TCV took nearly 100 years to be agreed (rail was relatively late compared, e. g., to the international agreements on postal service). One explication for goods transport agreements to have been signed decades before similar agreements in passenger transportation were made is that goods transportation was a commercially much more important issue than passenger transportation was (cf. revenue tables collected in Bagwell 1968: 300 f.). However, in the very early days of railways in Britain, passenger revenues prevailed (cf. Mitchell 1964)[24]. Nevertheless, on the long run, benefits of international coordination led railways into a voluntary system of mutual acceptance of their tickets.

In a recent Eurobarometer study, 75% of the Europeans reported to wish a single ticket for multi-operator journeys by rail (cf. Eurobarometer 2012: 93). When the European Commission plans legislation on integrated ticketing schemes both on the national and international level today, it focuses these direct network effects of following a fare standard:

> "In order to ensure that passengers continue to benefit from network effects, this provision gives Member States the possibility to establish information and integrated ticketing schemes common to all railway undertakings operating domestic passenger services in a way that does not distort competition. In addition, it provides for the adoption of coordinated contingency plans by railway undertakings to provide assistance to passengers if there is a major disruption of traffic" (European Commission 2013: 6).

The diffusion of tariff components such as target group discounts, predominantly for the young and the elderly, can be explained by coordination (or direct network) effects, too. In the epoch of state railways, networks of the operators were perfectly complementary to each other, thus, the size of the network could be easily expanded by agreeing on common standards for international rail travel.

The shady side of this development was that international fare standards strongly stabilised the persistent pattern of tariffing because any non-coordinated, individual action in the national fare policy would impair the attained through-tariffing effect with partner operators. Though the change might be beneficial on the domestic level, in sum, it would possibly turn out to be detrimental and in consequence be rejected. In other words, following the path could be rational due to coordination effects.

Complementarities

Complementarities are understood as synergies resulting out of the interaction between different resources, rules or practices. Sydow et al. (2009: 699 f.) name the example of Fordism, having evolved over time into an industry standard. Koch et al. (2009: 69) refer to indirect network effects as "complementary products and services accompanying a product". In the field of fare policy, complementarities can easily release self-reinforcement if a certain fare parameter requires other fare parameters to be compatible to it.

---

[24] See also chapter 4.3.1.

Mutually accepting their tickets, railways facilitated the transit across their networks – raising the question how to allocate the generated revenue to the different transport operators. For that purpose, the British Railway Clearing House employed distance tables for proportionally according revenue to its members (cf. Bagwell 1968: 51 f.). Thus, clearing and pricing were closely complementing interorganisational activities that reinforced the dominance of the distance standard.

The phenomenon of railcards can clearly be regarded as a case of positive feedback between distance fares and the complementary function of a railcard: Initially, railcards allowed for price discrimination. Yet unidentified when the first railcards where used, they also had the psychological effect of non-linear pricing (cf. Diller 2008: 249 f.). Both elements were prone to make railcards a success. Meanwhile, what railcards did not solve was the unequal utilisation of trains. Except for their interest of comfort and privacy, railcard holders have no incentive to switch to off-peak trains in a system of distance fares. Contrariwise, railcards permit passengers to travel at a reduced fare at peak time. Consequently, there were trials to introduce railcards with limited validity on peak days or differentiated percentage of discount according to travel days (e. g., by the NSB/Norwegian State Railways in 1988[25]). Though being priced at a lower rate with a railcard, the element of distance remained unchanged and even reinforced the standard: the more railcards spread, the more it was natural they had a base fare to refer to. If railways accepted railcards or discounts between each other, they provided stronger incentives to attract additional use of their offers. On the other hand, they unintendedly reinforced the existence of the base fare to which the discount was agreed to be applicable to. Nearly all European state railways have collected experience in introducing, amending, extending or – in some cases – removing railcards.

As a source of flexibility, supplements were compatible building blocks to a static base fare. They could reflect the quality or the speed of a train and be sold separately. Optionally selling a reservation with an open train ticket was a considerable, but initially modest source of extra revenue. This changed radically when electronic reservation systems were introduced nationally in the end of the 1960s and internationally in the mid-1970s (see the rich historical overview in Bieberstein 1979). Revenue generated from the complementing products "base fare ticket" and "reservation" increasingly formed a barrier to change to any alternative fare structure that would reduce the number of (payable) reservations. Additionally, an initially successful combination of ticket and reservation was likely to reinforce the basic pattern of a given tariff system because a reservation "naturally" requires the existence of a ticket it refers to. The typical fare of the state railway period even including TGV from 1981 until 1993 consisted in a

---

[25] The customer card entitled holders for a 30% reduction on the 2nd class fare on Fridays and Sundays, and 50% for all other days. Today the NSB railcard allows for a fixed 20% discount only.

distance-based fare, a product-dependent supplement and a complimentary or payable reservation, all of which affecting net income of a train operator.

Sales technology is another important issue that explains the stable outcome of distance fares. If sales technology was developed alongside with the standard railway fare, it increasingly limited the scope of technically feasible tariff measures. In other words, it increased the switching cost to any alternative. The Edmonson ticketing standard, which spread from the early 1840s on (cf. Bagwell 1968: 37 ff.) and which was applied for more than 100 years in Europe, was initially open for any kind of pricing. With the emerging fare calculation per line, ticket specimen, distribution facilities and book-keeping were adapted and incrementally improved for being used with distance fares. Sales technology increasingly emerged as a barrier to change. When electronic reservation systems spread in the 1960s, this consolidated the way of issuing ticket and reservation separately. Consumers had no incentive to buy their open kilometric tickets in advance, so sales had to concentrate on quick distribution before departure. The more sales activities were aligned with the standard fare, the more difficult (or less rational) it became to implement potential changes of the pricing strategy. SNCF's important investment for implementing an airline-like pricing for high-speed trains in 1993 shows how difficult it was to re-organise sales infrastructure for such purpose (cf. Mitev 1996; Bromberger 1993; Degenhard 1993).

When distance pricing became taken for granted, marketing activities of the firms were increasingly aligned with the pricing strategy. This was not limited to supplements and reservations as outlined above – gradually, a distance-based portfolio of complementing products was developed. Among those were rail passes with a sum of pre-purchased kilometres to be used upon travel as well as a similar offer for corporate customers (e. g., offered by DB/Deutsche Bundesbahn). These "kilometre books" with a defined number of kilometres to be travelled on the network of the carrier were not completely new as they had been offered by Badische Staatsbahnen since 1895 (cf. Schiefelbusch & Ziener 2013: 252), but they became a fixed complementing element to the fare portfolio of many railways. For instance, ÖBB and ČSD/ČD/ŽSSK developed the offers of "Grüne Bank" and "kilometrická banka".

Figure 10: A rebate in kilometres: Advertisement of DB in a German business periodical
Source: Manager Magazin 2/1979: 114

Learning

Learning effects in the context of fare policy can occur on the supply side as well as on the demand side of the passenger rail market.

On the supply side, railways learnt from the buying reaction of passengers. Initial benefits of an introduced fare or railcard were bound to conduct to exploitation, narrowing the perceived scope of possible alternatives. Evidence for that is found in the renewal and extension of scope of special offers that had the unintended effect of reinforcing the existence of a base fare to which the specials stood in relation to. European state railways developed an extensive body of passes, limited specials and discounts to cope with the disadvantages of static, uniform pricing. Most popular were lump-sum offers with various restrictions and percentaged reductions for accompanying passengers. Similar to railcards, many offers needed a distance-based fare to refer to, that is, to apply the discount to. Other railways, e. g. the SNCF, continuously extended their portfolio of railcards (cf. figure 11). However, special offers were never introduced to replace distance tariffs, but to cope with the limited capacity of distance prices to attract new demand without allocating discounts to existing demand. Special offers were evaluated by assessing their effect on the existing structure. If they were considered to cannibalise the status quo, they were withdrawn from the market with the learning effect to keep distance fares as the more revenue-efficient solution.

Figure 11: Reduced base fare for travel companions promoted by the SNCF in 1981
Source: Archives SNCF Le Mans, VDR2217_LD, VDR2216_LD

On the demand side of the market, learning involves price knowledge, price expectations and knowledge on the conditions of use or scope of services associated with a specific fare (cf. chapters 2.2, 2.3., 5). In that context, complexity of fare schemes is a widely discussed issue. Especially when there is a large choice of fares with various restrictions it can be more and more important to have a reference point that can be easily communicated and understood. The standard distance fare provided that notion of simplicity. Much about the critics on Deutsche Bahn's price experiments of 2002 was about confronting consumers with a fare structure they perceived as opaque. Considerable parts of the new fare policy had to be withdrawn (cf. Link 2004). Thus, the non-complex nature of the distance standard made it increasingly attractive from a price learning point of view. The less complex a fare scheme became, the easier it could be understood by stakeholders and implemented within the organisation. Put in other words: the more complex an alternative pricing approach was, the higher the probability for it to fail because it is more difficult to be communicated, understood and experienced by consumers. Moreover, price learning and learning about price reaction involve generating price and revenue expectations over time. In fact, learning effects on the supply and demand side are closely interlinked with the concept of adaptive expectations described in the following section.

Adaptive expectations

"[E]xpectations of expectations" (Luhmann 1995 [1984]) are also regarded as a source of incremental rigidity. Following this concept of expectations, individual preferences do not emerge until they are confronted with the expectations of others. Thus, they are conceived to be built interactively (cf. Sydow et al. 2009: 700). In the railway sector, presumed "best practices" have spread through this construction of expectations. The most explicit example for this is the diffusion of the Swiss *Halbtaxabonnement*, which was re-introduced in 1918 and copied by a large number of managers of European railways long before the concept of non-linear pricing was discussed. Therefore, railcards were not only a complementing product to the base fare, but also driven by a mimetic tendency among state railways.

Operators have restricted their way of pricing in anticipation or as a reaction of expectations of their stakeholders, e. g., passengers or governmental institutions. Evidence for this behaviour can be found in Sarter (1927) and Dobbin (1994) and for various special offers. Even though British Rail was a public service provider just as the SNCF, an SNCF manager considered the non-kilometric pricing approach gradually adopted in Britain as impossible to be applied in France:

> "Toute différente est la déréquation géographique, appliquée depuis plusieurs dizaines d'années en Grande-Bretagne où les prix sont variables suivant chaque relation, la notion de prix de base kilométrique ayant pratiquement disparue de la tarification ferroviaire. Une telle mesure, d'application difficile, serait tout à fait contradictoire avec la notion de service public et notamment avec les objectifs d'aménagement du territoire"[26].

Once a static, distance-based fare scheme was set up, it became more and more irreversible as other local investment decisions were made on the basis of an existing fare structure. This situation can be considered as a combination of complementarity between fares and the place of location of, e. g., housing or industrial facilities *and* adaptive expectations of entrepreneurs and workers that an existing fare scheme will be maintained in order to support their economic activities. When railways were challenged to adopt their fares to road competition, Rittershausen (1989 [1950]) noticed:

> "On the other hand, a total and immediate switch [in fare policy] to radical competition is impossible, because too many [...] people commute to their workplace at reduced rates [...], and too many factories and business lines owe their location to these fares. These sites cannot simply be dismounted at a glance" (Rittershausen 1989 [1950]: 30, translated by N. K.).

---

[26] Archives historiques SNCF, dossier 20LM925, Exposé de M. Weber, Directeur Commercial Voyageurs, relatif à la politique commerciale voyageurs à la S.N.C.F., dated 21 September 1983, p. 17

Thus, despite the purely economic network effect of a fare standard, setting a comprehensive fare on the whole network met the expectation of a coherent fare regime within and between railways (cf. chapter 4.2.1.). As railways fulfilled that stakeholder demand, consumers and business partners learnt about it and built expectations on a continuation of the way of pricing initially selected. Altogether, a path-dependent pricing of railways emerged by interaction between single train operating companies, their organisational field (the passenger transportation market) and the involved institutions (national and international railway associations, regulatory authorities). The specific self-reinforcing mechanisms underlying that path formation have been described above. The following list links self-reinforcing mechanisms and their empirical manifestation in the case of railway tariffing:

Self-reinforcing mechanism	Manifestation in passenger rail transport
Coordination effects	Through-tariffing on growing network Cross-border transit Diffusion of fare components (e. g., target-group conditions, Railplus rebate)
Complementarity effects	Clearing Interlinked fare policy and sales technology Compatible building blocks (railcards, supplements and reservations)
Learning effects	Renewal, cessation and extension of special offers Constitution of tariff knowledge and –expectations by passengers Non-complexity
Adaptive expectation effects	Anticipating stakeholder demands and regulation Best practices of passenger rail tariffing Housing and urban infrastructure

Table 9: Self-reinforcing mechanisms within the railway tariffing path

4.2.3. Lock-in: the point of no return

In the lock-in state of path dependence, "[o]ne particular choice or action pattern has become the predominant mode, and flexibility has been lost. "Even new entrants into this field of action cannot refrain from adopting it" (Sydow et al. 2009: 692). Though further decisions "are bound to replicate the path" (ibid: 694), in an organisational context, the lock-in stage is conceived as a period in which "an underlying core pattern" (ibid: 695) has gained dominance. In consequence, organisations are not expected to face total rigidity, but a certain "variance in the actual practicing of the organi[s]ational path" (ibid).

Lock-in in the railway tariffing case did not occur at a specific point of time because companies were nationalised in succession, but I argue that the foundation of state railways marks the threshold between closing and lock-in in the formation of the path. The essential reason for the lock-in of the standard railway tariff to emerge was its tremendous success. The self-reinforcing nature of network growth, simplicity of fare calculation, corresponding products and sales facilities allowed for highly profitable passenger operations. In that situation, there was no need to re-think fare strategy or to preserve other fare options. The main reason why I see nationalisation as a critical juncture is that with every disappearing private railway undertaking in Europe, diversity in the market including possible organisational slack (cf. Cyert & March 1963) was reduced. Before the automobile came up as a powerful competitor, nationalisation once again boosted profitability because it eliminated intramodal competitors and effectively harmonised the fares landscape. Subsequently, state-owned railways appreciated profit made by their passenger operations, but simply did not need to actively seek for increasing it because of their privileged market position. At the same time, nationalisation meant a point in which railways were partly insulated from the market forces (cf. European Commission 1996: 3) through generating revenue from subsidies.

Once the nationalisation process was completed in the time between 1920 and 1950, the standard railway tariff became an almost natural, persistent pattern of all state railways' pricing strategy. After the rail tariffing path entered the lock-in stage, as described in chapter 4.2.1., there was a period of decades in which a typical railway ticket comprised route, distance, optional rebate and the resulting fare out of these input factors. Applied to the phase model of path dependence proposed by Sydow et al. (2009), the path of the standard railway tariff based on distance can be described as follows: In the contingency phase between 1830 and the 1880s, mostly private railway operators collected experience with different forms of pricing, one of them being distance fares. When single railway lines expanded to networks, there was a need to harmonise fares among different operators and to find arrangements with public interest. More and more railways became controlled by governments between 1880 and the first half of the 20th century. With the support of self-reinforcing mechanisms, distance fares gained momentum. Distance fares became locked in as the predominant pricing pattern in a European territory after the event of nationalisation. That is, the founding of centrally administered organisations which bundled all railway operations in that area marks the final critical juncture in the path constitution process.

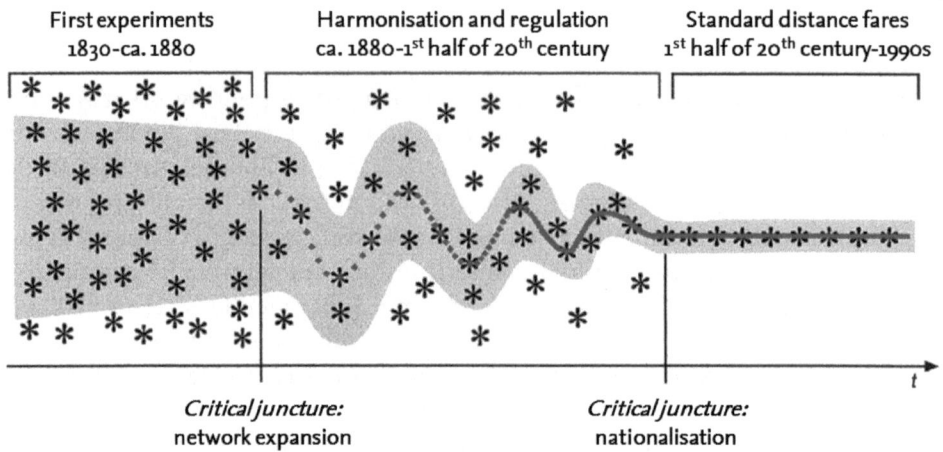

Figure 12: The path of the standard railway tariff
Source: derived from Sydow et al. 2009: 692

The phase model stated above will certainly raise the question what happened after the temporal frame it comprises – therefore, chapter 4.4. broaches the issues of path continuation, path dissolution and path breaking. As this study is aimed at reconstructing the path and investigating on its (potential) inefficiency, there will only be a short outlook to firms that have successfully broken the path after they entered the lock-in phase.

Being locked-in to a path doesn't necessarily mean that management of the railway undertakings did not reflect other options, but the self-reinforcing mechanisms in place mostly made it rational to continue the strategy or to only very slightly modify it. Effectively, managers may not realise that their organisation is locked-in before they engage in path-breaking initiatives. In the mid-1960s, Deutsche Bundesbahn had to experience that it could be forced by stakeholders to re-introduce discounts that had been removed from the market because they were not commercially justified (cf. Lampe-Helbig (1989 [1966]). It can also be observed that TOCs learnt that, on the short run, a deviation from the standard tariffing path even deteriorated their revenue situation instead of improving it. When Deutsche Bahn endeavoured to remove its 50% discount railcard from the market in 2002, there were not just fierce protests of passengers against that measure, but the company also observed a serious drop both in passenger numbers and revenue (cf. Link 2004; Brenck 2003). The partly failed path-breaking initiative of Deutsche Bahn in 2002 motivated Link (2004: 52) to ask whether "a yield-management type of fare scheme [is] sensible and feasible for rail at all". Again, the complexity argument is employed for explaining the failure of the pricing measure (cf. ibid: 54).

Within the framework of the SNCF study group on a new fare scheme for high-speed products, managers naturally reflected on the "combinabilité des tarifs"[27], speed, approaches in other industries etc.. But at the end, SNCF's managers found themselves in an environment that did not accept their suggestions, noting that "nous sommes victimes des habitudes acquises"[28]. There was a strong fear of excessively complicating the fare scheme[29]. In fact, when the TGV was inaugurated in end 1981, the fare structure for the new train was integrated into the traditional way of railway pricing by adding a compulsory reservation and supplements (cf. chapter 4.2.1.).

Simplicity of the mileage-based fare structure was the fundamental reason why first trials on selective pricing (i. e., fares for every route according to the competitive position of rail transit at different times of the day) were dropped in Britain in 1965. Facing the alternative involving business, off-peak and cheap ticket fares, the Management Committee of the British Railways considered that "the simplicity of the existing structure was an advantage" (Gourvish 1986: 480). However, concerning lock-in, Britain is somewhat of an exception. Though the nationalised British Rail did apply pure distance fares from the 1950s to the late 1960s, there was a tradition of trying to fill unused capacity. When the new product InterCity was launched, the related "strategy encouraged the replacement of British Rail's national, mileage-related tariff for season tickets, where there were substantial discounts over longer distances, to a route-by-route policy, with higher fares for higher quality services" (Gourvish 2002: 280). In fact, the introduction of selective pricing in 1968, "which meant an end to the practice of basing fares rigidly on the distance travelled" (Gourvish 1986: 471) was a major step other railways did not take. If the BR were in a lock-in, they successfully broke the path when introducing sector management for passenger operations, because there were more and more fares that radically stood in contrast to the standard railway tariff:

> "As sector management developed, there was a considerable growth in discounted fares, and in the first half of the 1980s British Rail tested the market with a series of radical, imaginative strategies. Railcards offering concessionary tickets were extended to families and the disabled (in 1981) and to all young people (in 1984). A special offer of free national travel on 10 June 1978 to holders of Senior Citizen Railcards was followed by a number of successful promotions, including a £1 Day Return in November 1980, and similar offers in March and November 1982, and annually from November 1984. The London and South East sector offered similar deals, including Party-Size 'Awayday' tickets of £1 in July–September 1982, a 'Go Anywhere' £2 Day Return for Senior Citizens in November 1983, and special offers to Network Card holders from 1986. There were also numerous leisure packages promoted on a local basis, notably those promoted by Scotrail in 1983 and 1984. Cheap discounted travel was also offered to small groups using voucher promotions, for example in association with Lever Brothers (Persil) and Kellogg's. Awareness of the strong competition offered by deregulated bus operators was the stimulus for much of this marketing effort, as it was in the provision of 'Saver' and 'Supersaver'

---

[27] Archives historiques SNCF, dossier 0026LM0465, minutes of a key meeting on fare policy, not dated (estimated from the context of neighbouring documents the meeting was held on 13 December 1971), p. 3
[28] Ibid: 6
[29] Ibid: 10

tickets from 1985, followed by a range of advance purchase tickets (Apex, SuperApex, Advance Return, Superadvance, Leisure First, etc.), from 1987. There were also special 'two for one' offers by InterCity made in association with retailers such as Boots and Shell [...]" (Gourvish 2002: 279).

4.3. Environmental change and inefficiency

The existence of immediate or latent (future) inefficiency is a constitutive element of path dependence (cf. Sydow et al. 2009: 695). Inefficiency is latent while, though being locked-in, an organisation is not yet forced to adapt to a changing environmental situation. The self-reinforcing mechanisms in action still contribute to a stable outcome of an appropriate setting of activities. The dark side of that rigidity is that an organisation will be unable to deviate from the path in case an environmental change occurs. Thus, path-dependence explains the counter-factual inability to adapt to changing market conditions. Being path-dependent in the field of passenger price-setting, railways were not flexible to adapt their pricing strategy to changes in the transport market. Outside observers could perceive this as omitted reaction to changing market requirements. In its 1996 white paper titled "A Strategy for Revitalising the Community's Railways", the European Commission addressed that issue by reporting:

> "The main reason [of the decline of railways' market share] is dissatisfaction with the price and quality of rail transport, despite encouraging examples of new services. Rail is felt not to respond to market changes or customers' needs, as other modes do" (European Commission 1996: 3).

Throughout this work, inefficiency is strictly considered in a business context. Thus, inefficiency means that a firm cannot generate a level of profit or revenue it could have generated if it were not path-dependent. This situation can coincide with the economics notion of inefficiency in markets, but not necessarily does.

4.3.1. A first unexpected rival: the automobile

Path dependence theory expects inefficiency to occur in the lock-in phase after a change in the environmental situation. In the railway case, the crucial environmental change was definitely the break-through of motor vehicles. This form of transportation appeared in the beginning of the 20th century and quickly became a means of mass transportation. With the development of cars and buses, rail transit gradually lost its monopoly status. Within a few years, the formerly extremely profitable companies changed from the main creditor of the state treasury to one of its main debtors (cf. Gall 1999: 62). Certainly, not even a maximally flexible pricing scheme could have prevented railways' market share from declining, but the question raised in this work is whether organisations being locked-in to a path could have performed better if they had been able to *adapt* their pricing to the new situation.

Already in the 1920s, the then largest train operating company of the world, Deutsche Reichsbahn-Gesellschaft, identified individual car transport as partly competitive with rail prices (cf. Sarter 1927: 44). In 1950, a contemporary author observed that the fare structure of railways in Germany with a uniform, static base fare, discounts and supplements, had been developed in a time when nobody could foresee competition:

> "What happened in the last 20 years [i. e. 1930-1950, N. K.] is nothing else but the clash of a sophisticated system of transport fare differentiation created when no human considered the occurrence of rivals, and a sudden competition from road transport" (Rittershausen 1989 [1950]: 29, translated by N. K.).

The citation above rather refers to goods transportation, but Rittershausen (ibid) did not explicitly separate passenger and goods fare policy. For passenger fares, it is not only the initial unchallenged position of the industry that led it into an irreversible situation, but also the predominance of goods transport in the beginning of the railway age. Bagwell's tables on the revenue proportions of passenger and goods transport support that the relative importance of passenger fare policy in Britain was relatively low compared to goods transport (cf. Bagwell 1968: 300 f.). Further research is needed for comparing the situation in different European countries, but it seems most likely that goods transport was the backbone of railways in the 19th century except for the very early days. It appears that the lock-in of passenger fares was not perceived as an efficiency problem because it emerged behind the back of actors who, for a possibly too long time, concentrated on goods transport (see also chapter 4.2.2 for the long timeframe of the international fare standardisation process).

Regulation of railway fares, which appeared necessary in the monopoly time, was certainly a stabilising factor for maintaining the path even under conditions of inefficiency. When the obligation to set up (static) fares and to publish them lost its primary justification, measures to protect passengers and forwarders from the overreaching power of railways were maintained (cf. Rittershausen 1989 [1950]: 31). In a report on options in transport tariff policy for the then six member states of the European Community, Allais et al. (1965) find the same out-of-time fare structures. Arguing that their insights are also applicable for passenger transport (ibid: 9, 116), they conclude:

> "All the six Community countries apply in one form or another fixed or maximum rates for goods transport by rail. These rates were originally designed to prevent the railways from taking improper advantage of the dominant positions which they had on almost all markets where there was no real competition [...]. However, the situation has changed considerably following the rapid development of road haulage. [...] However, the previous tariff systems have remained in force. But it might be asked whether their general maintenance is economically justified, in view of the present situation on the transport market. For the railways no longer occupy a monopoly position with regard to all their transport activities" (Allais et al. 1965: 106).

When state railways started to reflect stronger on their passenger operations, they observed that even rather unimportant changes could generate extra revenue. It was estimated that Deutsche Bundesbahn's fairly slight form of price differentiation for senior citizens in 1968 would have increased revenue by 8 million Deutsche mark during the limitation time of 4 months (Barthelmeß 1989 [1969]: 315). Building on minutes of the British Railways Board, Gourvish (1986) considered it unfortunate that the BR did not introduce selective prices before 1968, because "price changes were estimated to have increased income by £3.4 million in 1968 (1.9 per cent), £8.7 million in 19[6]9 (4.6 per cent) and £8.9 million in 1970 (4.3 per cent)" (ibid: 480 f.). These figures give an indication that there was significant potential for revenue in the context of road competition that could not be raised with pure distance pricing.

4.3.2. Another competitor: air transport

Motor vehicles having already a fatal impact on railways' modal share in regional transport, airlines started competing long-distance lines from the 1950s on. As described above, airline competition was responded by railways with product innovation, but not with a fundamental change of the pricing strategy. Marketing-driven offers of state railways introduced in the 1970s successfully stimulated demand but failed to sustainably produce the intended effects on the long run. A main characteristic of these offers was that they were not limited in quantity (see for instance critics on inefficient price differentiation and load factor management in Brunotte & Krämer 2003: 767).

Being part of a relatively young industry, airlines were not generally in advance to railways in the field of pricing. However, new comprehensive strategies for pricing in this sector were already begun to be explored in the 1960s (cf. Smith et al. 1992; also see more details on airline revenue management in chapter 5). Two major areas of that research were overbooking and discount allocation – a blind spot for railways. When RM practices were introduced by "a handful of major airlines in the post-deregulation era in the U. S." (Talluri & van Ryzin 2005: xxv) in circa 1978, the situation became more serious from the railways' point of view. The distance standard was very vulnerable towards advance purchase discounts. Railways bound with their standard fares faced extreme difficulty in responding to discounts of advance purchase prices made by airlines and bus operators if they did not want their revenue base to erode. It seems as if the founding myth of revenue management, which is the "destruction" of PeopleExpress by American Airlines through its yield management ability (Cross 1997: 125), happened in a similar way in Europe. Just that it was not a story of inter-airline competition, but of inert railway pricing vs. alternative approaches used by airlines. Besides the SNCF using SOCRATE since 1993, only the BR had a tool for introducing true advance booking rates in the 1990s:

"A move to pricing based upon specifying the train to be taken gained ground in the 1990s. This radical approach for railways took the form of airline-type Apex fares, booked in advance for travel on designated trains. Developed with the help of the new computer-based ticketing and seat reservation technology, and extended with the introduction of SuperApex fares in May 1992, the move produced a considerable erosion of the universal 'walk-on' fare. Price discounting was high because the fares could be offered to fill up capacity train by train in a fully managed way. It was also a response to the very low fares introduced by some of the coach operators and to discounting by the airlines. The revenue from Apex tickets increased from £3 million in 1990/1 to £26 million in 1992/3, and about 40 per cent of the business came from new customers. Advance purchase discounting then became a major element of passenger pricing over the rest of the decade" (Gourvish 2002: 282).

4.3.3. Neighbours becoming competitors: the opening of railway markets

Rigidity in price-setting did not only impede railways to defend their market share. Maintaining their fare strategy and fighting competitors by other organisational measures, railways risked to cut self-reinforcing mechanisms that once led to their expansion:

"Rail transport risks entering a vicious circle, if it has not done so already. Contractions in service lead to reductions in traffic flows, both directly and indirectly, because of the loss of network benefits; for example, cutbacks in regional services can reduce traffic flows on the main links. This in turn pushes up costs for the remaining traffic; in rail transport this effect will be strong because the sector is capital intensive and has a high level of fixed costs. The result will be a continuing spiral of price increases and of diminishing traffic or of losses met by subsidy or debt" (European Commission 1996: 8).

Already in the middle of the 1980s, the economic situation of the Western European state railways deteriorated in a way that made fundamental changes in the organisation of rail transport inevitable. Moreover, the post-communist railways in Eastern Europe came into similar financial trouble shortly after alternative transport modes were available. The gradual opening of European transport markets started with the 1985 judgment by the European Court of Justice[30]. This event paved the way for market entrance of other train operators than the legacy carriers. Liberalisation has been codified in different railway packages[31] affecting all EU member states. Key elements of the regulation are a separation of rail infrastructure and transport activity as well as discrete accounting for publicly funded and non-subsidised activities. With effect to January 1st, 2010, international passenger rail transport has been liberalised for all EU member states[32]. Many EU countries including Great Britain, Sweden, Austria, Italy and

---

[30] Decision in the Case 13/83 dated May 22, 1985, concluding that "the Council has infringed the European Economic Community Treaty [...] by failing to introduce a common policy for transport [...]" (p. 1583).
[31] Railway packages are a bundle of regulations and directives concerning European railway policy. 1st package: directives 2001/12-14/EC; 2nd package: directives 2004/49-51/EC, regulation (EC) 881/2004; 3rd package: regulations (EC) 1370-1371/2007, directives 2007/58-59/EC; a fourth railway package revisiting the previous ones is forthcoming.
[32] Exceptions apply on a limited timeframe.

Germany went beyond the minimum requirements and voluntarily opened their national markets, too.

The liberalisation process in the transport sector constitutes a rationality shift: while in the past, state railways had borne responsibility for providing transport services and for fulfilling governmental or social functions, they are now compelled to transparently calculate costs and benefits of their transport activity. This means that pricing must basically be aligned to economic reasons, if it is not, other market players will be able to expand their market share. From the legacy carriers' perspective, liberalisation on the one hand means loss of market share in their former monopoly areas; on the other hand it opens the opportunity for international expansion. Hence, internationalisation is the only way for state railways to keep overall performance stable. Therefore, legacy carriers are likely to transfer their historically grown competences into new markets.

As Sydow et al. (2009: 692) point out; even new market entrants can be affected by the predominant pricing pattern. Empirically, this can be observed with a long-distance market entrant in Austria. Starting operations in 2011, the TOC "Westbahn" has deliberately adopted strictly kilometric pricing and extreme flexibility for using a ticket with the argument of bringing simplicity back to rail travel.

4.3.4. Inter- and intramodal perspective on inefficiency

Train operating companies are agents in the competitive environment of road, rail and air transport modes. Derived from the understanding of inefficiency developed above, but more relying on revenue share than on nominal profit, the relative market position of firms in the railway industry can be compared to the one of their competitors. That notion of inefficiency implies that railway firms cannot reach a market position they would have attained if they were not path-dependent. More precisely, inefficiency can have two faces in passenger rail transport: an intermodal and an intramodal one. From an intermodal perspective, elaborating on inefficiency is analysing the railway operators' position (single or collectively) in regard to their position on the whole passenger transportation market. From an intramodal perspective, researchers focus on the position of a single railway operator within a geographically defined passenger rail market only.

Between 1970 and 1994, the performance of railway undertakings in the EU-15 increased by 25% from 216 to approx. 270 billion passenger-kilometres per year. Within the same timeframe, the volume of the passenger transport market doubled and usage of private motor cars increased by 120%. Despite of continuous growth in the transport market and important public subsidies, European state railways haven't realised more than marginal growth in their transport performance for decades (cf. European Commission 1996). This situation can be interpreted as intermodal inefficiency.

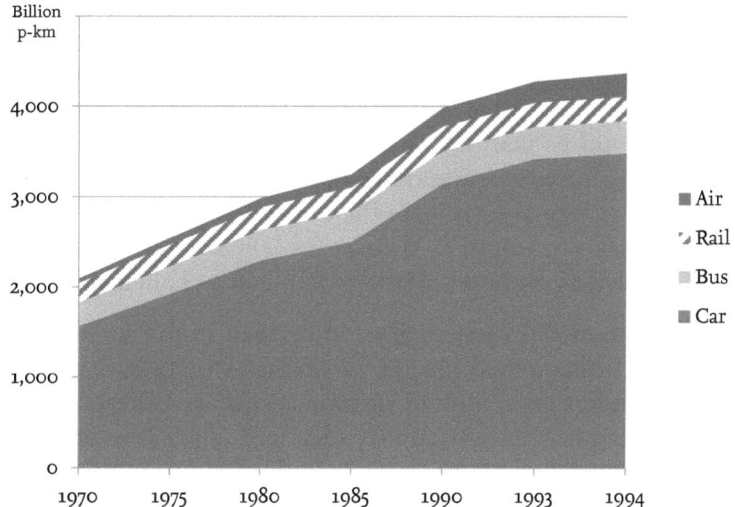

Figure 13: Growing transport market and passenger railways' performance in the EU-15
(in billion passenger-km)
Source: based on data of the European Commission 1996: 43

In his study on the British Railways, Gourvish (1986) comes to similar conclusions for the United Kingdom, except that there is even a slight decline in nominal transport performance.

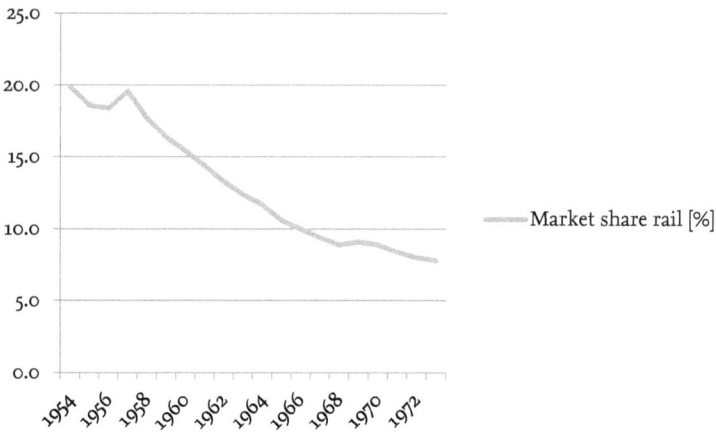

Figure 14: Railways' passenger market share in Britain 1954-1973
Source: based on data in Gourvish 1986: 617

The decline of European railways' market share is mainly due to the growth of individual car transport, but from the 1970s on, it is strongly reinforced by air transport expansion. Intermodal inefficiency of railways is seen here as the outcome of a systematically too low market share of railways in general or of a single railway operator in the transport market (including all means of individual and public transport). This type of inefficiency is characterised by non-exploitation of an existing revenue potential. As long as national territorial monopolies existed, any loss of market share to road or air transport was unwished, but still could be justified or explained by substantially different utility or better conditions for competing transport modes. In this epoch, comparative studies on the international level were the only possible attempt to track inefficiency of railways (cf. e. g., Oum & Yu 1994 for OECD railways). Because of specific national conditions, those results were frequently challenged.

Potential intramodal inefficiency can be seen in the following constellation: In case of a fundamental change of market structure, a path-dependent pricing strategy hinders expansion or restrains the scope of reaction against new competitors. Keeping the old system may even lead to a loss of pricing authority for a railway, if the company's performance in this field is judged inadequate. In other words, if a TOC in a situation of lock-in in its pricing loses market share (and most likely loses profit) to competing train operators that flexibly employ different pricing strategies in the same market, the former TOC faces intramodal inefficiency.

4.4. Distance fares today

Case study work in this chapter reconstructed the evolution of the standard railway tariff by collecting typical tariff parameters of passenger train operating organisations in Europe. It demonstrates the emergence of a path of railway tariffing with the outcome of an excessively stable fare standard. The development of passenger rail tariffication had its initial point at single organisations, as prices and conditions of carriage have been set by transport operating companies themselves. Hence, the role of railway operators as individual price-setters fits in the notion of organisational path dependence. It has been shown that, for a certain period of time, charging passengers individually according to the distance travelled has become an unquestioned commercial standard for rail travel in Europe.

Being a tremendous success at first place, that way of pricing backfired when motor vehicles and airlines changed the railway monopoly into intermodal competition. As the economic situation of the state railways deteriorated in the end of the 1960s (in some cases before), innovations in sales technology, intensified marketing effort with inventive commercial offers and international agreements helped to keep rail market share from eroding, but didn't remove the disadvantage of railway pricing towards to modal competitors. I conclude that railways' inertia in pricing had a strong influence on the decline of the industry's transport market share.

For many organisations in the railway sector, the process of rethinking distance fares is on-going. Though the situation among European train operating companies is diverse, it can be generally observed that high-speed branches of TOCs tend to having adopted at least airline-oriented models of pricing. Some have successfully broken the path when they introduced the new products (see the examples stated above). High-speed is closely linked with reports on the renaissance of railways. In the sector of regional transport by train, there is a tendency of fares being increasingly determined by transport associations offering a transport network of many cooperating carriers in space instead of pricing travel on a railway line (e. g., urban areas as RATP[33] in Paris and Transport for London, regional transport associations in Germany). Thus, even though distance pricing persists, there is dissolution of the path as fares for this market segment are now set differently by organisations other than the railway operators[34]. Nevertheless, there are some TOCs that continue to follow the path of static distance fares in our days. Many of them are Eastern European incumbents, but also the different Swiss railways (e. g., SBB, BLS, Rhätische Bahn) continue to apply kilometric fare calculation with elements of degression for longer distances. As noted above, also the recently founded Austrian TOC Westbahn has adopted purely distance-based fares.

Figure 15: Path continuity: distance fare ticket and optional railcard reduction in Romania
Source: original issued in May 2013

---

[33] Régie autonome des transports parisiens
[34] However, railway operators are generally members of transport associations. Public service obligations mostly require franchisees to participate in these associations.

It has been demonstrated that the standard railway tariff hindered train operating companies to defend their markets against modal competitors. As the transport market keeps developing, it is an open question what pricing strategy other than static distance fares is most promising for a contemporary train operator. By means of an agent-based revenue simulation model, the following part of this dissertation will elaborate on this issue.

5. Searching for more efficient railway prices

The key elements of the process of path creation being reconstructed, constitutive features of railway pricing in general are transferred in this chapter into an agent-based simulation model in order to be tested on possible more efficient alternatives.

As outlined in chapter 2, revenue management has spread to a variety of services since its implementation at different American airlines in the post-regulation U. S. transport market of the 1970s. This form of pricing may constitute an efficient alternative to static fares based on distance. Though air and rail transportation both offer – on an abstract level – similar services, many European railways have been reluctant to consequently introduce revenue management applications. Some exceptions to this are outlined in the previous chapter. As described in chapter 3, elaborating on the inefficiency question requires detailed investigation on a firm's markets and resources. Therefore, the assessment of a specific tariff structure to be more efficient than another one cannot be performed for the railway industry as a whole, but needs to be made for a focal train operating company. Thus, taking the perspective of an incumbent train operating company facing path dependence in its pricing, this part of the dissertation at hand uses RM methods to search for possible fare amendments. It applies a quantitative approach to elaborate in detail on the question what alternative or complementing tariff structure bears the potential of being more efficient than the standard railway fare based on distance. This search is performed by means of an agent-based simulation model.

5.1. Agent-based revenue simulation

It is the special characteristic of agent-based simulation models to consist of interacting individuals or entities. In order to adopt this method for revenue management in the focused industry, a precise representation of relevant agents in a revenue simulation model is needed. For building a revenue simulation model for a passenger TOC, I rely on studies in the field of social simulation and on operations research publications on revenue management models.

Computational modelling in general and agent-based objects in specific have gained broader acceptance among social scientists in recent years (cf. Miller & Page 2007; Gilbert 2010; Harrison et al. 2007). In cases where experiments in the actual target system are impossible (e. g., for complexity reasons), simulation as a method can be used to generate data of the empirical target and to compare it with statistically collected empirical data (cf. Gilbert & Troitzsch 2005; see also Arthur 1999 for complexity problems in the economy). Complexity in this context is defined by the feature that "the phenomena of interest result from the interaction of social actors in an essential way and are not reducible to considering single actors or a representative actor and a representative environment"

© Springer Fachmedien Wiesbaden GmbH, part of Springer Nature 2014
N. Kellermann, *Searching for a path out of distance fares*, Edition KWV,
https://doi.org/10.1007/978-3-658-23112-5_5

(Edmonds & Meyer 2013: 4). If a mathematical solution of a complex problem cannot be obtained, there is a need for "numerically exercising the model for the inputs in question to see how they affect the output measures of performance" (Law 2007: 5). This technique is referred to as simulation.

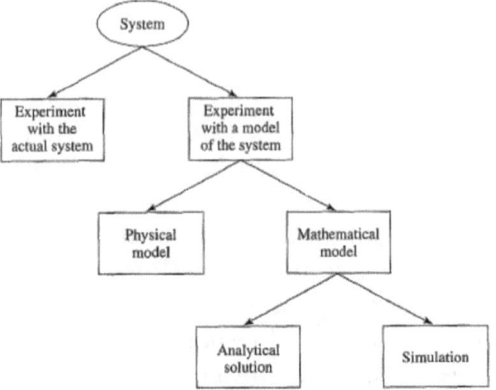

Figure 16: Ways to study a system
Source: Law 2007: 4

Generally, simulation enables the researcher to capture the processual dynamics of non-linear phenomena. Thus, it allows for moving from a cross-sectional to a longitudinal and dynamic perspective (cf. Davis et al. 2007; Harrison et al. 2007). Ihrig & Troitzsch (2013) see simulation modelling as the appropriate methodological approach for "exploring phenomena that are emergent and/or [...] complex and non-repeatable processes". For Carley (2002: 254), all "[s]ocial and organi[s]ational systems are complex non-linear dynamic" ones. Miller (1998) explicitly names management issues to be analysed with the help of "[c]omplicated, large-scale computational models" (ibid: 820). Hence, pricing and buying reaction are arguably among the fields that fit into this notion because real-world experiments in pricing can be very risky trials, and reactions to price measures by socially interlinked consumers can lead to emergent market outcomes. Applying the simulation method in the context of path dependence and pricing strategy clearly appears in line with the methodological recommendations made by Vergne (2013) and Vergne & Durand (2010) described above.

Simulation & philosophy of science

In his book on agent-based simulation, Axelrod (1997) refers to simulation as a third way of doing science which can be contrasted with the two standard methods of induction and deduction: "Like deduction, [simulation] starts with a set of explicit assumptions. But unlike deduction, it does not prove theorems. Instead, an agent-based model generates simulated data that can be analy[s]ed inductively. Unlike typical induction, however, the simulated data come from a rigorously specified set of rules rather than direct measurement of the real world" (ibid: 3 f.). Citing Axelrod (1997) and Waldrop (1992), Harrison et al. (2007: 1230) conclude that "[c]omputer simulation is now recogni[s]ed as a third way of doing science". Harrison et al. (ibid) see the method of computer simulation as a tool for theory construction because "[i]t renders irrelevant the deductive problem of analytic intractability [since] mathematical relationships can be handled computationally using numerical methods. It also partially overcomes the empirical problem of data availability, since a simulation produces its own 'virtual' data". Opposed to this perception of simulation being in-between induction and deduction, Ostrom (1988) titles simulation a "third symbol system". Ostrom (ibid) sees the potential of simulation, respectively, the reason for the "coming of age" (p. 381) of computer simulation in social psychology, in the fact that it can better express theoretical ideas than natural or mathematical language can. Again, in the end, simulation is supposed to aid developing theories on social phenomena.

While also Davis et al. (2007: 480) see the value of simulation modelling in the "creative experimentation to produce novel theory", Ihrig & Troitzsch (2013: 99) adopt a different view, arguing that "simulation is a way of deduction which is gone by means of an alternative symbol system and that it is not a way of doing science in the sense that it has a starting point of existing knowledge and ends up in new knowledge". In order to shed light the way new research insights can be gained from real-world problems, related theory, and a simulation model, Ihrig & Troitzsch (ibid) refer to the non-statement view (Sneed 1971; Stegmüller 1973).

The non-statement view is also referred to as the structuralist view. The central point of this conception is that a theory-element T is understood as a pair of a structural theory-core K and its domain of intended application I (cf. Küttner 1981: 165). While Popper's critical rationalism (see, for example Popper 2002 [1945]) considers any theory refutable, Kuhn (1996 [1962]) notices that "normal science [...] often suppresses fundamental novelties because they are necessarily subversive of its basic commitments" (p. 5). Normal science means "research firmly based upon [...] achievements that some particular scientific community acknowledges for a time as supplying the foundation for its further practice" (ibid: 10). This community doesn't only have common assumptions and rituals, but also shares a set of techniques and practices for generating new knowledge. Kuhn introduces the notion of a scientific paradigm which is subject to a transition from one to another through a revolutional challenge of the old paradigm if the contradictions or the tensions of the old paradigm become too large. Kuhn's central point is that new paradigms are incommensurable with the old ones, thus, there is no accumulation of knowledge. Lakatos (1970; 1976) tries to establish a moderating position between Popper and Kuhn by defining theory to consist of a theory-core which is more protected from being refuted and a theory "front court" or protecting belt. In "Mathematics, science and epistemology", which is a post-mortem published collection of papers written by Lakatos, Lakatos suggests a possible experimental scientific research programme which stands in line with the simulation method (cf. Lakatos 1978: 96).

Now, is simulation itself a way to construct theory and what is the theoretical status of a simulation model? According to Ihrig & Troitzsch (2013: 100), a model "describe[s] the contents of a theory" and can be grouped into three classes. The first class comprises measurable or observable terms of the theory, regardless if the theory has been yet formulated, the second class consists of terms that only have a meaning once the theory is formulated, and the third class consists of axioms linking class one and two. Ihrig & Troitzsch see simulation as a way of conducting *theoretical* research, differentiating between a more deductive part (which is a theory-based simulation environment and an executable simulation model) and a more inductive part (which are the runs of a simulation with the data generated at these runs). They write:

> "More often than not, simulated data cannot be compared to purely theoretical assessments as a classical mathematical formulation of the axioms of the theory has no analytical solution (and a numerical solution of, for instance, a system of non-linear differential equations is also the result of a computer simulation for a specific combination of parameters), such that simulation sometimes is the only possibility to generate deductions from theoretical assumptions. This simulation exercise will result in theory-driven hypotheses that are empirically testable. Although an executable simulation model is a full model of the theory and makes all **T**-theoretical terms (as in 'theory-element' of the non-statement view) and their values visible, it also generates hypotheses from which the **T**-theoretical terms were eliminated. Subsequently, the **T**-non-theoretical simulated data can be compared to empirical data. In an empirical follow-up study, the real world issue that is being investigated can be further examined by obtaining empirical data through *systematic data gathering* on a basis that is informed by the previous simulation research, and perhaps ways can be found with the help of a link to another theory to measure terms which are theoretical with respect to this theory **T**, but not to the other (linked) theory **T'**" (Ihrig & Troitzsch 2013: 103, emphasis and bold in the original).

In sum, Ihrig and Troitzsch (2013: 102) conclude a research architecture which involves simulation as a new pillar of theoretical research linking purely theoretical modelling without simulation to empirical research. Thus, simulation is at first place non-empirical research and needs to be compared to empirical findings. In this work, I follow the "core logic of simulation" stated by Gilbert & Troitzsch (2005), which is to firstly define a real-world target to be studied, then modelling it with the help of abstract features of it and finally run simulations for generating simulated data (see also Ihrig & Troitzsch 2013: 100). Thus, I do not see simulation as a different way of doing science, but as a method of building an abstract model, running artificial experiments with it by manipulating its parameters, and subsequently analysing the resulting data.

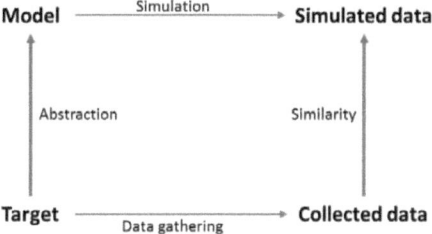

Figure 17: Simulation as a method
Source: Gilbert & Troitzsch 2005: 17

In line with this perspective on simulation, Weber (2004) summarises the key features of simulation relevant to philosophy of science: From an epistemological view, the simulation method bears the advantage of representing complex processes, namely, phenomena of emergence. Simulations make theoretical assumptions explicit and can help to overcome the problem of non-observable processes, thus, they extend the limits of scientific research. Simulation studies are notably useful when real experiments are impossible. However, usefulness and credibility of simulations depends on the input data used. Assumptions in simulations being considered as hypotheses, results of simulation experiments cannot replace empirical validation – all of them remain falsifiable.

Historical aspects and types of the simulation method

The use of computational methods in science can be considered as old as the computer technology itself. Formalisation of social science was already one of the contributions of the computer science pioneer John von Neumann (cf. Troitzsch 2013: 13). Concerning first applications of simulations, Harrison et al. (2007: 1230) write: "The first well-known computer simulation involved the design of the atomic bomb in the Manhattan Project during World War II". While subsequently, simulation became "an accepted and widely used approach" (ibid: 1231) in the natural sciences, especially in physics and in biology, the social sciences did rarely adopt it. Though there was pioneering work by Forrester (1961), Cohen et al. (1972) and Cyert & March (1963) using computer simulation methods, the methodology played a peripheral role in the social sciences in the first decades of its appearance (cf. Harrison et al. 2007: 1231; Gilbert 2008: xi).

Troitzsch (2013) provides a concise review of the historical development of the simulation method which also helps to understand the emergence of the four major terms associated with simulations: *system dynamics, microsimulation, cellular automata* and *agent-based simulation.*

Publications on system dynamics are mostly associated with Jay W. Forrester who extended his 1961 book on industry dynamics to urban dynamics (Forrester 1969) and even world dynamics (Forrester 1971). Thereby, "[t]he general idea behind system dynamics was, and is, that a system, without considering its components individually, could be described in terms of its aggregate varia-bles and their changes over time" (Troitzsch 2013: 14). The second term associat-ed with simulations, microsimulation, is defined by Gilbert (2008: 17) as a pro-cess that "starts with a large database describing a sample of individuals, house-holds, or organi[s]ations and then uses rules to update the sample members as though time was advancing". Microsimulation was first mentioned by Orcutt (1957) who built models used for predicting demographic changes and the effects of economic policy decisions, e. g., on taxation. In contrast to agent-based mod-els, microsimulation models "[u]sually do not take into account that the overall changes of the aggregated variables of the population (or the sample) may affect individual behaviour" (Troitzsch 2013: 15). Cellular automata as a third simula-tion term are defined as "a composition of finite automata which all follow the same rule, are ordered in a (mostly) two-dimensional grid and interact with (re-ceive input from) their neighbours" (Troitzsch 2013: 17). Well-known early exam-ples of those automata are Gardner's game of life (Gardner 1970) and Schelling's segregation model (Schelling 1971).

The Monte Carlo method and discrete event modelling are two other terms associated with simulations. Monte Carlo simulations are a stochastic method for determining an approximate solution for a problem which cannot be solved analytically (or which takes too much resource to be solved analytical-ly). This solution is obtained by performing a large number of runs of the simu-lation model and subsequently doing a probabilistic analysis of the outcome. Hence, Monte Carlo simulations are not used as a tool for experiments but re-produce a large number of output values for a given scenario. OR researchers categorise simulations according to the representation of time and state. In ad-dition to the types of simulations described above, this categorisation leads to the use of the term *discrete event models*. Differing from Monte Carlo simula-tions, which "require[] state sequencing, but no explicit representation of time" (Nance & Sargent 2002: 161 f.), discrete event simulation models "specify state changes at discrete points in time" (ibid: 162). In that sense, agent-based simula-tion models can be considered as a subgroup of discrete event models. The spe-cial characteristics of agent-based simulations will be described in more detail below. Altogether, the development of the simulation approach over time shows that there is a continuous effort to represent more heterogeneous objects and to allow interaction between them. Thus, there is a tendency to incorporate more social interaction and (intrinsic) learning behaviour to agents (cf. Troitzsch 2013).

Approach	Used since	Characteristics
System dynamics	Mid-1950s	Only one object (the system) with a large number of attributes
Microsimulation	Mid-1950s	A large number of objects representing individuals that do not interact, neither with each other nor with their aggregate, with a small number of attributes each, plus one aggregating object
Cellular automata	Mid-1960s	Large number of objects representing individuals that interact with their neighbours, with a very restricted behaviour rule, no aggregating object, thus emergent phenomena have to be visualised
Agent-based models	Early 1990s, with some forerunners in the 1960s	Any number of objects ("agents") representing individuals and other entities (groups, different kinds of individuals in different roles) that interact heavily with each other, with an increasingly rich repertoire of changeable behaviour rules (including the ability to learn from experience and/or others, to change their behavioural rules and to interact differently to identical stimuli when the situation in which they are received is different)

Table 10: Approaches in computational social science
Source: Troitzsch 2013: 19

Special characteristics of agent-based objects

Within the framework of the simulation method, the idea of agent-based modelling is to directly represent individual entities and their interactions (Gilbert 2008). Axelrod (1997: 4) writes that "[a]gent-based model[l]ing is a way of doing thought experiments. Although the assumptions may be simple, the consequences may not be at all obvious". Axtell & Epstein (1994: 28) state that "[t]he defining feature of agent based models is precisely that fundamental social structures emerge from the interaction of individual agents".

Specifically, agent-based modelling and simulation allows for incorporating individual heterogeneity, feedback mechanisms and social interaction into a market model (cf. Rand & Rust 2011; Kamakura et al. 1996). Such a model forms the starting point for quasi-experimentation by parameter manipulations (cf. Wu & Hamada 2009). Formalisation of an abstract agent-based model makes sure that all assumptions are made explicit. Clear declarations have to be made about the environment, the agents, and the rules of behaviour they follow. Other than system dynamics modelling, agent-based simulation helps to expose the relationships between the levels of analysis, for instance, between individual decision-making and market outcomes. Therefore, North & Macal (2007: 3) consider it as "one of the most exciting and practical developments in business model[l]ing that has occurred since the invention of relational databases". The agent-based method appears notably useful when it comes to applications of choice models (McFadden 1986; Ben-Akiva & Lerman 1985; Ben-Akiva et al. 1997) and thoroughly corresponds to the micro-foundation thinking in marketing science.

This is not only because economic processes are simulated "from 'the bottom up'" (D'Alessandro & Winzar 2014: 3), but also due to the fact that "[e]ach entity in the model can be different, with different behaviours and attributes" (Edmonds & Meyer 2013: 6). Rand & Rust (2011) suggest considering agent-based models "[i]f the question emphasi[s]es groups of autonomous, heterogeneous entities that operate in a dynamic environment and if the measure of interest is an emergent result of these entities' interactions" (ibid: 184). Briefly, agent-based simulation "opens the world of social complexity to formal representation in a more natural and direct manner" (Edmonds & Meyer 2013: 6).

Altogether, the research agenda for the simulation part of this dissertation involves the set-up of a simulation model, the testing and calibration of the model, running virtual experiments by varying its parameters and statistically analysing the generated simulation data.

5.1.1. A generic mobility market model

Generally, a market is defined by interacting agents on the supply and demand side. Transferred to the context of a revenue simulation model for passenger railways, a market consists of transport operators including individual transport as a quasi-self-transportation and consumers with mobility demand. Starting with a pre-committed – in other words, scheduled – transportation offer, a model of that transportation market needs to incorporate different transportation options available for each individual consumer. Consumers perform a utility calculation and choose the offer which rewards them with the highest utility value based on their personal preferences. This generic view on a mobility market is outlined below:

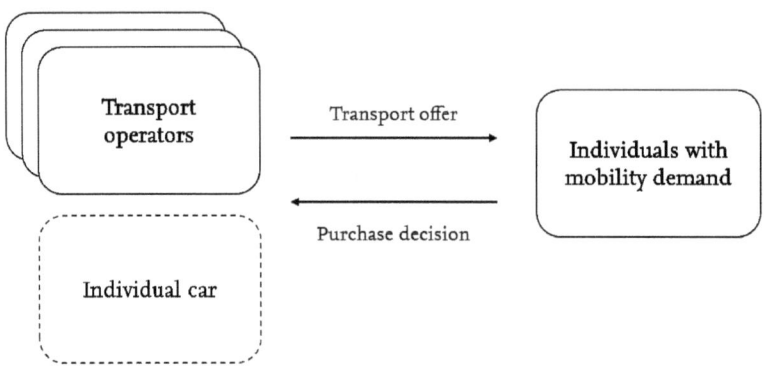

Figure 18: A generic mobility market model

The simulation method allows for a "repeated use of artificial demand" (Cleophas et al. 2009: 334) over a longer timeframe. The basic characteristics of the focal mobility market are implemented through individualising consumers' preferences and rules of behaviour as well as through attributing the empirical features of real-world transport offers to operator agents.

5.1.2. Role-model RM applications

Revenue simulation models have been implemented by airlines as tools for analysing the outcome of different pricing strategies and options (cf. the example of REMATE in Cleophas 2012a; see also Zimmermann et al. 2011). In that sense, revenue simulation models constitute an environment for performing "serious games" in the field of pricing. Simulating transactions in a mobility market including railways with the aim of measuring effects generated by airline-oriented pricing implies to model a simplified RM process. Therefore, this section describes the basic functions of classical RM models. In their seminal book on the theory and practice of revenue management, Talluri & van Ryzin (2005) outline a typical revenue management flow.

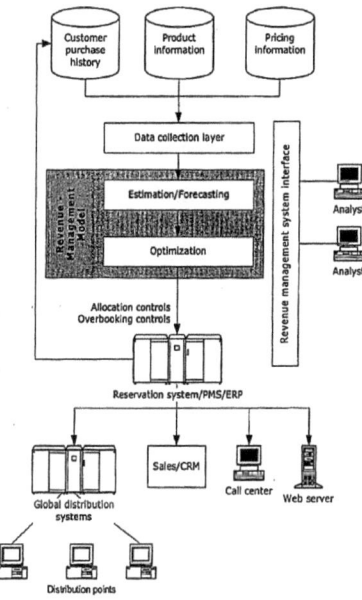

Figure 19: Flow of a RM model
Source: Talluri & van Ryzin 2005: 19

The core element for a quantity-based RM approach is located in the centre of the illustration above. It is the allocation control with the help of a reservation system derived from demand estimation and optimisation. Though the revenue simulation model for the present research cannot provide a complete model to be used for revenue management, it needs to include a simplified capacity control module in order to simulate the outcome of introducing quantity-based RM.

Besides the documentation on SNCF's airline-oriented system SOCRATE (cf. chapter 4.2.1.), one of the rare publications on revenue management for railways is the paper of Ciancimino et al. (1999). However, the latter work does not contain a full railway RM model, but concentrates on mathematically solving a single-fare multi-leg problem. Similarly, Gopalakrishna & Rangaraj (2010) propose a capacity management model for railways. Harti et al. (2010) describe elements and conditions for a RM model which was specifically set up for the German railway market, Dutta & Ghosh (2012) propose a RM system for an emerging Asian market.

Frank et al. (2008) provide a general design for a revenue simulation model in the airline industry and basic principles for setting it up. Similar to the flow chart proposed by Talluri & van Ryzin (2005), an inventory control system stands in the centre of the revenue simulation model. Special attention has to be paid when building a module for generating artificial demand because "[a]n airline does not have reliable information about the basic principles of [a buying] decision and therefore a booking appears stochastic. This stochastic demand and its prediction establish the basis of [RM] and are therefore essential for a simulation" (ibid: 9).

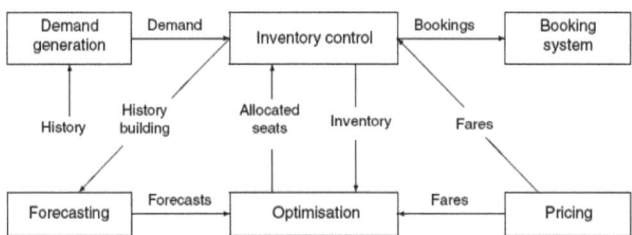

Figure 20: Elements of an airline revenue simulation model
Source: Frank et al. 2008: 9

Cleophas et al. (2009) propose to use the "stable and fully controllable conditions" (ibid: 331) in revenue simulation environments for evaluating different demand forecast approaches employed by airlines (see also Cleophas 2009). Along with this, they present an overview how to implement the simulation of artificial demand in revenue management models. As the design developed by Cleophas et al. (ibid) has the objective of evaluating the quality of demand forecasting, in the illustration below, artificial demand is channelled into two simulated reservation systems and their respective inventory controls.

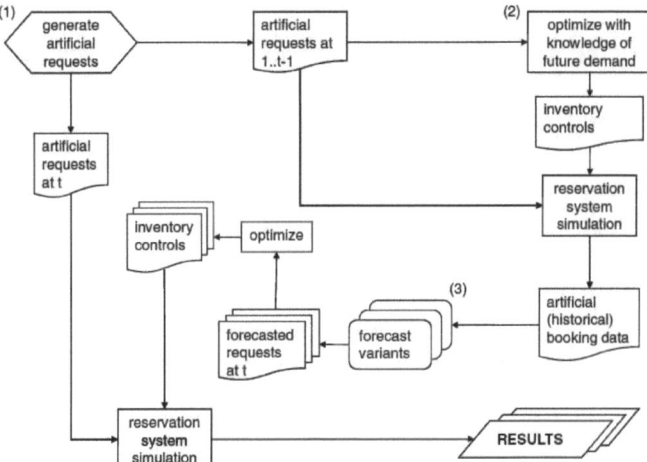

Figure 21: Simulation of demand for RM studies
Source: Cleophas et al. 2009: 334

Following the role model designs outlined above, in the simulation model at hand, demand generation is conceptualised as an artificial mobility need consumer agents are triggered with. This mobility need is the source of artificial requests both for car and public transportation. To meet these requests with available seats, a reservation system representing the factual inventory is needed. As the purpose of the simulation model is testing the performance of pricing options, the forecasting and optimisation features typical for RM simulation models are implemented in a simplified way. Transport operators follow specified rules of seat allocation depending on the measured occupancy of their trains.

5.1.3. Choice of platform and premises

The concrete agent-based simulation model displayed in the following is conceptualised as a representation of a passenger transportation market including intramodal competition and private car transit. Though the observer level can be used for any kind of market analysis, it is designed for being employed for analysing revenue generated by a focal train operating company.

Ihrig & Troitzsch (2013) differentiate between multi-purpose toolkits and theory-related toolkits as simulation environments. While multi-purpose toolkits (e. g., AnyLogic, Repast, NetLogo) "can be used for nearly all simulation approaches developed for the social sciences at large" (ibid: 100), theory-related toolkits (e. g., EMIL-S, SimISpace) are pre-defined for a certain group of research questions around a specified concern such as knowledge or learning. Revenue simulation models being a relatively new field of agent-based modelling, there is no theory-related toolkit involving behavioural pricing available. The purpose of this dissertation being a study on specific options and outcomes of railway pricing, building a new theory-related toolkit incorporating all theoretical aspects of behavioural pricing would be out of scope. Existing revenue management simulation toolkits could be extended with behavioural consumer reaction to the price stimulus, but have predominantly been developed for an airline context. Therefore, building a new simulation model on a multi-purpose toolkit appeared most adequate. The present simulation model is set up on the NetLogo platform (Wilensky & Resnick 1999; Tisue & Wilensky 2004), which is a fully programmable environment developed at Northwestern University, Evanston (USA). Netlogo has initially been used as a simple educational tool in schools, but has found wide acceptance in the scientific social simulation community. The motivation for choosing this simulation environment is described below.

Why NetLogo?

When Railsback et al. (2006) compared five different simulation platforms (Swarm, Java Swarm, Repast, MASON, and NetLogo), they originally wanted to exclude Netlogo for being too limited in scope (cf. ibid: 610). It turned out that out of the five platforms compared, NetLogo was "the highest-level platform, providing a simple yet powerful programming language, built-in graphical interfaces, and comprehensive documentation" (ibid: 609). The authors conclude:

> "NetLogo clearly reflects its heritage as an educational tool, as its primary design objective is clearly ease of use. Its programming language includes many high-level structures and primitives that greatly reduce programming effort, and extensive documentation is provided. The language contains many but not all the control and structuring capabilities of a standard programming language. Further, NetLogo was clearly designed with a specific type of model in mind: mobile agents acting concurrently on a grid space with behavio[u]r dominated by local interactions over short times. While models of this type are easiest to implement in NetLogo, the platform is by no means limited to them. NetLogo is by far the most professional platform in its appearance and documentation" (Railsback et al. 2006: 613).

Gilbert (2008: 48 ff.) compares the four platforms Swarm, Repast, MASON, and NetLogo. He writes: "NetLogo stands out as the quickest to learn and the easiest to use" (p. 49) and dedicates a good dozen of pages to describe it in more detail. In a recent dissertation, Ghorbani (2013) evaluates different platforms for implementing agent-based simulations comprising among others Repast, MASON, and Anylogic. She concludes that:

> "None of the mentioned tools (except MASON to some extent) support conceptual modelling. Therefore, an agent-based model is directly implemented as a simulation. This makes the management of more complex simulations difficult because the model is represented in low-level languages. Direct implementation also makes reusability and redevelopment of models more complicated" (Ghorbani 2013: 150).

Concerning NetLogo and its applicability to the simulation of organisations and other entities than individuals, Ghorbani states:

"Netlogo [...] is one of the frequently used platforms for ABM[s]. This tool is not limited to social systems and agents (turtles) do not necessarily represent human beings. Therefore, Netlogo is abstract enough to model almost any kind of system. Compared to other ABM[] platforms Netlogo is relatively easy to learn and use. Another benefit of Netlogo is the visuali[s]ation of the simulation and results which make it also suitable for educational purposes" (Ghorbani 2013: 150).

An additional feature of Netlogo is that it offers an integrated tool for collecting, storing and organising simulated data with the BehaviorSpace application. This integrated function allows determining all settings of variables to be tested and respectively collects selected output measures. There can be a single output only or multiple outputs to be recorded. Together with the number of repetitions (determining how many times each combination of parameters shall be run), BehaviorSpace automatically calculates the total number of runs necessary for the experiment. Optionally, stop conditions or a time limit in ticks can be defined. Outputs can either be written into a comma-separated values file (.csv file) after each tick or stored in memory until the end of the experiment in order to be written into a spreadsheet .csv file. The latter facilitates the calculation of mean values across a single run, making it a suitable option for longer series of revenue experiments.

The separate programme BehaviorSearch builds on an existing Netlogo model and allows for finding local optima with the help of genetic algorithm search. That is, BehaviorSearch allows for finding a possibly optimal combination of parameters for a defined output (which can be specified to be either a minimum or a maximum) instead of simply measuring large sets of parameter combinations and thereby eventually finding an optimum. In Netlogo terms, BehaviorSearch offers an "inverse search" option to BehaviorSpace. For one of the very applications of BehaviorSearch published so far, see Olaru & Purchase (2014). In the work at hand, BehaviorSearch is used in version 1.0.0 which was released in January 2013. The search encoding representation used in the subsequent BehaviorSearch experiments is GrayBinaryChromosome[35].

---

[35] BehaviorSearch documentation states that GrayBinaryChromosome encoding is "[s]imilar to StandardBinaryChromosome, except that numeric values are encoded to binary strings using a Gray code, instead of the standard 'high order' bit ordering. Gray codes have generally been found to give better performance for search representations, since numeric values that are close together are more likely to be fewer mutations away from each other" (BehaviorSearch version 1.0.0 help function).

5.2. The modelling process

Gilbert (2008: 21 ff.) provides a rough structural framework for creating agent-based models. First, the model itself, relevant agents, assumptions as well as the chosen parameters have to be described clearly. Second, the key procedures in the model need to be described in plain language. It is of specific importance what rules agents follow – in other words, what agents seek to achieve – and what actions they take based on these rules. Furthermore, it has to be defined what information agents receive from their environment and/or other agents and how they keep record of their current state. Finally, the properties of the model which shall be measured are to be described. Once the model is programmed, parameters can be manipulated. Through running the model repeatedly, outcomes of these manipulations can be analysed statistically. This section provides a description of the revenue simulation model built, an outline of its procedures and describes the efforts made for verifying and validating it.

In a first step, the structure of airline revenue simulation models such as the one of Frank et al. (2008) cited above is adapted to the special characteristics of a passenger railway. For simplicity, if a TOC's activity involves a public service obligations (PSO) contract, it is assumed that it bears the economic risk of revenue, thus, that it has an interest to maximise revenue. The model considers timetable and rolling stock as fixed features, and infrastructure does not contribute to profit. As Cleophas (2012) points out, learning is a crucial issue in revenue simulations. Within this dissertation, all agents are modelled with the ability of learning from and reacting to other agents' actions.

Gilbert & Troitzsch (2005) advise scholars to let potential users of the simulation model participate in the process of modelling: "Rather than merely presenting the results of simulation to potential users at the end of a project, it is becoming increasingly common for the stakeholders to become involved at all stages, from the formulation of the initial research question to the synthesis of the research conclusions" (ibid: 214). For this reason, the set-up of the model is closely aligned with the revenue management branch of a TOC. There is a central advantage of having a stakeholder firm closely involved: practitioners are a "rich source of knowledge about the phenomenon being modelled" (ibid) and therefore increase validity. As the characteristics of the empirical target are as much as possible included in the present model, this dissertation follows an empirical embeddedness strategy (cf. Boero & Squazzoni 2005).

5.2.1. Conceptual design and documentation of the model

Implementation of Prospect Theory and the reference price concept

As described in chapters 2.2.5. and 2.3., there has been extensive effort in marketing and operations research to explore the buying reaction depending on deviations to an internal reference price p_{ref}. Thus, a central conceptual issue for building a revenue simulation model for this dissertation is to adequately implement Prospect Theory and reference price learning from simulated (i. e., "actual") transactions. For this purpose, in equations 3 and 4, I basically employ the mathematical operationalisation of Prospect Theory as formulated by Nitzsch (1998):

Let $U(p)$ the utility in function of the price,
Let l_a the individual loss aversion factor,
Let $c = 2ln\left(\frac{1}{r} - 1\right)$, where r represents the extent of sensitivity of consumers to losses compared to gains; r is a sensitivity parameter 0.5<r<1. The higher r is, the faster sensitivity decreases to the function of perceived "gains" of price.
Let *norm* be a parameter that allows aligning the utility values to $U(p_{ref} - norm = 1)$ (cf. Nitzsch 1998: 629). This variable is used for generating a standardised representation of utility values according to Prospect Theory. However, *norm* can be set to any other value except 0, too.

For $p \leq p_{ref}$

$$U_{rail,car}(p) := \frac{1-e^{-c\left(\frac{p_{ref}-p}{norm}\right)}}{1-e^{-c}} \quad (3)$$

For $p > p_{ref}$

$$U_{rail,car}(p) := -l\_a\left(\frac{1-e^{-c\left(\frac{p-p_{ref}}{norm}\right)}}{1-e^{-c}}\right) \quad (4)$$

Represented graphically, the two mathematical equations show that, depending on the individual's loss aversion factor, utility of price is stronger negatively affected by a price increase than there is a positive utility assessment for a lower observed price compared to the individual reference price. Though it is precisely corresponding to the equations listed above, the mathematical operationalisation provided by Nitzsch (1998) uses slightly different parameter labels. Nitzsch (ibid) calls the point in which the expected price exactly corresponds to the observed price "BP", i. e., the reference point to which values for perceived gains and losses caused due to a different price than the expected one are calculated. If an observed price fits the reference price, the resulting utility value (v) is 0. Furthermore, Nitzsch (ibid) simply uses the label *la* for loss aversion instead of the denomination l_a outlined above. Note that the variable "p" in Nitzsch's graphic quoted below does not represent price, but the sensitivity parameter needed as an input for calculating c. For reasons of clarity, this parameter controlling the extent of an individual's sensitivity to losses is described by "r" throughout this work. Despite these differences to the notation presented above, the following graphic cited from Nitzsch's original work is a precise formalised version of Kahneman's and Tversky's conceptual drawing outlined in chapter 2.2.5. It is therefore reproduced in its original form.

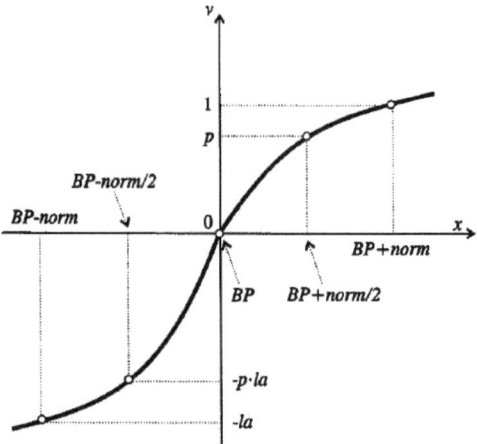

Figure 22: Mathematical operationalisation of Prospect Theory
Source: Nitzsch 1998: 629

Diller (2008: 146) provides a slightly amended operationalisation of Nitzsch's work explicitly dedicated for calculating the utility of a given price as a function of the reference price. For this purpose, the utility of price function is turned 90 degrees to the right so that price modifications can be captured on the axis of abscissae.

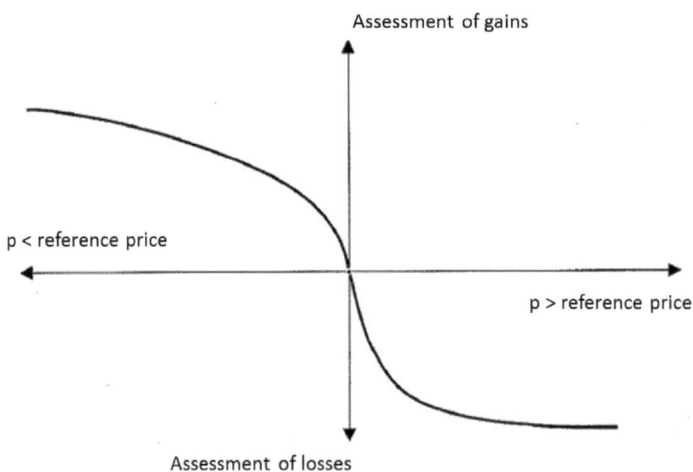

Figure 23: A utility function with price as an independent variable
Source: Diller 2008: 146, legend on axis translated by N. K.

However, though bringing the practical characteristic of having price on the x-axis, the graphical illustration cited above does not exactly correspond to the respective mathematical equations in terms of convexity and concavity.

Therefore, the utility of price function implemented in the present simulation model is shaped in the form corresponding to Nitzsch (1998). It arranges price as an independent variable with a point at which an observed price equal to the reference price separates gains and losses.

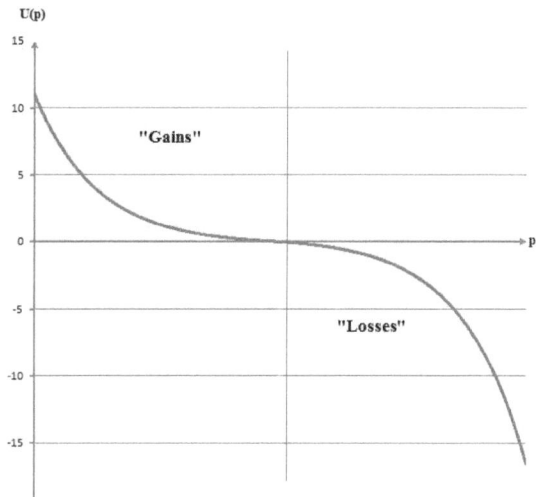

Figure 24: Operationalisation of Prospect Theory for a given set of input values
Source: based on Nitzsch 1998: 629

Assuming the speed of decrease of sensitivity to be r=0.7 as a result of testing the parameter with empirical prices and possible deviations, I follow Nitzsch's suggestion to generate a standardised representation of utility values according to Prospect Theory (cf. Nitzsch 1998: 629). Therefore, the specification of the "norm" parameter is chosen in the manner of equation 5:

$$U(p_{ref} - norm) \equiv 1 \qquad (5)$$

Drawing on the findings of reference price research described in chapter 2.2.5., particularly on Mazumdar et al. (2005), price learning is generally conceptualised in the following way:

Let α the learning parameter with $0 <= \alpha <= 1$. Then, the reference price p_{ref} is defined in equation 6 as

$$p_{ref} = p_{ref(t-1)}(1 - \alpha) + p_t \alpha \qquad (6)$$

If there can be implicit mental accounts for food, poker gains, cars and holiday houses, I interpret Thaler (1985) in the way that consumers can mentally distinguish a standard fare and a discounted one (cf. Mayhew & Winer 1992). Thus, consumers may be treating gains and losses separately for each category of fare. Full separation of all prices paid being a rather theoretical case; I introduce a control parameter for manipulating the influence of special offers to the overall reference price. This "degree of mental accounting" ranges from 0 (i.e., consumers only construct a single reference price regardless what fare they bought) to 1 (i. e., consumers perfectly compartmentalise standard fares and specials, thus, price experience with specials does not affect the reference price). Apart from this basic reference price learning, reference prices can be affected and changed by social interaction, or a between-consumer-communication process, as described below in the standardised protocol for simulation models.

Concerning the supply side of the transportation market represented in the model, there is a simplified, yet realistic, schedule of transport offers. The transport capacity of the trains is derived from the actual number of seats available on the trains. As their individual means of transport, consumer agents are equipped with cars according to statistical figures. As a basis for fare calculation, public transport offers of railways involve a base fare and a railcard fare. Firms have the option of introducing inventory-managed special fares. Additional or deviating strategies and options in pricing will be described in more detail in the experiments section.

ODD protocol

Besides the detailed outline of the implementation of Prospect Theory presented above, the description of the simulation model in this dissertation follows the guidelines developed by Grimm et al. (2006) and Grimm et al. (2010), who have developed a standard protocol for characterising agent-based simulation models. Because this standard comprises seven steps grouped into three blocks – which are model overview, design and details – it is referred to as the "ODD protocol". The ODD protocol of simulation models shall "make reading and understanding [of models] easier" (Grimm et al. 2006: 116) by considering and guiding readers' expectations. The following steps describe the nature of the present simulation model according to the ODD protocol.

Overview	Purpose
	State variables and scales
	Process overview and scheduling
Design concepts	Design concepts
Details	Initialization
	Input
	Submodels

Figure 25: Seven elements of the ODD protocol
Source: Grimm et al. 2006: 117

1. Purpose

The purpose element is generally stated in the introduction of a publication (as it is the case in the present work). Nevertheless it is a part of the ODD protocol because it informs the reader about the reasons why a complex model is needed and for what specific research the simulation method is used (cf. Grimm et al. 2006: 117). In this work, a simulation model is needed to represent pricing behaviour of transport operators and buying behaviour of consumers in the context of an individual price reaction function derived from Prospect Theory. The simulation model is used as a tool for quasi-experimentation involving the manipulation of several price parameters. It comprises a very broad scope of possible parameter settings that can be directly controlled from the model interface. This allows the model to be used as a general tool for transport firms investigating on the effects of pricing measures – ranging from a simple price increase to, for instance, a different allocation policy for special fares.

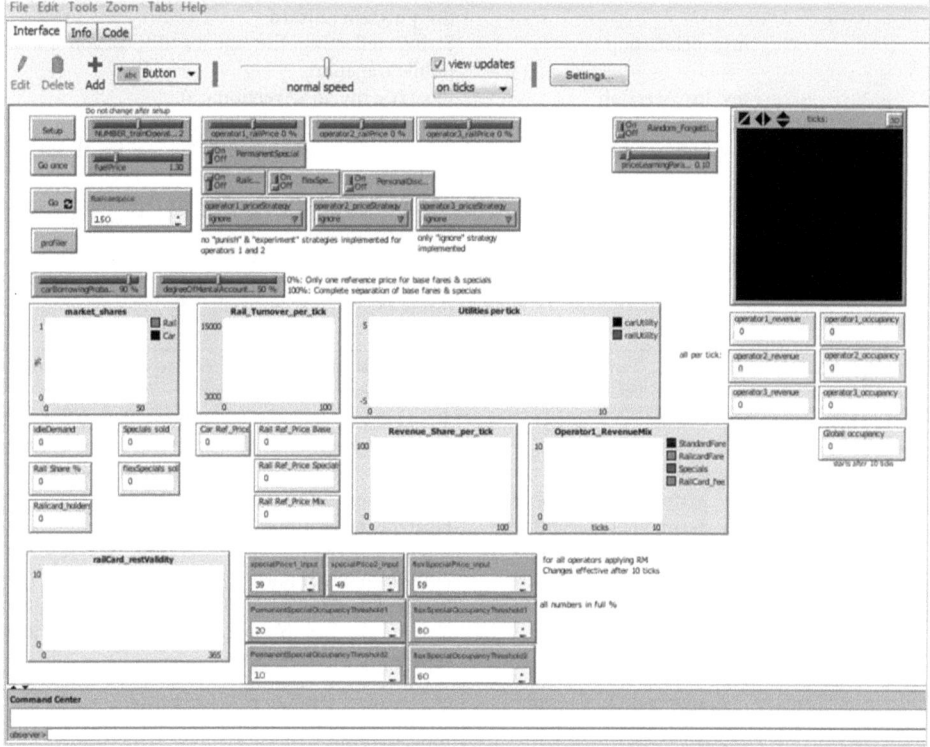

Figure 26: Screenshot of the model interface

2. State variables and scales

State variables are "low-level variables that characteri[s]e the low-level entities of the model, i. e. individuals or habitat units" (Grimm et al. 2006: 117 f.). In their update on the ODD protocol, Grimm et al. (2010) specify "that state variables can include behavio[u]ral attributes and model parameters" (ibid: 2762).

Though there is a spatial dimension of the simulation model at hand (transport occurs from cities A to B), there is no spatial unit attributed to it. Physical distance is represented by a fixed kilometre value implemented in the code. As there is a large number of low-state variables attributed to the different agents in the model, the respective variables are listed and described in a table.

Agentset	Low-scale variables	Type of variable/description
Consumers (passengers)	my_car	Boolean stating whether the consumer owns a car
	my_publicTransportAccess	Boolean
	my_age	Integer
	my_degreeOfFlexbility	Integer (%)
	my_preferenceForFlexbility	Float 0<=p<1; reflects the consumer's attitude to restrictions for the use of a ticket
	my_railcard	Boolean determining whether the consumer initially owns a railcard
	my_socioGroup	String reflecting the agent's disposition to use public transport
	my_lossAversion	Float (1 < my_lossAversion < 2)
	my_railcardValidity	integer in days from 365 to 0
	my_budget	Integer of monthly mobility budget for all variable mobility cost (e. g., petrol)
	my-links	Links to other consumer agents representing family and friends
	my_personalDiscount	Current level of loyalty discount
		Represents a discount for loyalty; integer for each full %
TrainOperators	RM	Boolean stating if the operator applies quantity-based revenue management
	my_trains	String list of trains (i. e. transport offers at a specific time, not physical trainsets) run by an operator
	my_schedule	Departure time of the trains run by the operator
	my_permanentSpecialPrice1	Float (observer input)
	my_permanentSpecialPrice2	Float (observer input)
	my_permanentSpecialQuota	Integer (observer input)
	my_flexSpecialPrice	Float (observer input)
	my_flexSpecialQuota	Integer (observer input)
	my_pricingStrategy	String; pricing behaviour toward competitors' agency
Trains	my_capacity	Integer; number of seats available in that train
	my_baseFare	Integer; cents
	my_category	Comfort category of the train
	my_travelTime	Float; speed of the train
	railcardAllowed	Boolean determining if railcards are accepted in the specific train

Table 11: Low-state variables in the model

Grimm et al. (2006: 118) recommend to subsequently describing the higher level entities, such as "a population consisting of individuals" (ibid). This is not necessary for the present model because the next higher level is the market outcome accessible to the observer. The socio-demographic groups passengers are associated with are an exception to this. Passengers in the same group share a common attitude towards public transport that directly influences the outcome of the utility calculation they effectuate in case they have the choice whether to use a car or a train. One socio-demographic fraction will never use public transport even if it were free of charge.

In a last step, scales of the model are to be defined. Scales involve the length of a time step as well as the time horizon. Generally, the length of a time step in this revenue simulation model is conceptualised as one day. This is because every train number is defined as a transport offer running from an origin to a destination once a day. An infrastructure provider would call this a train path. The time horizon of the simulation is determined by the model sensitivity analysis and practical considerations (how long will a pricing decision generally be effective before it is replaced by another one?). Basically, it is thought to capture a timeframe between approximately six months and two years, or 180 to 730 steps respectively.

3. Process overview and scheduling

This ODD element is to provide "a verbal, conceptual description of each process and its effects" (Grimm et al. 2006: 118). From their 2010 review on the use of the ODD protocol, Grimm et al. specify that processes shall only be listed instead of being described in plain text at this step (cf. Grimm et al. 2010: 2762). Again, due to the large number of functions used in the present model, processes are presented here in the form of a table. Verbal descriptions are added in case the process names are not self-explaining.

Process	Effects
Setup	

set-trainOperatorIDs
initialise-supply
  • generate-trainInventory
  • generate-trainSchedule
initialise-demand
set-trainDetails
	Creates an inventory and a schedule, attributes individual characteristics to consumers
	
	Attributes characteristics to each train

Go	
Calculate-occupancy	Get information on the least utilised trains

Set-prices
  • every 100 ticks: generate-specials
    ○ get-occupancy-list
    ○ get-occupancy-list-flex
check-railcards
  • consider-railcard
    ○ buy-railcard
Generate-demand
  • search
  • decide
    ○ if only train available
      ▪ get-prices
        ▪ get-baseFare
        ▪ get-railcard-acceptance
        ▪ get-specialRailPriceCoordinates
        ▪ get-flexSpecialRailPriceCoordinates
      ▪ book-rail
    ○ if train+car available
      ▪ calculate-utility
        ▪ get-prices
        ▪ get-travelTimeRail
	Decide to buy a railcard or to renew an expired railcard
	
	Consumers search for a transport offer; they may borrow the car of another consumer agent they are linked with.
	Consumer agents generally choose the cheapest offer they can find. According to their degree of flexibility, they search up to 3 times around their initial mobility demand time. They do not wait strategically. Passengers with a strong preference for flexible tickets will consider the standard offer as the cheapest one. As preference for flexibility is uniformly distributed, thresholds to switch from a standard price to a special or from a flexible special to a restrictive special work as probability gates. Thresholds have to be manipulated in the model code.

calculate-referencePrices	A simple calculation of the resulting reference price out of price memory according to the setting of the mental accounting slider.
align-referencePrices	All *n* ticks, interlinked individuals reveal and share their reference prices to each other. Technically, they share items of their transaction lists.

Process	Effects
calculate-personalDiscount	In case that individuals are offered a discount depending on their travel expenses, this discount is calculated here based on the amount of expenses made. For complexity reasons, this feature has only been implemented for a one-operator scenario.

move
organise-booking-data
do-clearing
observe-competitors
report-transactions
   •   get-turnover-data (for export to file)
   •   monitor-referencePrices
refill-budget	

Reporters

budget-check-rail-passed? [who_number]
budget-check-car-passed? [who_number]
get-ticket []
get-baseFare [train_number]
get-railcard-acceptance [train_number]
get-permanent-specialPrice1 [operator_identificator]
get-permanent-specialPrice2 [operator_identificator]
get-permanent-specialQuota1 [operator_identificator]
get-permanent-specialQuota2 [operator_identificator]
get-flex-specialPrice [operator_identificator]
get-flex-specialQuota [operator_identificator]
get-specialRailPriceCoordinates [train_number_day]
get-occupancy-list [operator_identificator]
get-occupancy-list-flex [operator_identificator]
get-turnover-data
get-repetition-info
get-others-referencePriceRail
get-competitors-baseFares
get-referencePriceCar
get-referencePriceRailBase
get-referencePriceRailSpecials
get-referencePriceRailMix
get-travelTimeRail (for ratio with car travel time)
get-roundFare

Table 12: The simulation model processes and their effects

The scheduling of the model's processes "deals with the order of the processes and, in turn, the order in which the state variables are updated" (Grimm et al. 2006: 118). In their 2010 version, Grimm et al. find "schedule descriptions based on pseudo-code most useful" (Grimm et al. 2010: 2762). Therefore, a short flow of one time step ("tick") of the functions and updates is provided here:

1. Transport operators set their prices. Some or all of them may generate special offers.
2. Passengers fulfil their mobility demand by choosing the offer rewarding them with the highest utility.
3. Passengers memorise their transactions and update their reference prices.
4. Modal split is calculated and turnover for all operators is cleared from the bookings records.

Congruently to the model descriptions outlined in the second element of the ODD protocol (the *state variables and scale* element), time is divided into discrete time steps. Consumer agents seek to fulfil their mobility demand (whether the demand is for the present time step or a future time step within the booking horizon) right in the time step they get affected with that demand. Consumers with a mobility demand are selected randomly and in a random order, all transactions are executed subsequently, i. e. passenger after passenger. Due to this order and to an instant inventory control for any transaction, special offers can be sold out for the last passengers while the first one selected had the opportunity to buy one. Global variables are only updated ex post after all transactions and revenue clearing have been executed. A possible extension of the model could comprise more strategically thinking passengers who may postpone their buying decision in case they expect a better price to be offered in the future (cf. Cleophas & Bartke 2011; Cleophas 2012).

4. Design concepts

Design concepts refer to a common language to communicate agent-based models that was developed for individual-based ecology models in Grimm & Railsback (2005). For the ODD protocol, Grimm et al. (2006: 118 f.) and Grimm et al. (2010: 2764 ff.) provide a checklist from which the relevant features for the present model have been selected. A general concept underlying the design of the present model is the generalisation of reference prices (cf. Monroe 1973; Kalyanaram & Winer 1995; Mazumdar et al. 2005; Popescu & Wu 2007; Nasiry & Popescu 2011). The reference price is memory-based (cf. Briesch et al. 1997) in the sense that it emerges out of the transaction experience individuals make. Another central underlying concept is the loss-averse price response suggested by Kahneman & Tversky (1979).

In the conceptual field of *emergence*, price experience made by individuals truly emerges from the individual traits of consumers and the price-setting activity manipulated by the observer (or a BehaviorSpace research setting). Individual experience in one timestep shapes buying behaviour in the following ones and thus can produce emergent buying experience made by the individual.

Learning and adaptation is the part Grimm et al. (2010: 2762) wish to be highlighted in this section of the ODD protocol. Depending on their pricing strategy, operator agents can react to a pricing decision of their competitor(s).

Moreover, every operator following the revenue management approach reacts to low occupancy of its trains by specifying trains where special offers are available. Yet, only an appropriate quota of specials will improve their fitness measured in revenue. Therefore, classical revenue simulations will use an optimiser after each tick. In the present work, Netlogo's BehaviorSearch extension is employed for finding an optimal long-term quota for specials. In sum, learning of consumer agents is somewhat limited in the present model. It is strictly focused on building a memory of transactions.

Concerning *fitness seeking*, or the *objectives* of the agents, all consumer agents follow the objective to choose the means of transport that rewards them with a maximum utility. In the theoretical case of an equal utility value being calculated, consumers prefer the more flexible use of private cars.

Due to their close relationship in this simulation model, *Sensing* and *Interaction* are grouped together. Generally, consumer agents do not know each other's reference prices, whereas operator agents continuously observe each other and know about their actual prices (this represents the empirical fact that transport fares must be easy to assess in order to find travellers). By sharing their price experience once every defined number of time steps, consumer agents learn from each other and align their price expectations. Technically, every individual calls exactly one of its links to transfer its last price experience item to the other end of the link, where it is inserted as the newest price experience. If only one side has used a railcard, the information is ignored in order to avoid unrealistic price perceptions. This process can be repeated for a defined number of loops. Individuals also interact by borrowing their cars to each other if a car is available. In the situation of a mobility need and non-availability of an own car, a passenger will ask a defined number of links (two in the present model) whether the other link-end is ready to borrow her or his car (which in reality can mean to travel together). The sharing is also reflected in an average load factor of a car of 1.5.

Stochasticity. Every timestep in the model, consumer agents stochastically get affected with a mobility need within a certain day in the booking horizon. This is because not all inhabitants of a city will have to travel at the same instant; some may plan their journey while others will face an immediate necessity to leave. As the model does not explicitly incorporate seasonal variation of demand, a fixed average travel demand fits the needs of representing the characteristics of a partial transport market. I assume a generally independent demand for mobility, but demand for a specific means of transport depends on the prices of all other means of transport (e. g., a fuel price increase will switch demand from car transit to public transport and vice versa). Thus, from a consumer agent's perspective, mobility demand is stochastic, while it is deterministic in quantity and price-dependent in allocation to operators from the observer's perspective.

Concerning *collectives*, the human network of links is randomly defined in the setup procedure and remains static over the simulation run. Conversely, an individual's characteristic of being part of a socio-demographic group has been set by the modeller based on market research data. There are no dynamics or switching between these groups.

For *observation*, revenue and traffic data generated in the simulation model are displayed with the help of various plots and monitors (see the screen-shot in the overview section of the ODD protocol). For statistically analysing the data, specified input settings and output variables are recorded in comma-separated values files with the help of Netlogo's BehaviorSpace extension.

5. Initialisation

This step in the ODD protocol deals with the following questions: "How are the environment and the individuals created at the start of a simulation run, i. e. what are the initial values of the state variables? Is initialization always the same, or was it varied among simulations? Were the initial values chosen arbitrarily or based on data?" (Grimm et al. 2006: 119).

The present revenue simulation model always uses the same initialisation procedure. Initial values have been chosen according to empirical figures (e. g., schedule, fuel price) or as a part of the experimental design (e. g., railcard on/off). Many of the settings are self-explaining (e. g., the price level change slider), therefore, only the settings with need for some explication are listed below.

The degree of mental accounting slider refers to the seminal work of Thaler (1985). It involves the possibility to activate a certain separation of reference prices for standard and special offers. If set to the position "0%", it means that consumer agents create their reference prices out of all the transactions they have made for a means of transport. If set to "100%", there is a full mental separation between prices for standard offers and for special offers. The variable car-BorrowingProbability involves the disposition of consumer agents to borrow (or effectively share) their cars if they are asked to. This sharing feature represents the fact that consumers may have access to a car although they do not own one. Every tick, consumers can ask two randomly selected members of their network whether they have a car or whether they would borrow it. If random forgetting is activated, the price memory list is manipulated by extracting parts of the memory. The (price) learning parameter represents the importance of the most recent price experience compared to the older ones. The model uses an exponential smoothing approach by setting a learning parameter alpha which reflects the importance of the previous reference price compared to the last transaction price (cf. von Massow & Hassini 2013). Though the learning parameter can be set to any value between 0 and 1, in part, reference price theorists assume it to be generally between 0.2 and 0.35 (cf. Mazumdar et al. 2005). As transactions occur very frequently in the present model, and learning takes place in a fast way, the value is determined at the minimum of this range. Special fares can take any value; there are permanent specials allowing to use a specific train only and flexSpecials that entitle a consumer to use a group of trains. The model simplifies permanent special prices into two possible amounts – a cheaper and a more expensive special fare. All special fares are subject to a seat quantity limitation. The seat allocation rules represent the empirical practice and can be set with the help of the quota variables. Quotas are derived from a train's occupancy every 5 ticks.

Interface variable	Setting/Range of Settings
Degree of Mental accounting	50%; 0-100% in steps of 10%
Railcard	on; on/off
PermanentSpecial	on; on/off
FlexSpecial	off; on/off
carBorrowingProbability	90%; 0-100% in steps of 10%
RailcardPrice	[monetary value based on empirical figure]
LearningParameter	0.2; 0<=alpha<=1
RandomForgetting	off; on/off
SpecialPrice1_input SpecialPrice2_input	[monetary value based on empirical figure]
FlexSpecialPrice_input	[monetary value based on experimental design]
Operator1_pricing_strategy Operator2_pricing_strategy	"ignore"; "ignore"/"follow" "ignore"; "ignore"/"follow"
PermanentSpecialOccupancyThreshold1 PermanentSpecialOccupancyThreshold2	[Percentaged value set according to empirical allocation practice]
PermanentSpecialSmallQuota1 PermanentSpecialSmallQuota2	[Percentaged value set according to empirical allocation practice]
PermanentSpecialLargeQuota1 PermanentSpecialLargeQuota2	[Percentaged value set according to empirical allocation practice]
FlexSpecialOccupancyThreshold1 FlexSpecialOccupancyThreshold2	[Subject to experimental design]
FlexSpecialSmallQuota FlexSpecialMediumQuota FlexSpecialLargeQuota	[Subject to experimental design]

Table 13: Initial parameter settings of the model

6. Input

There is a close link between the initialisation step and the input step of the ODD protocol, where information is provided on the input data processed in the model in order to generate the outputs. However, this section of the ODD protocol refers to external input data such as files which are used to represent the target processes. The present model uses simplified schedule data for initialisation. This external data consists of operator identification, the number of train pairs running between the end points of the line every day and the frequency of trains. For example, an input of "1, 20, 1" would mean that operator 1 runs 20 train pairs between city A and city B with an hourly frequency. For a possible extension of the model, inventory data can be attained from an external file, too. That file would simply indicate an operator identification and the number of physical train sets (or other type of transport vehicle) available for that respective operator.

7. Submodels

"Here, all submodels representing the processes listed above in 'Process overview and scales' are presented and explained in detail, including the parameteri[s]ation of the model" (Grimm et al. 2006: 119). For this detailed description of the model, Grimm et al. recommend to firstly providing a "mathematical skeleton" of the model, which is to be followed by a verbal description of the equations in the same order. Additionally, the ODD protocol requires authors to provide "justification for why and how formulations were chosen" (Grimm et al. 2010: 2766). For this dissertation, please see the sections on Prospect Theory and the validation section for more detailed information on the modelling choices made. The model processes and respective details are once again presented in the form of a table.

Model element listed in step "Process overview and scheduling"	Equations Verbal description / Literature reference
Setup	

set-trainOperatorIDs initialise-supply
  • generate-trainInventory
  • generate-trainSchedule
	All inputs represent the situation in the target market in terms of number of train pairs, frequency, and capacity of trains.

initialise-demand	Consumer agents are proportionally grouped into six sociological groups representing their affinity to public transport (source: market research of the empirical partner train operating company). Consumers CarAddicted in % Consumers Traditionalist in % Consumers Commuter in % Consumers Situative decision maker in % Consumers CalculatingYoung in % Consumers NetworkMobilists in % Consumers undefined in % 75% of the individuals get access to urban public transport (e. g., bus stop).
set-trainDetails	Trains get their specific travel time from empirical figures.
Go	

Calculate-occupancy Set-prices
  • every 100 ticks: generate-specials
    ○ get-occupancy-list
    ○ get-occupancy-list-flex
check-railcards
  • consider-railcard
    ○ buy-railcard
	Checks if a railcard is expired.
	The renewal rate is derived from empirical figures, the decision to buy a new railcard stochastically affects the same number of agents who did not renew it (subject to experiments), keeping their number stable and excluding extremely car-preferring consumer agents.

Generate-demand
  • search
  • decide
    ○ if only train available
      ▪ get-prices
        ▪ get-baseFare
        ▪ get-railcard-acceptance
        ▪ get-special-railPriceCoordinates
      ▪ book-rail
    ○ if train+car available
      ▪ calculate-utility
      ▪ get-prices
      ▪ get-travelTimeRail
	Individuals calculate their utility of price out of the fare they found for their specific mobility demand. They always chose the offer with the highest utility value for themselves.

Model element listed in step "Process overview and scheduling"	Equations Verbal description / Literature reference
	For this, Prospect Theory is operationalised according to Nitzsch 1998 (p. 630). Note: Because they follow the rule of always chosing car transport, consumer agents who are members of the "car addicted" subgroup do not effectuate the utility calculation.

- let $U(p)$ the utility of rail and car transport in function of the price (calculated *separately* for rail reference and car reference values)
- let l_a the individual loss aversion factor
- let $c=2\ln\left(\frac{1}{r}-1\right)$
- let r a sensitivity parameter $0.5<r<1$. The higher it is, the faster sensitivity decreases
- let *norm* a parameter that allows to align the utility values to U(reference price ./. norm) = 1 (however, *norm* can be set to any other value except 0, too).

For p <= reference price

$$U_{rail,car}(p) := \frac{1 - e^{-c\left(\frac{P_{ref}-P}{norm}\right)}}{1 - e^{-c}}$$

For p > reference price:

$$U_{rail,car}(p) := -l\_a\left(\frac{1 - e^{-c\left(\frac{p-p_{ref}}{norm}\right)}}{1 - e^{-c}}\right)$$

Individuals additionally account for a rail utility bonus or malus in function of the speed ratio between rail and road travel.

$$t = \frac{t_{car}}{t_{rail}}$$

If r>1, thus, the selected train is faster than car transport:

$$U_{car} := \begin{cases} \frac{U_{car}}{r}, & U_{car} > 0 \\ U_{car} - (|U_{car}| - \frac{|U_{car}|}{r}), & U_{car} < 0 \\ U_{car} - (1-r), & U_{car} = 0 \end{cases}$$

If r<1, thus, the selected train is slower than car transport:

$$U_{car} := \begin{cases} U_{car} + U_{car}(1-r), & U_{car} > 0 \\ U_{car} - \left(|U_{car}| - \frac{|U_{car}|}{r}\right), & U_{car} < 0 \\ U_{car} + (1-r), & U_{car} = 0 \end{cases}$$

The distance between the nominal prices for car and rail transport is accounted for in the following way:

Model element listed in step "Process overview and scheduling"	Equations Verbal description / Literature reference
	Let $d = p_{rail} - p_{car}$ $$U_{rail} := \begin{cases} U_{rail} - \dfrac{p_{rail}}{p_{car}} + 1, & d > 0 \\ U_{rail} + \dfrac{p_{car}}{p_{rail}} - 1, & d < 0 \end{cases}$$ The *absence* of public transport access is represented as follows: $$U_{car} := \begin{cases} 2U_{car} + 2, & U_{car} > 0 \\ U_{car} + |U_{car}| + 2, & U_{car} < 0 \\ U_{car} + 2, & U_{car} = 0 \end{cases}$$ According to the individuals' membership to a sociological group, some bonus and malus additions apply: For all agents of the "traditionalist" subgroup: $$U_{car} := \begin{cases} 1.5U_{car} + 2, & U_{car} > 0 \\ U_{car} + 0.5|U_{car}|, & U_{car} < 0 \\ U_{car} + 2, & U_{car} = 0 \end{cases}$$
calculate-referencePrices	The calculation of reference prices is based on the price experience derived from the actual transactions made (cf. Briesch et al. 1997). let α learning parameter o<=α<=1 $$p_{ref} = p_{ref(t-1)}(1 - \alpha) + p_t \alpha$$ The last item of the transaction list represents the latest price experience of an individual.
align-referencePrices	A consumer agent asks one of her/his links and transfers her/his last price experience to the other end of the link. In case only one of the two ends holds a railcard, the reference price is unchanged to avoid illogic transactions stored in the transactions lists. The loop is repeated n times.
move	Moves of trains are programmed for illustration only.
organise-booking-data do-clearing	Revenue is allocated to operators. This is possible because transactions are stored in an array including train number and transaction amount and every train is associated with a specific operator.
observe-competitors	Operator agents call the prices of a randomly selected train of eventual competitors.

Model element listed in step "Process overview and scheduling"	Equations Verbal description / Literature reference
report-transactions	
• get-turnover-data	Collects data for a possible export to file.
• monitor-referencePrices	Displays reference prices on the interface.
refill-budget	Monthly filling of the budget according to official transport statistics.

Reporters

budget-check-rail-passed?	
budget-check-car-passed?	
get-ticket	Creator of unique identificators.
get-baseFare	
get-railcard-acceptance	Determines whether a railcard discount is applicable.
get-permanent-specialPrice1	
get-permanent-specialPrice2	
get-permanent-specialQuota1	
get-permanent-specialQuota2	
get-specialRailPriceCoordinates	For internal processing only.
get-flexSpecialRailPriceCoordinates	
get-occupancy-list	
get-occupancy-list-flex	
get-turnover-data	
get-repetition-info	Probabilitistic function determining whether a process is repeated.
get-others-referencePriceRail	
get-competitors-baseFares	
get-referencePriceCar	
get-referencePriceRailBase	Calculates the weighted actual reference price for rail travel
get-referencePriceRailSpecials	according to the DegreeOfMentalAccounting setting out of
get-referencePriceRailMix	the referencePriceRail and referencePriceRailSpecials values.
get-travelTimeRail	Reports the travel time associated with a specific train for building a ration with car travel time.
get-roundFare	Rounds the fare up to full 10 cents.

Table 14: Mathematical representation and description of submodels

5.2.2. Verification

According to Gilbert & Troitzsch (2005: 25), "verification concerns whether the program is working as the researcher expects it to, [whereas] validation concerns whether the simulation is a good model of the target". Considering the literature on building a credible simulation model, in a first step, verification effort for the present simulation model is described.

Code verification

Following Rand & Rust (2011), methodological rigor in verification of a model not only implies documenting the conceptual design, but also programmatic testing of the model and running test cases and scenarios (cf. Rand & Rust 2011: 187 f.). Because of the building block approach (cf. Harrison et al. 2007) used when programming the model, unit testing and debugging was performed at every programming step. A proof of verification by formal logic did not appear relevant for the present model. Some bugs could be eliminated through observing the model's behaviour in corner cases or small sample scenarios. Moreover, the model has been presented at various doctoral colloquia and at meetings with the empirical partner firm from which I collected advice for improvements. Specific scenarios (i. e. inputs for which outputs are already known) have been performed for a limited price increase.

For Midgley et al. (2007), establishing "assurance" of agent-based models concerns verification and empirical validation. For the critical issue of software verification, they recommend to publish the code and let software experts test it. Though the code of this work can only be published in parts complemented by pseudo-code for confidentiality reasons, the full code has been made available for testing by the programming experts of the supervisory team of this dissertation.

Sensitivity analysis

To achieve a credible model, Gilbert (2008: 44 ff.) advises researchers to conduct systematic sensitivity analysis of model behaviour toward central input factors. The question is whether this step of methodological rigour is to be regarded as an initial part of model calibration or whether it rather belongs to basic testing in the verification process. I report sensitivity analysis before calibrating the model because I regard this step as a check whether the model's output variables behave in a way they are supposed to given different numbers of agents and different time horizons. Thus, sensitivity analysis is not performed to find an *adequate* extent of demand or of ticks the model needs to be run, but instead to settle some minimum requirements that have to be taken into account for generating valid data.

A major decision in interpreting the revenue results generated by the model is determining the number of timesteps the model shall be running. For this, it has to be clear on what timeframe buying reactions occur, in other words, how sensitive simulated data is to the number of steps the model is run. There is also a relationship to step 2 of the ODD protocol, where the time horizon the modeller has in mind, called the scales of the model, is described. While there can be a pragmatic decision to limit the timeframe, there is also a mathematical approach to define the minimum number of timesteps by the point where a stabilised variance is attained. Lorscheid et al. (2012: 33 f.) propose a dimensionless measure of variance for the model – the variance coefficient. The coefficient is simply calculated as the ratio of the standard variation and the mean of the output measure, as described in equation 7:

$$c_v = \frac{s}{\mu} \quad (7)$$

I use this approach to test whether the planned analytical timeframe of 180 to 730 ticks holds from a variance coefficient perspective. In order to test the model's sensitivity to that number of ticks, I chose the 2-operator-scenario in the base-case settings listed in chapter 5.3.1. Subsequently, the mean revenue per tick for every operator at a certain number of ticks was calculated. The scenario was run 100 times for every time horizon ranging from 10 steps to 2,000 steps.

	Steps									
	10	20	50	100	200	300	400	500	1,000	2,000
variance coefficient operator1_revenue	0.019	0.026	0.020	0.019	0.024	0.021	0.021	0.019	0.020	0.019
variance coefficient operator2_revenue	0.028	0.041	0.032	0.025	0.029	0.024	0.027	0.026	0.023	0.028

Table 15: Model sensitivity to ticks

As a result, the simulation model is rather stable in terms of the variance coefficient beginning at 100 model steps. At 300 steps, there can be nearly no change of the coefficient observed in what concerns operator 1's revenue, whereas there is still a slight variation of the coefficient of operator 2. Consequently, simulation experiments can be performed with any runtime larger than 300 model steps (i. e., ticks). This number represents the point where a sufficiently high level of variance stability is reached.

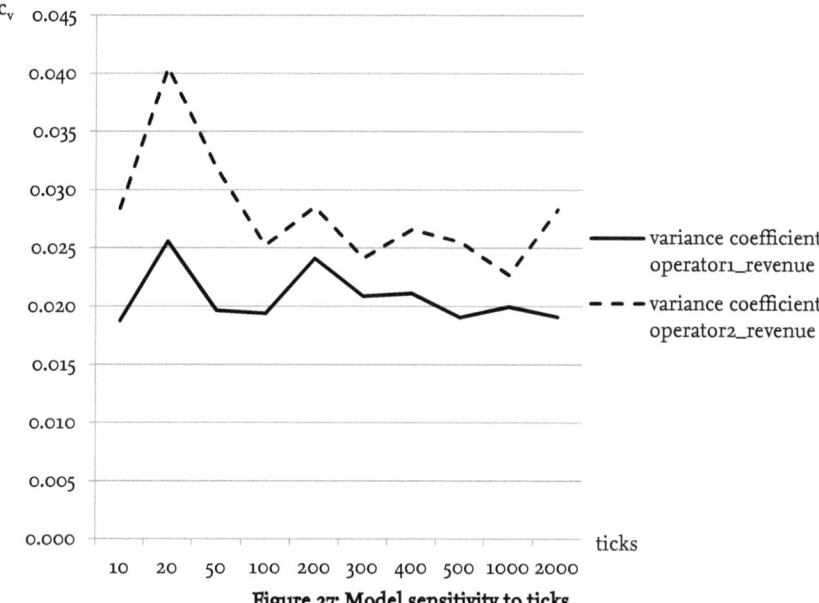

Figure 27: Model sensitivity to ticks

As the extent of total demand in the artificial transportation market determines demand for public transport operators in an almost linear manner, it does not appear fruitful to analyse sensitivity of the model to the number of agents for the simulation model at hand. However, I tested whether a multiplication of agents really leads to the expected multiplication of revenue for public transport operators and to a respectively higher observed load factor. As the graphic below computed from 50 runs per scenario shows, there is an almost linear relation between aggregated demand on the one hand and total generated revenue and occupancy across all operators on the other hand. Mean revenue is calculated out of a population range of consumers receiving a need for mobility starting with 100 and ending with 30,000 individuals.

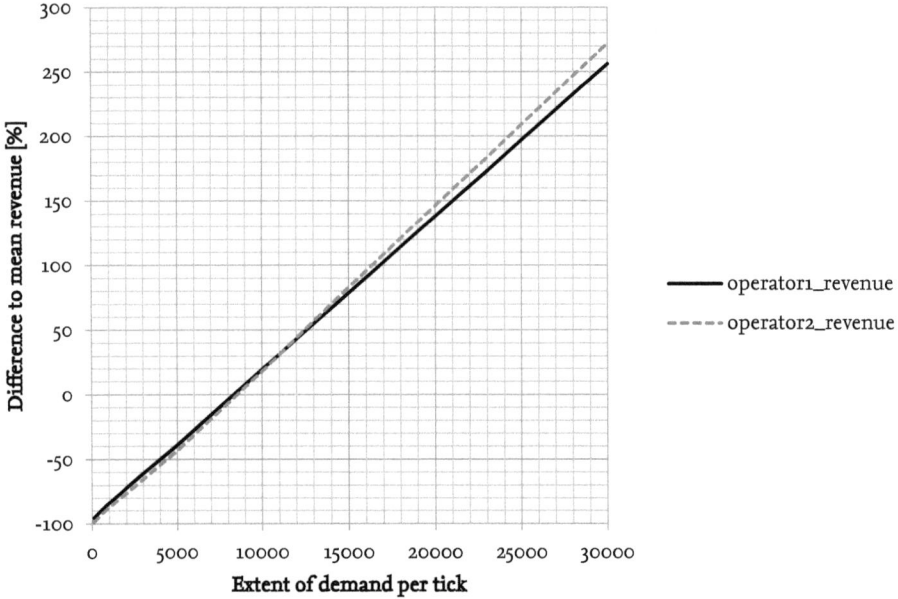

Figure 28: Testing the linearity of model output with regard to aggregated demand

The last general aspect of model sensitivity studied is the model's sensitivity to the overall population. As Netlogo has a limitation in processing very large numbers of agents, the model population cannot be scaled in a 1-to-1 manner to the target market population. Because fractions of seats cannot be processed in the RM inventory control module, the population is also not fully represented in the model in relation to agents affected with mobility demand per tick (each tick, a higher fraction of the model population than the real-world fraction is affected with mobility demand). Thus, it had to be observed how a limited population size influences revenue outputs. Despite all programming effort for efficiently running the code supported by Netlogo's profiler function, the model's processing behaviour does not allow for a population of more than 100,000 individuals if the model is run singularly on one computer. If run in parallel, according to the experiences made in this work, Netlogo can fluently process the present simulation model with a maximum population of up to 40,000 individuals and their respective links. The model setup runs more smoothly with a population of 30,000. With any population larger than 60,000 individuals, transactions in the model are performed at a very low speed and frequently cause runtime errors. In order to make sure that this restriction does not too strongly affect the performance measures, I conducted an experiment involving the effects of different population sizes combined with a fixed number of agents receiving a mobility demand every tick. The experiment was run 1,100 times in total for a population between 10,000 and 60,000 agents, the results are analysed with simple descriptive statistics.

Descriptive Statistics				
Population		Mean	Standard Deviation	N
Difference to operator1 mean revenue [%]	10,000	-2.540	2.9163	100
	15,000	-2.260	2.3932	100
	20,000	-1.833	2.3905	100
	25,000	-1.361	2.2661	100
	30,000	-.237	2.1431	100
	35,000	-.279	2.2162	100
	40,000	.686	2.2840	100
	45,000	1.010	1.8909	100
	50,000	1.652	1.6595	100
	55,000	2.244	2.1615	100
	60,000	2.924	1.6044	100
	Total	.001	2.8226	1100
Difference to operator2 mean revenue [%]	10,000	-4.403	3.4418	100
	15,000	-2.981	2.6416	100
	20,000	-2.343	2.5859	100
	25,000	-1.265	2.3386	100
	30,000	-1.097	3.1576	100
	35,000	.445	3.2802	100
	40,000	.915	2.4374	100
	45,000	1.707	2.6531	100
	50,000	2.564	1.9094	100
	55,000	2.981	2.1197	100
	60,000	3.471	2.0126	100
	Total	-.001	3.6215	1100

Table 16: Descriptives of the population size experiment

				Hypothesis			Partial Eta
Effect		Value	F	df	Error df	Sig.	Squared
Intercept	Pillai's Trace	.000	.000[b]	2.000	1088.000	1.000	.000
	Wilks' Lambda	1.000	.000[b]	2.000	1088.000	1.000	.000
	Hotelling's Trace	.000	.000[b]	2.000	1088.000	1.000	.000
	Roy's Largest Root	.000	.000[b]	2.000	1088.000	1.000	.000
Population	Pillai's Trace	.671	54.940	20.000	2178.000	.000	.335
	Wilks' Lambda	.339	78.191[b]	20.000	2176.000	.000	.418
	Hotelling's Trace	1.927	104.712	20.000	2174.000	.000	.491
	Roy's Largest Root	1.912	208.262[c]	10.000	1089.000	.000	.657

Multivariate Tests[a]

a. Design: Intercept + Population

b. Exact statistic

c. The statistic is an upper bound on F that yields a lower bound on the significance level.

Table 17: Influence of population size to revenue outcome

As expected, there is a significant effect of the overall population size on the levels of revenue because the probability for individuals in the model to be affected with a need for mobility rises with a diminishing population size they are selected from. Consequently, different dynamics of reference price learning arise. With a spread of standard deviations of 1.3119 for operator1 revenue and 1.5324 for operator2 revenue, the 11 different population sizes tested displayed a rather equal effect on the revenue generated by operator2 compared to the one of operator1.

Altogether, the standard deviation arising from the different population sizes tested remains on a tolerable level. In case the simulation model is used as a decision support tool in practice, and more extensive computing capacity is available, the overall population size can easily be increased in order to obtain more precise outputs. Displayed graphically, the spread of revenue generated by the two operators in the experiment based on standard deviation is the following:

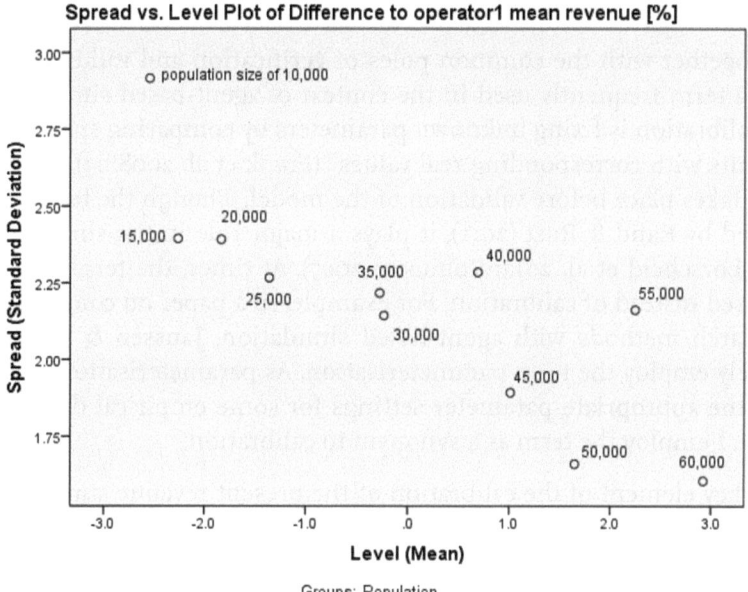

Figure 29: Spread analysis of operator1 revenue outcome for different model population sizes

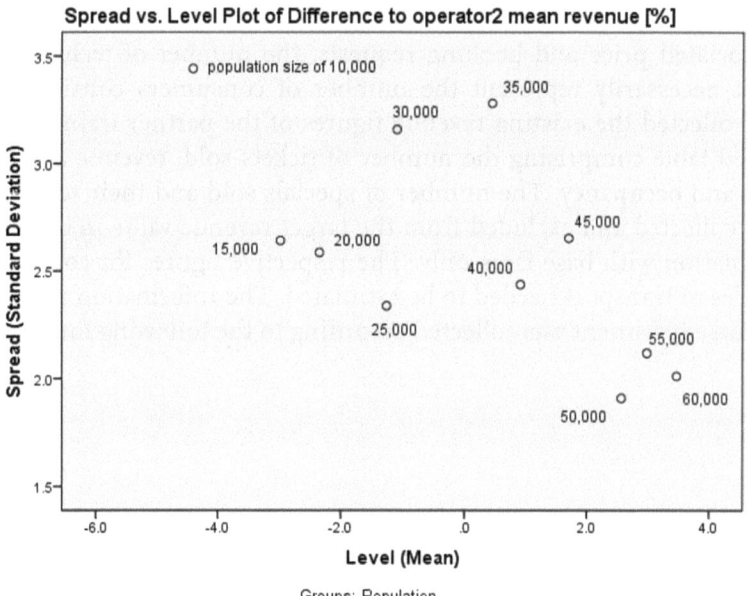

Figure 30: Spread analysis of operator2 revenue outcome for different model population sizes

5.2.3. Calibration/parameterisation

Together with the common poles of verification and validation, "calibration" is a term frequently used in the context of agent-based simulations. "The aim of calibration is fixing unknown parameters by comparing specified simulation results with corresponding real values" (Frank et al. 2008: 13), therefore, calibration takes place before validation of the model. Though the term calibration is omitted by Rand & Rust (2011), it plays a major role in the simulation literature (cf. Lorscheid et al. 2012; Robinson 2007). At times, the term parameterisation is used instead of calibration. For example, in a paper on combining empirical research methods with agent-based simulation, Janssen & Ostrom (2006) exclusively employ the term parameterisation. As parameterisation also refers to finding the appropriate parameter settings for some empirical distributions or outcome, I employ the term as a synonym to calibration.

A key element of the calibration of the present revenue simulation model is to find the appropriate figure of overall demand generated each time step that produces a revenue level similar to the empirically observed one in a known fare parameter setting. This is necessary because a specific railway has no information on the number of potential passengers who considered to travel, but did not make a booking. It can only observe its own revenue figures and conduct market research on potential demand. Even in a context of exclusive online sales with associated price and booking requests, the number of technical requests does not necessarily represent the number of consumers considering a trip. Thus, I collected the existing revenue figures of the partner train operator in a structured table comprising the number of tickets sold, revenue attributable to the line, and occupancy. The number of specials sold and their respective revenue was collected and excluded from the target revenue value in order to simulate a situation with base fares only. The respective figures for competing TOC and modes of transport needed to be estimated. The information needed for the calibration experiment was collected according to the following form:

Carrier specific parameter	Unit / description	Line A-B
Number of trains operated by operator A on the line		[empirical value]
Number of trains operated by operator B on the line		[empirical value]
Number of passengers transported by operator A		[empirical value]
Number of passengers transported by operator B		[estimation]
Average capacity of trains operated by operator A	*number of seats*	[empirical value]
Average capacity of trains operated by operator B	*number of seats*	[empirical value]
Average seat load factor of operator A	*in %*	[empirical value]
Average seat load factor of operator B	*in %*	[estimation]
Gross revenue of operator A on the line	*in € per day*	[empirical value]
Gross revenue of operator B on the line	*in € per day*	[estimation]
Number of specials sold	*number of tickets*	[empirical value]
Average revenue of specials	*in € per ticket*	[empirical value]
Availability of public transport (e. g., bus stop)	*in %*	[estimation]
Revenue mix of operator A	*in % of total revenue generated on the line*	
Base fare		[empirical value]
Railcard fare		[empirical value]
Special		[empirical value]
Revenue mix of operator B	*number of tickets*	
Base fare		[estimation]
Railcard fare		[estimation]
Special		[estimation]
Travel time	*in hh:mm*	
Operator A product 1		[empirical value]
Operator A product 2		[empirical value]
Operator B product 1		[empirical value]
Operator B product 2		[empirical value]
General parameters		**[Country]**
Railcards	*in % of the country's population*	[empirical value]
Railcards sold per day	*Number of railcards*	[empirical value]
Mobility budget per month	*in [currency]*	[estimation]

Table 18: Collection of calibration data for the target line

Calibrating demand on the existing level of revenue can only build on the base of assumptions on consumer buying behaviour. While some consumer characteristics could be implemented with the help of results from prior market research, some aspects of consumer behaviour remained unknown. For this reason, a special market research project was conducted to shed light on the reference price building and consumer preferences on the empirical target line and a second line to be examined in future research. This research focused on the prices users of public transport have in mind and their attitude towards restrictions in the use of tickets. This information is necessary to fine-tune consumer buying behaviour before calibrating the demand level to the known status quo outcome. The respective market research questionnaire was developed by the author of this dissertation in close cooperation with the partner train operating company. Because of the specific content of the questionnaire referring to the railway lines under investigation, the questions can only be displayed in a anonymised version in the appendix of this work (cf. Appendix B). Market research was performed and analysed by a professional market research service provider. It comprised 200 online interviews of passengers who have travelled either by car or public transport on one of two selected lines, one of them being the target line of this work. Data was collected between October 11th and 21st, 2013.

Structure of interviewees		
	Number of cases	Percent
Total	200	100 %
Gender		
Male	88	44.0
Female	112	56.0
Age		
16-30 years	51	25.5
31-50 years	84	42.0
51-70 years	65	32.5
Means of transport		
Individual (i. e., car)	100	50.0
Public	100	50.0
Residence		
City A	120	60.0
City B	40	20.0
City C	40	20.0
City A		
Individual	60	30.0
Public	60	30.0
City B		
Individual	20	10.0
Public	20	10.0
City C		
Individual	20	10.0
Public	20	10.0

Table 19: Structure of interviewees for calibrating the revenue simulation model

A striking result of the survey is that consumers have a relatively exact memory of the prices paid and clearly differentiate base fares and specials. Thus, reference price generation in the model can be considered adequate. A field of calibration the present market research was specifically designed for is the degree of mental accounting. As described in the ODD protocol above, the parameter can be set from non-existing to a full mental separation of standard and special fares. The relatively limited number of cases does not allow for a precise definition of the extent of mental accounting. However, consumers using public transport offers on the target line appear to perform a certain differentiation of base fares and specials, as they revealed differences between the usual price for travel on the line and eventual special offers. Reference price research on promotional offers grounded in the fast-moving consumer goods branch support a parameter avoiding the two extreme values (cf. Kalwani & Yim 1992; Kalwani et al. 1990). For this reason, the mental accounting parameter was set to a medium position of 50%. Two thirds of the respondents stated that they share the prices they paid for their tickets with their family and friends, 10% of them reported to do so after every transaction. This information is parameterised in a way that a reference price exchange occurs every 14 ticks in the model. It also had to be determined what share of (potential) passengers would be ready to switch from a base fare to more restrictive offers including innovative ones that do not yet exist on the market. Market research revealed that approximately 50% of the consumers living in the area of the target line are very reluctant to buy a ticket that can only be used on a single specified train. For an eventual semi-flexible offer, a respective threshold for consumers accepting a restriction to use a group of trains only had to be estimated. This threshold is set to 80%, meaning that a share of 20% of consumers would not choose a cheaper offer which incorporates limits in the choice of trains. A certain number of secondary parameters needed to be estimated by experts or to be taken from industry averages. For instance, the price learning parameter was set according to the pricing literature on fast-moving consumer goods. The learning parameter is set to the lowest value stated in the literature (cf. von Massow & Hassini 2013) because transactions in the simulation model occur rather often, which would lead to a very fluctuating price perception.

After the collection of internal revenue data and market research information, technically, calibration was performed through increasing the number of demand per tick while observing the revenue per tick and occupancy output parameters for all operators. This procedure is followed to find the demand level that fits to the status quo revenue level and the load factor known. For computational reasons, this revenue level is subsequently scaled at a 1:2 relation; consequently, seat capacity in the model is adapted, too. Revenue and occupancy outcomes in this calibration experiment are calculated out of the mean of 100 simulation runs for 11 different levels of demand. Please note that no actual figures of total demand per tick can be displayed for confidentiality reasons. Instead, all graphical displays of the results show the percentaged deviation to the target revenue or the target occupancy.

As they both refer to a percentaged deviance from a target value, revenue and occupancy can be combined as one in a meta-measure. Consequently, this meta-measure represents the equally weighted percentaged deviation from the target value across all generated revenue and occupancy data. The value for demand per tick to be calibrated shall be the one that comes closest to the target revenue and occupancy. As the graphic below shows, the most adequate extent of demand for representing the empirical target revenue and occupancy is an aggregated need for mobility of 15,000 agents per tick.

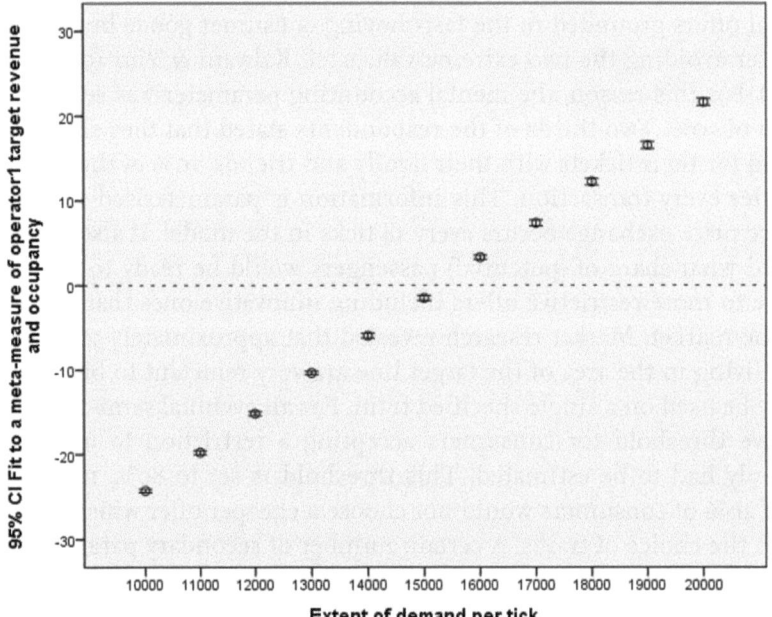

Figure 31: Calibrating demand per tick

The resulting parameter settings from this calibration constitute the base case setting for the experiments performed with the simulation model. In case the model is to be used for other lines or for a network, the same calibration procedure can be performed.

5.2.4. Validation

Once a model of the empirical target has been set up, researchers will face the question whether or not their model really represents the research problem and how far it can be applied to real situations. Once simulated data is generated, it is open how this data corresponds to the target problem under investigation. This section summarises the general possibilities for validating a model discussed in the literature and describes the measures taken for validating the present revenue simulation model.

Cleophas (2012: 242) points out that "[] the usefulness and success of simulations are determined by their credibility". Marks (2007) addresses two central problems of validating simulation models: complexity arising with the degrees of freedom in a high-dimensional space and the difficulty to prove necessity of model outputs. For agent-based simulations, already in 1994, Axtell & Epstein identified a necessity of "understanding our creations" (ibid: title). They name four different levels of agent-based model performance and analysis, ranging from a simple visualisation of reality up to full quantitative accordance of the model to empirical microstructures:

Level	Description
0	The model is a *caricature* of reality, as established through the use of simple graphical devices (e. g., allowing visualisation of agent motion)
1	The model is in *qualitative agreement with empirical macro-structures*, as established by plotting, say, distributional properties of the agent population
2	The model produces *quantitative agreement with empirical macro-structures*, as established through on-board statistical estimation routines
3	The model exhibits *quantitative agreement with empirical micro-structures*, as determined from cross-sectional and longitudinal analysis of the agent population

Table 20: Performance levels of an agent-based model
Source: adopted from Axtell & Epstein 1994: 29, emphasis in the original

As outlined above, generally, Gilbert & Troitzsch (2005: 214) recommend to closely integrating stakeholders into the process of building and validating a simulation model. Law (2007) adopts a similar view on validation as a processual issue ending up in credibility of a model. He defines validation as the "*process of determining whether a simulation model is an accurate representation of the system, for the particular objectives of the study*" (Law 2007: 244, emphasis in the original). Thus, validation comes into play at different stages of model development and is always connected to the purpose of gaining acceptance by stakeholders. Law (ibid: 245) illustrates that view with an example of the verification and validation process in the U.S. Department of Defence. In this thinking, validation is not limited to be the final part of methodological rigour in modelling, but is also embedded in the very beginning of the modelling process when assumptions on the real-world target are collected.

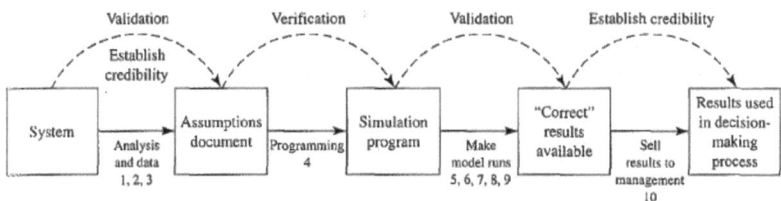

Figure 32: Validation in the process of establishing model credibility
Source: Law 2007: 245

Rand & Rust (2011) describe two basic steps for assuring methodological rigor in agent-based simulations: verification and empirical validation of the model. "Verification determines how well the implemented model corresponds to the conceptual model" (ibid: 187), whereas validation "is the process of determining how well the implemented model corresponds to reality" (ibid: 188). For rigorously validating the model, they propose four steps beginning with a micro and macro-face validation followed by an empirical input and output validation. I apply this procedure for demonstrating validation effort made in this work.

Steps 1 and 2: Micro-face and macro-face validation

The first two steps of validation are concerned with micro-structures and the macro-outcomes of a model. Micro-face validation means "the process of making sure that the mechanisms and properties of the model 'on face' correspond to real-world mechanisms and properties" (Rand & Rust 2011: 188). Similar to the definition provided by North & Macal (2007), Rand & Rust (2011) refer to macro-face validation as "the process of showing that the aggregate patterns of the model 'on face' correspond to real-world patterns" (ibid: 188). Concerning these two forms of validation, Rand & Rust list the following questions to be answered:

- "[D]o the individuals in the model correspond in a meaningful way to real-world individuals?
- Do the actions possessed by a consumer agent correspond to real-world actions?
- Do consumer agents possess a realistic amount of information? [...]
- [D]o the dynamics of the model correspond to the real world?
- Does the theory of the model correspond to our current understanding of the real world?" (Rand & Rust 2011: 188, bullet points added)

As the present model represents a very simplified transportation market, the relationship between the model and real-world transactions can be considered valid if the key practices performed by market participants are equally performed in the model. Individuals in the present model collect fare information if they are affected with demand for travel. They compare the offers available to them and chose the one rewarding them with the highest utility value. Utility is re-calculated at every instance based on personal preferences and varying reference prices. This basic procedure corresponds to the assumption of choice of means of transport employed in operations research and in the transportation industry. Thus, I assume correspondence of the model in the flow of logic leading from mobility demand to purchasing transactions of means of public transport or the use of individual cars as a means of transport. Concerning aggregate patterns of behaviour, basic empirically observable dynamics such as an increased market share for public transport at a fuel price increase are replicated by the model outputs. As Prospect Theory has been validated in a large number of research projects (cf. chapter 2.2.5.), I can assume correspondence of the theoretical assumptions of the model to actual consumer behaviour.

Step 3 Empirical input validation

"Empirical input validation [...] is the process of ascertaining that the data being input into the model are accurate and bear a correspondence to the real world" (Rand & Rust 2011: 189). Because Rand & Rust do not use the word calibration, this "validation" activity has a close relationship to the model calibration (or parameterisation) described above. If real-world parameters are known and do not have to be defined with the help of other known parameters, I consider the use of real-world inputs as an elementary modelling activity to be performed with the very first set-up steps. The overall research design of this modelling project and the building block programming approach constantly involved empirical input data and market research activities. That is why empirical input validation is not fulfilled in a separate step, but achieved as an underlying principle throughout the modelling activities.

Step 4 Empirical output validation

This step is the most important part of testing a model's validity. It "involves showing that the output of the implemented model corresponds to the real world" (Rand & Rust 2011: 189). If simulation models are to be used as a support in business decision making, they definitely need to undergo such process of validation (cf. North & Macal 2007, chapter 11, p. 1).

The empirical partner train operator played a major role in validating the simulation design and results. There were continuous meetings at which the author of the present work and representatives of the TOC's revenue management and marketing branches discussed the assumptions underlying the model, the functions to be implemented and the inputs needed for experimenting with the simulator. Once data was gathered, meetings were held on interpreting and challenging the findings. However, Marks's argument concerning the difficulties with the practical use of economic simulation models remains in place: although simulations can provide evidence for the existence of a phenomenon and allow explaining it, "it is difficult for simulation to derive the necessary conditions for models to exhibit the specific behaviour" (Marks 2007: 285). In line with the methodological restrictions of simulations described in chapter 5.1., model outputs cannot be finally considered valid before the same experiment is performed in the real-world and this real-world experiment proves to be consistent with the predictions derived from the simulated data.

5.3. Experiments

Once the revenue simulation model was set up according to the guidelines of methodological rigor, it could be used for generating experimental revenue data. Subsequently, this data was analysed statistically. The present section describes the details of the experiments performed and interprets their results.

5.3.1. Procedure of experimental data analysis

The experiments performed generally follow the principles outlined by Wu & Hamada (2009) and Lorscheid et al. (2012). Technically, experiments were effectuated in a high-performance computing environment provided by Freie Universität Berlin using Netlogo's headless mode. In accordance with the guidelines of Lorscheid et al. (2012), experiments did not generally follow a "one manipulation at a time" approach, but were performed in a factorial design where appropriate. Nevertheless, computational and practical limitations made it necessary to split up fields of experiments. This is because Netlogo is limited to a one-node mode, in other words, experiments cannot be computed on different nodes at a time. This limits the maximum number of runs that can be performed in parallel. As also described in chapter 5.1.3., there are two general types of experiments available for Netlogo simulation models:

1. BehaviorSpace
2. BehaviorSearch

BehaviorSpace experiments involve a controlled variation of selected parameters and the measuring of the outcome. I use the BehaviorSpace extension already included in Netlogo 5.0.3. BehaviorSearch is a separate programme requiring an existing Netlogo model and performing a genetic algorithm search on a previously defined scope of parameters as well as a unique fitness measurement variable. Genetic algorithms are an optimisation approach with roots in biology (cf. Davis et al. 2007). This experimental approach is particularly useful for finding (locally) revenue-optimal allocation rules for special offers and for finding prices of newly introduced fare products[36].

All changes in the parameters of the experiments described below refer to the initialisation parameters of the ODD protocol (cf. chapter 5.2.1.) which have been calibrated as outlined in chapter 5.2.3. as a reference, or base case. This base case setting comprises the following parameters:

---

[36] See chapter 5.1.3. for more details on this Netlogo extension.

Parameter (interface variable)	Base setting
`Operator 1-3 railprice`	[representing no change to the empirical base fare in a "o" position]
`Degree of mental accounting`	50%
`Railcard`	on; on/off
`PermanentSpecial`	on; on/off
`FlexSpecial`	off; on/off
`carBorrowingProbability`	90%; 0-100% in steps of 10%
`RailcardPrice`	[monetary value based on empirical situation]
`Learning parameter`	0.2; 0<=alpha<=1
`Random forgetting`	off; on/off
`SpecialPrice1_input` `SpecialPrice2_input`	[monetary value based on empirical situation]
`FlexSpecialPrice_input`	[monetary value based on experimental design]
`Operator1_pricing_strategy` `Operator2_pricing_strategy`	"ignore"; "ignore"/"follow" "ignore"; "ignore"/"follow"
`PermanentSpecialOccupancyThreshold1` `PermanentSpecialOccupancyThreshold2`	[Percentaged value set according to empirical allocation practice]
`PermanentSpecialSmallQuota1` `PermanentSpecialSmallQuota2`	[Percentaged value set according to empirical allocation practice]
`PermanentSpecialLargeQuota1` `PermanentSpecialLargeQuota2`	[Percentaged value set according to empirical allocation practice]
`FlexSpecialOccupancyThreshold1` `FlexSpecialOccupancyThreshold2`	[Subject to experimental design]
`FlexSpecialSmallQuota` `FlexSpecialMediumQuota` `FlexSpecialLargeQuota`	[Subject to experimental design]

Table 21: Base case scenario

Hence, the term "base case" corresponds to the initial parameter settings listed above. However, though the results of the experiments can be compared to average revenue generated with the base case settings, they do not necessarily need a base case to refer to. The following experiments form independent units within which outcomes of different parameter settings are compared. Thus, the experiments are studies in the context of absence or of specific parameter values contrasting other settings of parameters which, in some cases, can correspond to the base case setting. Every possible combination of parameters in an experiment constitutes a *scenario*. The effects of price manipulations across all scenarios of an experiment are analysed statistically. Troitzsch (2014) argues that a simple significance test on the manipulation is not enough for analysing simulation results, mainly because the sample size can be arbitrarily increased. Instead, revenue results in this project are analysed in their nominal effect on revenue as well as the statistical effect size that can be attributed to them. This factorial design approach is more appropriate than a simple significance test because the effect size estimation helps to identify the extent of explained variance excluding noise and the effects of other parameters that have been varied in the experiment. The timeframe chosen for all experiments is 465 ticks, corresponding to an initial price and occupancy learning time of 100 ticks plus one year of operations.

5.3.2. Scenario 1: General price variations

In the first experiment, effects of base fare variations performed by the focal train operator are observed under the existence of inventory-managed special fares (permanent specials) for less utilised trains. The manipulation consists in activating and deactivating those fares. Additionally, outcomes are measured for the competitor train operator choosing an "ignore" or "follow" strategy towards the incumbent operator's pricing behaviour. If the competitor follows, it keeps its base fare exactly on a 50% level of the one of the focal TOC. The experiment involves the manipulation of the parameters listed below:

Manipulation	Settings
operator1_railprice (change of operator1 base fare)	-40 % to +40% in 2% steps
Introduction of the price change	after 100, 200, and 300 ticks
operator2_pricing_strategy	"ignore", "follow"
permanentSpecial (availability of inventory-managed special fares)	true, false

Table 22: Manipulations in the first experiment

Due to the broad scope of parameters changed, the experiment comprises a very large number of 24,600 runs (calculated out of $41 \times 3 \times 2 \times 2 = 492$ combinatorial options repeated 50 times each). Data is collected with the Netlogo BehaviorSpace tool.

As expected, a later introduction of the other manipulations either after 200 or 300 ticks does not lead to non-linear outcomes. Reference prices adapt in any of the settings. Therefore, "introduction of the price change" is excluded from the effect size analysis outlined below. The effects of the remaining manipulations were computed as follows:

Tests of Between-Subjects Effects						
Dependent Variable:	difference to operator1 mean revenue					
Source	Type III Sum of Squares	df	Mean Square	F	Sig.	Partial Eta Squared
Corrected Model	2751804.007[a]	163	16882.233	1041.602	0.000	.874
Intercept	1.015E-06	1	1.015E-06	.000	1.000	.000
operator2_pricing_strategy	505.004	1	505.004	31.158	.000	.001
permanentSpecial	10230.678	1	10230.678	631.214	.000	.025
operator1_railprice	2698695.768	40	67467.394	4162.613	0.000	.872
operator2_pricing_strategy * permanent_special	848.139	1	848.139	52.329	.000	.002
operator2_pricing_strategy * operator1_railprice_change	26157.324	40	653.933	40.346	.000	.062
permanent_special * operator1_railprice_change	3680.225	40	92.006	5.677	.000	.009
operator2_pricing_strategy * permanent_special * operator1_railprice_change	11686.869	40	292.172	18.026	.000	.029
Error	396057.299	24436	16.208			
Total	3147861.306	24600				
Corrected Total	3147861.306	24599				
a. R Squared = .874 (Adjusted R Squared = .873)						

Table 23: Effect size analysis of experiment 1

The factors of the first experiment account for most of the variance in the model measures, leaving less than 13% of the variance unexplained. As the key regulating instrument for a railway's pricing, base fare changes alone show a strong effect with an 87% share of the explained variance. With a 2.5% share of the explained variance, there is a relatively limited but significant effect of introducing special fares.

Differing from conventional elasticity analysis based on a quantity reaction of demand, the model's output data is used for determining the influence of base fare variations to generated revenue per tick. This can be observed as revenue elasticity to price. For base fare *increases* at a runtime of one simulated year, the model shows a revenue elasticity of ca. 0.5. This model behaviour illustrated in the graphic below means that for every full percent of base fare increase, revenue per tick generated by operator1 increases by 0.5%. However, for price reductions, two thresholds can be identified around which revenue increases despite lower prices. These appear because of traffic attained from car transportation once rail fares reach the level determined by out-of-pocket cost for car transit. Due to this effect, revenue elasticity for base fare *decreases* emerged to be ca. -0.4, meaning that a full percent of base fare reduction results to -0.4 percent of revenue per tick from the perspective of operator1. Thus, in absolute values, revenue elasticity is slightly lower for price reductions.

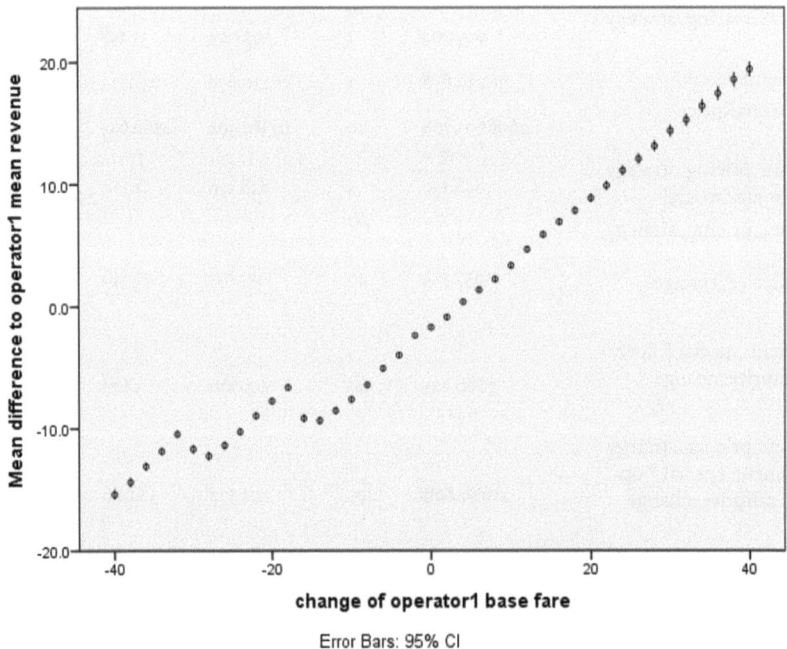

Figure 33: Observed revenue elasticity to price manipulations

The simulated data shows that across the experiment as a whole, introducing inventory-managed special offers does not necessarily increase revenue within the set of prices taken from empirical practice. According to the graphical display below, the confidence interval of a situation with activated specials is clearly lower than the one without those offers. This is due to the fact that the model does not measure advertising effects or newly induced traffic. However, as the further output analysis below shows, there are situations in which RM effectively increases revenue within the scope of the model, especially in case operator2 ignores base fare decisions made by operator1 (cf. figure 36). The subsequent experiment elaborates on the question whether there are other situations in which RM pays off given the same prices associated to the special offers.

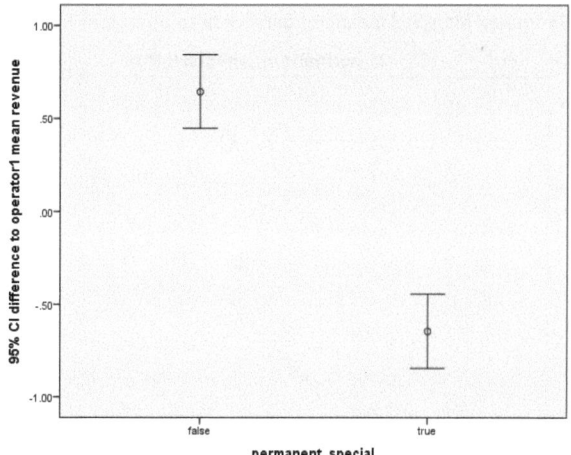

Figure 34: Overall revenue effect of introducing permanent specials

As the 95% confidence intervals are smaller than 1% in revenue scope, they are neglected for the following more detailed parts of the experiment analysis. Across all measures, a competitor who ignores the focal operator's pricing decisions appears marginally more beneficial (from the incumbent's point of view) than a one following the focal operator's price steps. Meanwhile, if the focal operator applies quantity-based RM, there is a stronger advantage of an "ignoring" competitor if it comes to price cuts. This observation is reflected in the following two graphs, one illustrating the revenue outcome across all base fare manipulations and one particularly focusing on a 30% base fare decrease. Please note that if there is a line between two binary or discrete values of a parameter, this is for the purpose of illustration only. The connecting line must not be interpreted as a representation of intermediate values of that parameter[37].

---

[37] This note equally applies for all following experiments.

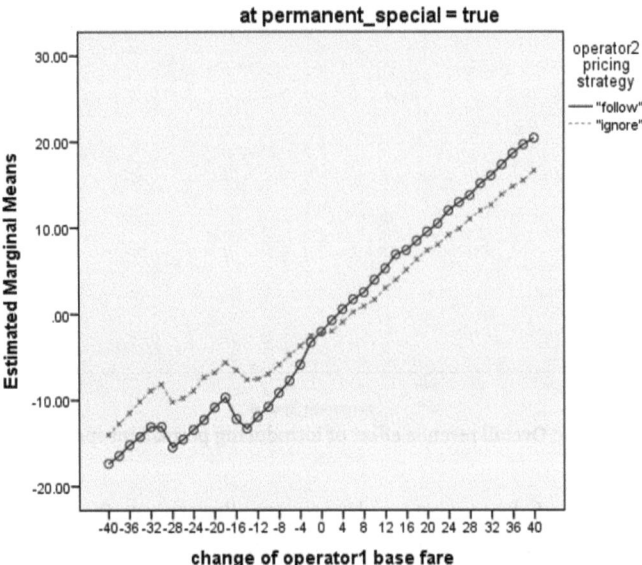

Figure 35: Revenue depending on competitor's pricing strategy

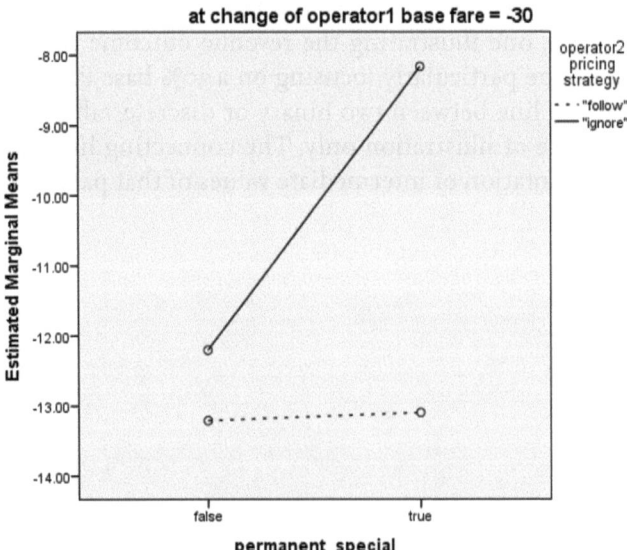

Figure 36: A situation in which RM increases revenue

One interaction effect sticks out: the factors of operator1 deciding on a change of its base fare occurring *together* with the strategy adopted by operator2 amount to a 6.2% share of the explained model output variance. From this it can be concluded that in practice, revenue estimations should be sub-grouped by expectations about competitor reactions.

5.3.3. Scenario 2: Finding the optimal allocation of seat quotas

In this BehaviorSearch experiment, different numerical combinations for allocating special fare seat quotas are tested in order to find an at least locally optimal one. The allocation policy implemented in the simulation model involves a decision rule for creating either a small or a large seat quota for permanent specials. The large quota applies for very weak occupancy rates of a train, while the small quota is dedicated to increase the load factor of moderately occupied trains. Differing from the empirical situation, the model only contains two generic price levels.

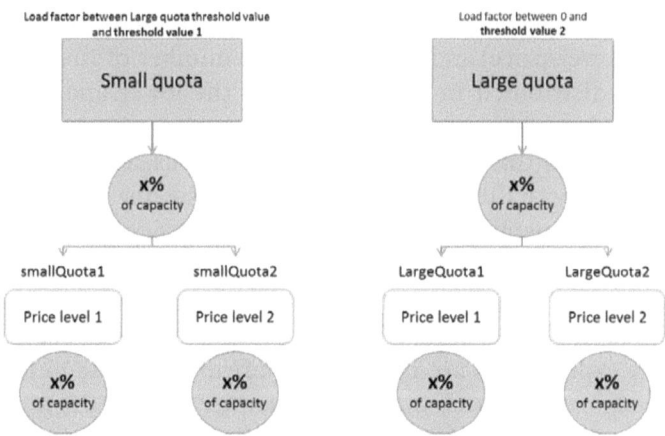

Figure 37: Seat allocation rules for discounted offers

The quota is updated every five ticks according to the simulated occupancy rate of the train. In contrast to the real-world situation, the artificial reservation system in the model allows to measure the exact occupancy of each train at any tick. With the maximising goal of finding the highest mean across 465 model steps in a sample of five runs and one best checking replicate, the number of model runs is limited to a total of 5,000. The following range of parameters is specified for the search:

Variable	Parameter space searched
permanentSpecialSmallQuota1	0-5% (in steps of 0.5%)
permanentSpecialLargeQuota1	2.5-10% (in steps of 0.5%)
permanentSpecialSmallQuota2	0-5% (in steps of 0.5%)
permanentSpecialLargeQuota2	2.5-10% (in steps of 0.5%)

Table 24: Parameter search of experiment 2

Though the fitness landscape in the graphic below does not show extreme fluctuation of revenue outcomes, compared to the status quo allocation of quotas, a higher fitness value can be reached. For confidentiality reasons, the fitness values and parts of the quotas cannot be displayed in absolute numbers. The highest fitness value found in the specific search of this experiment is generated by tripling the seat capacity for the small quota (distributed almost equally to the higher and the lower price) and increaseing the number of the seat capacity for the large quota (distributed in a 3:1 manner to the lower and higher price) by 25%.

The meaning of this result is that ceteris paribus, a superior level of revenue can be reached with differing seat quotas than the ones currently used. This finding clearly demonstrates the potential of inventory-managed fares to increase revenue. The revenue gain for operator 1 corresponds to a ca. 4% increase compared to the revenue generated in a simulation with the current empirical settings outlined in chapter 5.3.1.. If these findings were to be used for RM decisions, auxiliary experiments are needed to confirm them due to the limitations of the genetic algorithm search method (cf. chapter 6.2.). As the model only uses two generic price levels, RM tools need to replicate the tests for a set of actual prices used for cheap advance-purchase offers. The genetic algorithm search procedure could additionally include the prices for these specials as an extension.

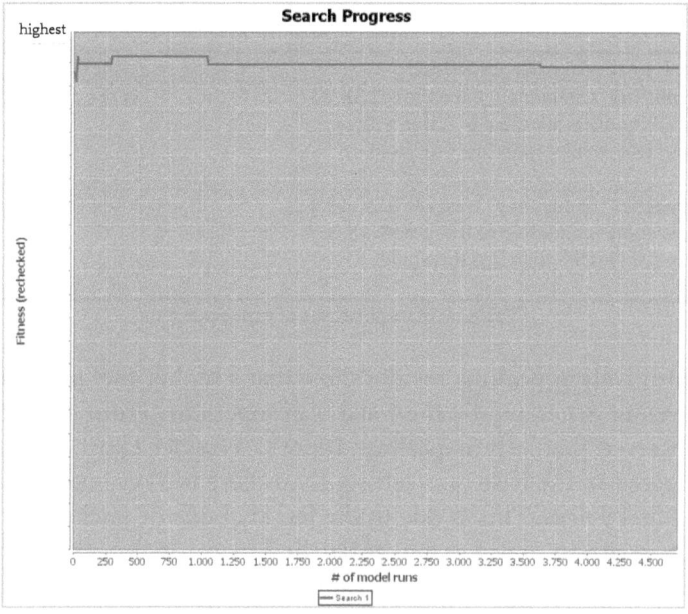

Figure 38: Fitness landscape of experiment 2 at 4,500 runs

5.3.4. Scenario 3: Fuel price shocks and rail operators' reaction

The third scenario focuses on fuel price variations and possible price reactions performed by railway operators. In case a temporarily stable change of
the fuel price level occurs, it appears in the first instance useful to react by a
change in the allocation of special fares. As mentioned above, permanent specials are allocated according to the average occupancy of a train. Depending on
this occupancy value, a small or a large quota can be allocated following the
scheme listed in chapter 5.3.3..

The experiment at hand involves the variation of these allocation rules in
different fuel price contexts with a focus on the threshold aspects. Thus, there is
no direct manipulation in terms of the quantity of seats allocated, but in the rule
for allocating the large or the small quota only. The fuel price parameter is initially set at 1.30 currency units. The fuel price change gets effective after 100 ticks
in the simulation model. Thus, if the parameter remains at 1.30 per litre, no fuel
price change occurs. Please note that the fuel price is to be understood as a me-
ta-parameter representing all combustibles available on the market. Using
Netlogo's BehaviorSpace extension, the experiment is run 50 times for each
combination of figures amounting to 1,800 simulation runs (calculated out of
$3 \times 4 \times 3 = 36$ combinatorial options repeated 50 times each).

Manipulation	Settings
Fuel price (in currency format)	1.10; 1.30; 1.50
Permanent_special_occupancy_threshold1 (in %) (a small specials quota is allocated to trains with an occupancy rate smaller than this threshold)	75 / 80 / 85 / 90
Permanent_special_occupancy_threshold2 (in %) (a large specials quota is allocated to trains with an oc- cupancy rate smaller than this threshold)	50 / 60 / 70

Table 25: Manipulations of experiment 3

As intuitively appealing, results show that a higher fuel price positively influences revenue generated by the focal train operator. From the graphic below
it can be observed that, ceteris paribus, there is a higher effect of a fuel price increase compared to the base case setting than there is a revenue decrease in case
of a drop of fuel prices. This is due to the fact that out-of-pocket cost of car travel is already relatively low for the initial fuel price of 1.30, thus, an additional
drop in that cost does not lead to a strong demand reaction. Furthermore, simulation results show that there is no one-to-one relation between a percentaged
increase in fuel prices and revenue increase for a public transport provider.

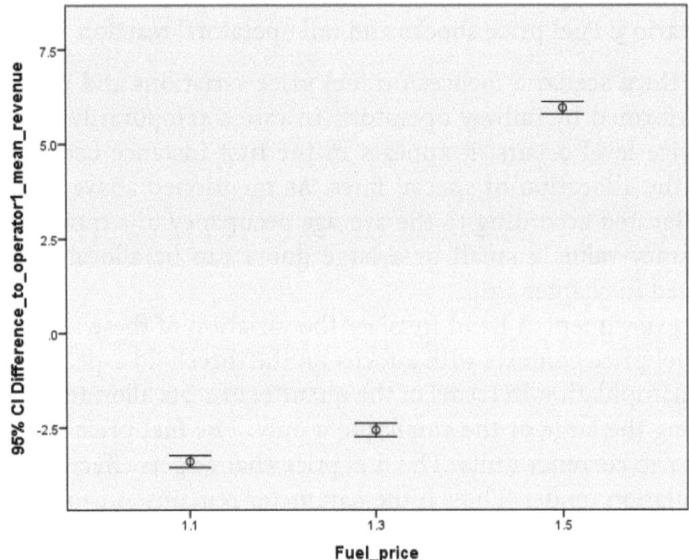

Figure 39: Fuel price changes and revenue

However, as shown in the table below, there is almost no variance in the
statistical model explained by the manipulation of threshold values for allocating either a small or large quota of permanent specials to trains. Only the second threshold value accounts for a significant, but small, share of the explained

variance. All the rest is explained by the fuel price factor. There are two reasons explaining this observation: first, relatively few trains hit the high average occupancy rate defined in the model, thus, any allocation decision for these few trains is limited in effect. Second, there is a very small amount of seats allocated to the special prices in the current allocation practice of the partner train operator. Despite this relative null result, the learning of this experiment is that effectively, it is the allocated quantity of seats which is most important for an effective reaction to fuel price changes. Leaving the allocated number of seats stable and only manipulating occupancy threshold values does not appear promising for a fuel price reaction strategy.

Tests of Between-Subjects Effects						
Dependent Variable:	Difference_to_ operator1_mean_ revenue					
Source	Type III Sum of Squares	df	Mean Square	F	Sig.	Partial Eta Squared
Corrected Model	32242.660[a]	35	921.219	211.969	0.000	.808
Intercept	5,556E-06	1	5,556E-06	.000	.999	.000
PermanentSpecialOccupancyThreshold2	35.670	2	17.835	4.104	.017	.005
PermanentSpecialOccupancyThreshold1	2.323	3	.774	.178	.911	.000
Fuel_price	32080.024	2	16040.012	3690.74	0.000	.807
PermanentSpecialOccupancyThreshold2 * PermanentSpecialOccupancyThreshold1	23.376	6	3.896	.896	.496	.003
PermanentSpecialOccupancyThreshold2 * Fuel_price	27.428	4	6.857	1.578	.178	.004
PermanentSpecialOccupancyThreshold1 * Fuel_price	21.705	6	3.617	.832	.545	.003
PermanentSpecialOccupancyThreshold2 * PermanentSpecialOccupancyThreshold1 * Fuel_price	52.134	12	4.345	1.000	.447	.007
Error	7666.370	1764	4.346			
Total	39909.030	1800				
Corrected Total	39909.030	1799				
a. R Squared = .808 (Adjusted R Squared = .804)						

Table 26: Statistical analysis of experiment 3

5.3.5. Scenario 4: Market maturation

The fourth scenario involves the hypothetic removal from the market of the railcard allowing for a 50% discount on the base fare. As compensation, the incumbent railway operator would cut the price for base fare travel. The competing operator has the option to keep its price level unchanged or to adopt its base fare to the new prices of operator1. Data generated in the experiment is collected with Netlogo's BehaviorSpace extension. Measuring the two operators' revenue and occupancy, the simulation model is run 50 times for each setting in a two-competitor-scenario, totalling to 2,200 runs (calculated out of $2 \times 11 \times 2 = 44$ combinatorial options repeated 50 times each).

Manipulation	Settings
railcard	true/false
operator1_base_fare_change	-50% to +/- 0% in 5% steps
operator2_pricing_strategy	"ignore"/ "follow"

Table 27: Manipulations of experiment 4

The manipulations listed above proved to have a significant effect on both operators' revenue and occupancy measures; additionally, the extent of explained variance is very high across all measures. From the high partial load factors, it can be interpreted that there is considerable interaction between the two suppliers' pricing policy and demand reaction.

Tests of Between-Subjects Effects							
Source		Type III Sum of Squares	df	Mean Square	F	Sig.	Partial Eta Sqd.
Corrected Model	operator1 mean revenue	392189.831[a]	43	9120.694	2263.111	0.000	.978
	operator1 mean occupancy	39695.502[b]	43	923.151	1255.126	0.000	.962
	operator2 mean revenue	503214.750[c]	43	11702.669	1299.901	0.000	.963
	operator2 mean occupancy	379990.394[d]	43	8836.986	5582.831	0.000	.991
Intercept	operator1 mean revenue	3.682E-06	1	3.682E-06	.000	.999	.000
	operator1 mean occupancy	2.841E-05	1	2.841E-05	.000	.995	.000
	operator2 mean revenue	2.909E-06	1	2.909E-06	.000	1.000	.000
	operator2 mean occupancy	2.618E-05	1	2.618E-05	.000	.997	.000
operator2_pricing_strategy	operator1 mean revenue	725.915	1	725.915	180.121	.000	.077
	operator1 mean occupancy	2.488	1	2.488	3.383	.066	.002
	operator2 mean revenue	47803.403	1	47803.403	5309.875	0.000	.711
	operator2 mean occupancy	19492.682	1	19492.682	12314.645	0.000	.851
operator1_baseFare_change	operator1 mean revenue	302748.300	10	30274.830	7512.073	0.000	.972
	operator1 mean occupancy	8338.185	10	833.818	1133.668	0.000	.840
	operator2 mean revenue	176567.988	10	17656.799	1961.270	0.000	.901
	operator2 mean occupancy	4623.448	10	462.345	292.090	0.000	.575
railcard	operator1 mean revenue	23474.506	1	23474.506	5824.713	0.000	.730
	operator1 mean occupancy	12320.946	1	12320.946	16751.685	0.000	.886
	operator2 mean revenue	644.591	1	644.591	71.599	.000	.032
	operator2 mean occupancy	84004.000	1	84004.00	53070.143	0.000	.961
operator2_pricing_strategy * opertor1_baseFare_change	operator1 mean revenue	2076.615	10	207.661	51.527	.000	.193
	operator1 mean occupancy	307.495	10	30.750	41.807	.000	.162
	operator2 mean revenue	25975.022	10	2597.502	288.524	0.000	.572
	operator2 mean occupancy	66265.135	10	6626.514	4186.349	0.000	.951
operator2_pricing_strategy * railcard	operator1 mean revenue	25553.934	1	25553.934	6340.680	0.000	.746
	operator1 mean occupancy	3917.238	1	3917.238	5325.917	0.000	.712
	operator2 mean revenue	65814.165	1	65814.165	7310.463	0.000	.772
	operator2 mean occupancy	147373.217	1	147373.217	93104.111	0.000	.977
operator1_baseFare_change * railcard	operator1 mean revenue	34846.550	10	3484.655	864.645	0.000	.800
	operator1 mean occupancy	14451.023	10	1445.102	1964.776	0.000	.901
	operator2 mean revenue	118496.165	10	11849.617	1316.224	0.000	.859
	operator2 mean occupancy	35584.469	10	3558.447	2248.075	0.000	.912
operator2_pricing_strategy *operator1_baseFare_change * railcard	operator1 mean revenue	2764.010	10	276.401	68.583	.000	.241
	operator1 mean occupancy	358.127	10	35.813	48.691	.000	.184
	operator2 mean revenue	67913.416	10	6791.342	754.364	0.000	.778
	operator2 mean occupancy	22647.444	10	2264.744	1430.769	0.000	.869
Error	operator1 mean revenue	8689.018	2156	4.030			
	operator1 mean occupancy	1585.748	2156	.736			
	operator2 mean revenue	19409.897	2156	9.003			
	operator2 mean occupancy	3412.703	2156	1.583			
Total	operator1 mean revenue	400878.848	2200				
	operator1 mean occupancy	41281.250	2200				
	operator2 mean revenue	522624.647	2200				
	operator2 mean occupancy	383403.097	2200				
Corrected Total	operator1 mean revenue	400878.848	2199				
	operator1 mean occupancy	41281.250	2199				
	operator2 mean revenue	522624.647	2199				
	operator2 mean occupancy	383403.097	2199				

a. R Squared = .978 (Adjusted R Squared = .978)
b. R Squared = .962 (Adjusted R Squared = .961)
c. R Squared = .963 (Adjusted R Squared = .962)
d. R Squared = .991 (Adjusted R Squared = .991)

Table 28: Effect analysis of experiment 4

The graphical display of selected groups of measures shows that there are revenue-neutral combinations of parameters. Depending on the competitive strategy chosen by operator2, the focal train operator can realise a stable level of revenue if it decides a withdrawal of the railcard together with a base fare decrease. If the competitor ignores the decision made by the incumbent instead of following it, a chosen decrease can lead to an estimated revenue loss of 10% compared to the mean of all measures in which railcard availability is switched off. Thus, the competitor's reaction to the incumbents' pricing decision strongly influences the revenue outcome. Compared to the average revenue generated with the basic settings outlined in chapter 5.3.1. (which are also one of the combinatorial options in the present experiment), an equal revenue level is reached within a base fare decrease of 20-25% in case the competitor follows, and within 10-15% of decrease in case the competitor ignores the decision. Being very small in the output measure of revenue, confidence intervals are not displayed here in order to increase visibility.

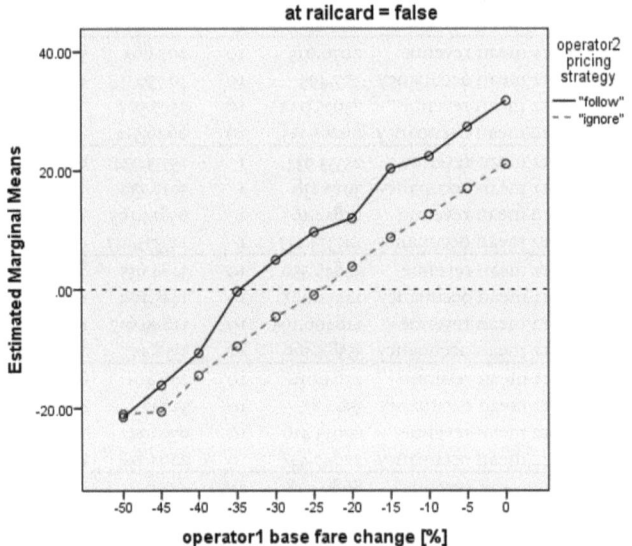

Figure 40: Levels of equal revenue level depending on competitor strategy

Concerning occupancy figures, the expectation that lower fares increase occupancy is generally confirmed. A withdrawal of the railcard constituting an indirect price increase, the mean differences mostly result from a comparison of a railcard vs. non-railcard situation. The larger the base fare decrease, the higher is the variance of the occupancy outcome for operator1. Ignoring the pricing decisions made by operator1 means a precisely estimable occupancy loss for the competing operator2, whereas adopting a "follow" strategy leads to a larger confidence interval. For operator 2, the interval is floating around +10% occupancy

compared to the mean value across all settings for a price cut decided by opera-
tor1 in the range of 30 to 50%.

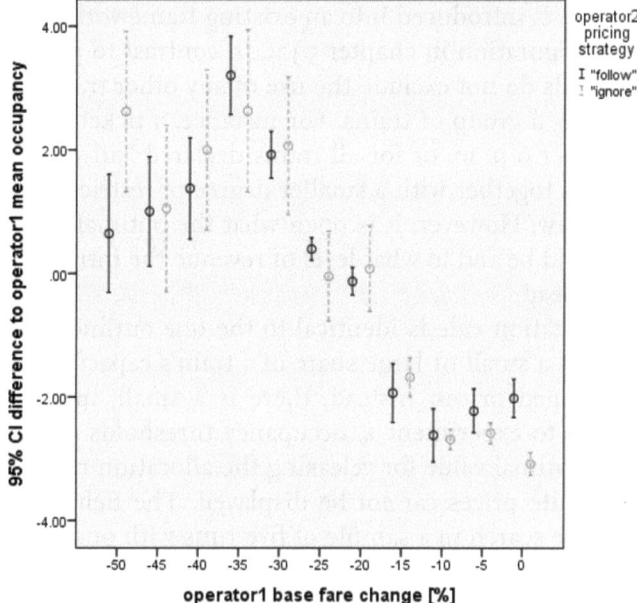

Figure 41: Occupancy effects for operator1

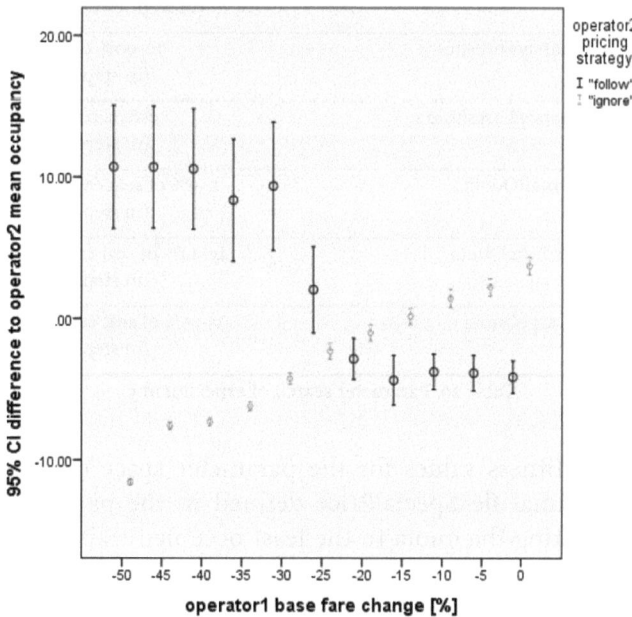

Figure 42: Occupancy effects for operator2

5.3.6. Scenario 5: Introduction of a new fare product

In this fifth experiment, a new offer named *flexSpecial* with a respective price and seat quota is introduced into an existing framework of fares represented by the base configuration in chapter 5.3.1.. In contrast to permanent specials, semi-flexible specials do not exclude the use of any other train than the booked one, but allow using a group of trains. For instance, a ticket can be valid for all trains departing after 6 p. m. or for all trains declared "off-peak" ones. Thus, a flexible special goes together with a smaller degree of restrictions from the consumer's point of view. However, it is open what the optimal price for this kind of special offer would be and to what level of revenue the introduction of a semi-flexible fare would lead.

The seat allocation rule is identical to the one outlined in experiment 2, except that not only a small or large share of a train's capacity is made available for inventory-managed prices. Instead, there is a small, medium and a large quota. Also similar to experiment 2, occupancy thresholds are manipulated in order to find the optimal value for releasing the allocation rule. For confidentiality reasons, absolute prices cannot be displayed. The BehaviorSearch experiment comprises one search in a sample of five runs with one best fitness checking replicate. The total number of model runs for the search is limited to 5,000.

Variable	Parameter space tested
flexSpecialPrice	[0-x currency units] (in steps of 1 currency unit)
flexSpecialOccupancyThreshold1	70-90% occupancy (in steps of 5%)
flexSpecialOccupancyThreshold2	0-65% occupancy (in steps of 5%)
flexSpecialSmallQuota	0-9% of seat capacity of a train (in steps of 1%)
flexSpecialMediumQuota	10-14% of seat capacity of a train (in steps of 1%)
flexSpecialLargeQuota	15-25% of seat capacity of a train (in steps of 1%)

Table 29: Parameter search of experiment 5

The highest fitness values for the parameter space described above are found for the maximal flexSpecialPrice defined in the parameter scope. The threshold for allocating the quota to the least occupied trains was assessed 0%, thus, the allocation of a large quota is irrelevant. In the optimal combination of parameters, trains are only equipped with a "medium" or small quota, the small one being allocated at an occupancy rate of more than 85%. For the medium quota, which in fact, represented the large quota, 12% of a train's capacity are to be allocated, while 8% of the seats shall be made available for the small quota.

This fitness plateau reached after 2,000 simulation runs is represented in the graphic below.

In practice, the identified parameter combination means that the nominal price for a semi-flexible ticket offer should be tested by market research in its upper bound, relatively close to the base fare price. If a flexSpecial is to be introduced, results of the present experiment suggest that a quota of those fares should be available in all trains including the ones running at peak times. A division into small, medium and large quotas appears unnecessary. Instead, the current practice of allocating a small and large quota can be maintained.

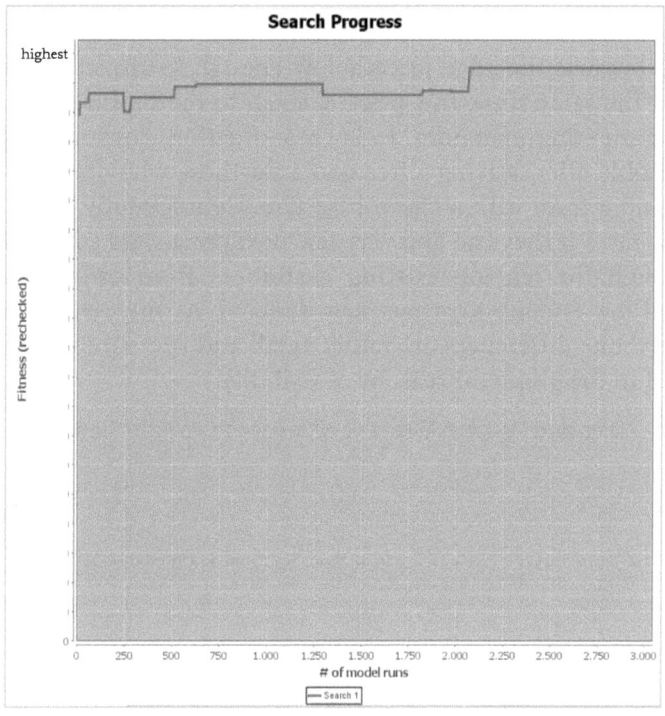

Figure 43: Fitness landscape of experiment 5 at 3,000 runs

Robustness check

As the experiment is performed with the assumption that 80% of consumers would generally accept semi-flexible restrictions (or technically, not ignore them if they were cheaper than non-restrictive offers), the robustness of the findings towards other shares of the population willing to buy the new offer is to be tested.

For different possible thresholds of consumers accepting the semi-flex restriction, revenue outcome is tested for a range of prices between the price for a restrictive ticket (accepted by 10% of the population) and the base fare. The BehaviorSpace experiment comprises 3,850 runs including 50 runs per combination. This number is calculated out of the combinatorial options of 10 prices and 7 thresholds with activated flexSpecials ($10 \times 7 \times 50 = 3{,}500$) plus 350 runs with deactivated flexSpecials. For confidentiality reasons, the nominal prices used cannot be displayed. The small quota was set 5%, the medium quota 10%, and the large quota 15% of the seat capacity of a train. The small quota is allocated for trains with an average occupancy of more than 85%, while the medium quota applied for occupancies between 60 and 85%. As the graphic below shows, there are situations in which a defined price for the introduced flexSpecial is too low to maintain a mean level of revenue. However, there is a similar pattern across all variations.

The drop of revenue between the lowest and the second lowest flexSpecial price occurs because the edge price is low enough to attract demand from car transport. At the same time, this price is equal to the railcard fare and the base fare of the competing operator2. In such a situation, consumer agents choose the more flexible offer, leaving a free quota for those who do not own a railcard or did not find a train with a cheap base fare. Consequently, individuals rather choose those fares if they can and very few flexSpecials are sold. Thus, the price is high enough for fencing existing customers from cannibalising existing products and low enough to attract new demand. As the 95% confidence intervals of the revenue differences are rather small and very rarely overlapping, they are neglected in the graph for reasons of visibility.

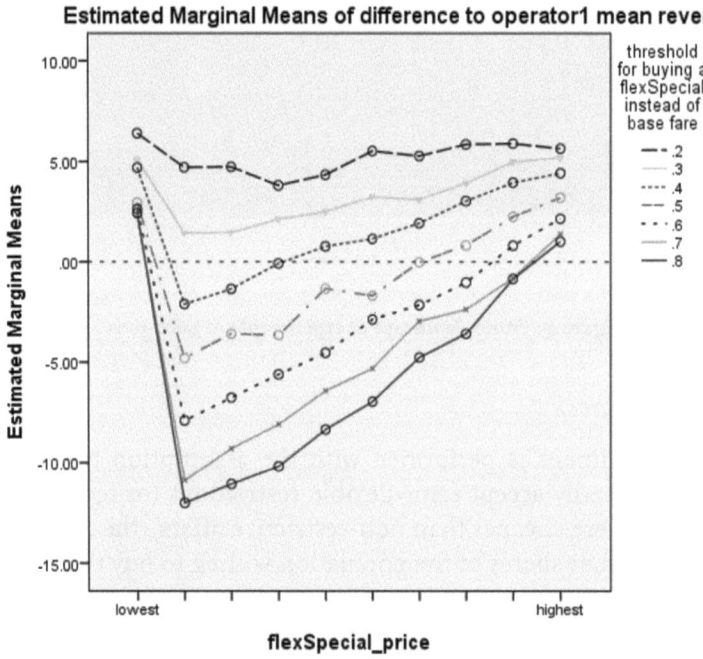

Figure 44: Demand potential and different prices for flexSpecials

5.3.7. Scenario 6: Searching for the optimal railcard price

The sixth experiment made with the simulation model at hand involves the following question: Given a consumer price experience in the status quo, what would be the long-term effect of a significant change of the price for purchasing a railcard? A railcard is assumed to allow for a 50% base fare reduction and needs to be purchased in advance. Railcard fees are credited to the incumbent operator's revenue account at the moment of purchase. Consumers holding a railcard are automatically offered the reduced price until their card expires. If a railcard expires, consumers can decide whether to renew it or not. This situation is modelled probabilistically based on the actual renewal rate. Every tick, a number of randomly selected consumer agents buys a new railcard. As there is no reference price for the railcard implemented, I rely on expert estimations and assume an elasticity of demand of -0.75 effective on the group of agents who purchase a newly issued railcard only. Consumers simply renewing their old railcard are charged the increased price.

Manipulation	Settings
railcard_price_change (increase in %)	0-55 (in steps of 5)

Table 30: Manipulations of experiment 6

The empirical railcard price being rather beneficial from a consumer point of view, the effects of a price change are only measured for price increases. The experiment comprises 100 runs per combinatorial option, that is $12 \times 100 = 1,200$ runs. The statistical results for this number of runs are listed below:

Tests of Between-Subjects Effects						
Dependent Variable:	difference to operator1 mean revenue					
Source	Type III Sum of Squares	df	Mean Square	F	Sig.	Partial Eta Squared
Corrected Model	127.259[a]	11	11.569	2.551	.003	.023
Intercept	0.000	1	0.000	0.000	1.000	0.000
railcard_price_change	127.259	11	11.569	2.551	.003	.023
Error	5386.900	1188	4.534			
Total	5514.158	1200				
Corrected Total	5514.158	1199				
a. R Squared = .023 (Adjusted R Squared = .014)						

Table 31: Statistical analysis of experiment 6

Variance explained by the railcard price factor is 2.3%, which is in line with the relatively limited number of expiring railcards that are not automatically renewed. Though the confidence intervals do not allow for definitive conclusions on the optimal railcard price, according to the graphic below, two bottom points appear at a moderate price increase of 10% and at a 35% price increase. If a change of the railcard price is to be considered, a more detailed analysis of the parameter space can help to avoid these observed revenue gaps.

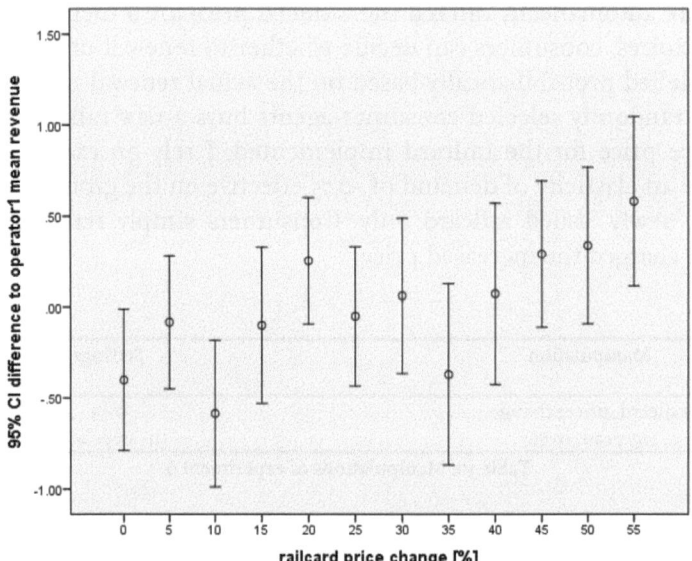

Figure 45: Revenue effects of different railcard prices

5.3.8. Scenario 7: Personal discount

In this experiment, the effects of introducing a personal discount regime instead of a railcard are analysed. Due to the complexity of clearing processes necessary, the personal discount option has only been implemented in the simulation model code for a 1-operator-scenario. Thus, the generated data does not include competitor revenue effects. The experiment consists in introducing a gradual personal discount depending on the revenue an individual generates during a period of 365 ticks. The personal discount level is updated every 5 ticks and is calculated according to the following scheme:

Purchase volume (in currency units)	Discount level
0-100	5%
101-150	15%
151-200	25%
201-250	35%
251-300	45%
301-350	55%
more than 350	60%

Table 32: Personal discount calculation scheme

The scenario is run 200 times in the base case configuration of chapter 5.3.1. with deactivated personal discount against 200 runs with the personal discount activated. As a difference to most of the prior experiments, occupancy figures are collected in addition to the revenue generated by the single railway operator.

Manipulation	Settings
personal_discount (activated after 100 ticks)	true/false

Table 33: Manipulations of experiment 7

The manipulation explains nearly all the revenue variance in the model and 28.5% of the variance in occupancy. Though the introduction of a personal discount in the scope described above leads to an average increase of occupancy amounting to ca. 1%, it can be observed that the discount leads to a nearly 28% decrease of revenue compared to the base case. At the same time, an activated personal discount reduces the confidence interval of the occupancy outcome. From this it can be concluded that personal discounts are appropriate as an element for controlling the load factor of a defined inventory. However, more research is needed to reduce the negative revenue effects arising with this benefit. The details of the statistical analysis of the experiment as well as the graphical revenue and occupancy plots are outlined below.

		Type III Sum of Squares	df	Mean Square	F	Sig.	Partial Eta Squared
		Tests of Between-Subjects Effects					
Corrected Model	difference to operator1 mean revenue	105398.921[a]	1	105398.92	28614.15	0.000	.986
	difference to operator1 mean occupancy	441.441[b]	1	441.441	158.573	.000	.285
Intercept	difference to operator1 mean revenue	0.000	1	0.000	0.000	1.000	0.000
	difference to operator1 mean occupancy	2.250E-06	1	2.250E-06	.000	.999	.000
personal_discount	difference to operator1 mean revenue	105398.921	1	105398.92	28614.15	0.000	.986
	difference to operator1 mean occupancy	441.441	1	441.441	158.57	.000	.285
Error	difference to operator1 mean revenue	1466.014	398	3.683			
	difference to operator1 mean occupancy	1107.968	398	2.784			
Total	difference to operator1 mean revenue	106864.936	400				
	difference to operator1 mean occupancy	1549.409	400				
Corrected Total	difference to operator1 mean revenue	106864.936	399				
	difference to operator1 mean occupancy	1549.409	399				

a. R Squared = .986 (Adjusted R Squared = .986)

b. R Squared = .285 (Adjusted R Squared = .283)

Table 34: Effect analysis of experiment 7

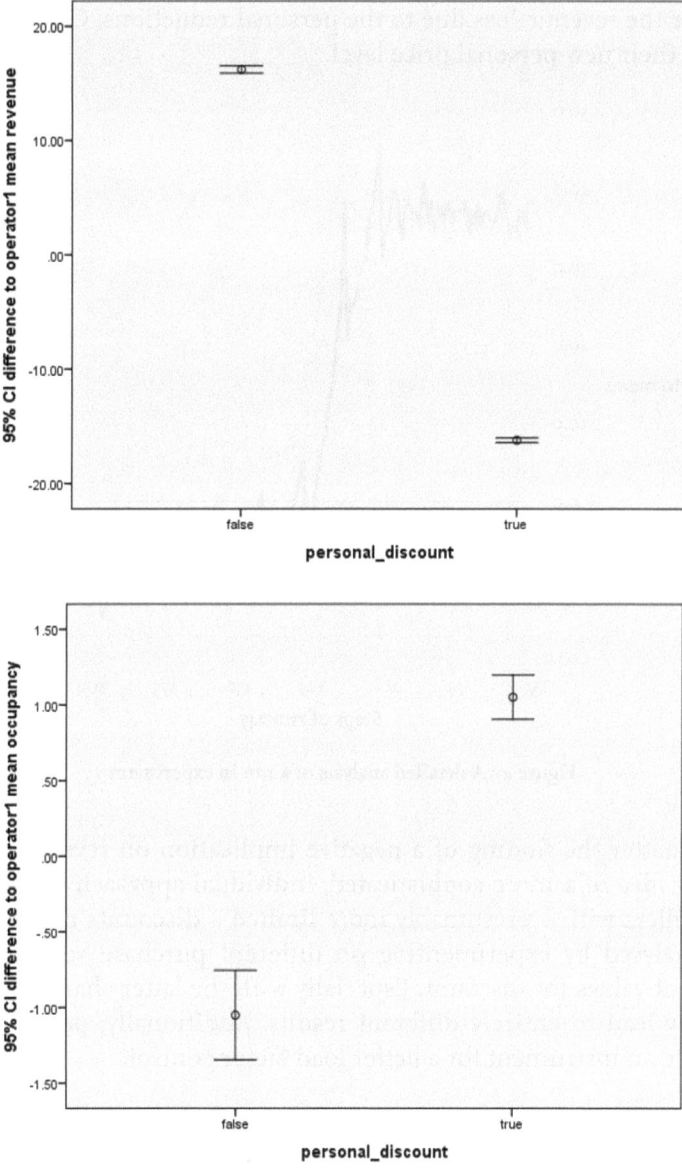

Figure 46: Profile plots of experiment 7

Despite the severe decrease of average revenue for the parameter setting under investigation, there is a characteristic observable pattern of revenue per tick. This pattern is illustrated here with the example of run no. 247 involving an activated personal discount. It is especially interesting that there is an initial increase of revenue due to the removal of the railcard, which is quickly succeeded by a gradual decline. Thus, the stimulating effect of increased discounts cannot compensate the revenue loss due to the personal reductions. Consumers rapidly get used to their new personal price level.

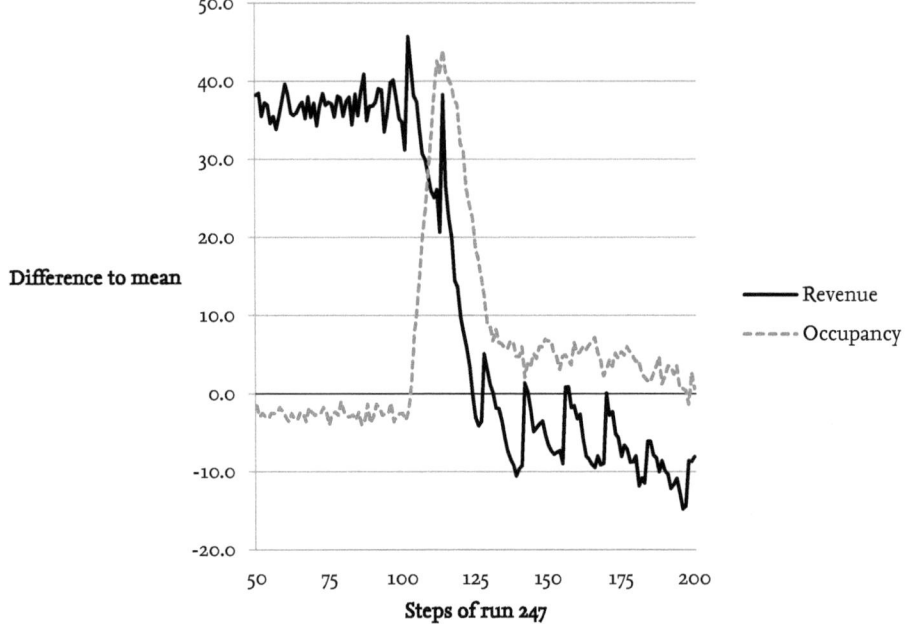

Figure 47: A detailed analysis of a run in experiment 7

No matter the finding of a negative implication on revenue in the given setting, the idea of a more sophisticated, individual approach of rewarding frequent travellers with – presumably more limited – discounts may be more profoundly analysed by experimenting on different purchase volume thresholds and different values for discount. Especially with the latter changes, these experiments may lead to entirely different results. Additionally, personal discounts may provide an instrument for a better load factor control.

5.4. Summary and interpretation of simulation results

The simulation model set up for this thesis is used for artificial price experiments. Selected price parameters are manipulated and respective revenue and occupancy outputs are measured in compact scenarios. Additionally, for target-oriented searches, realistic parameter spaces are tested for optimal combinations with the help of a genetic algorithm search.

Drawing from the first scenario on base fare variation, two revenue gaps are identified from which both a price increase and decrease is beneficial in terms of revenue generation for the focal railway operator. Across the entire base fare variations tested, simulation results of the first experiment show that revenue generated by the focal train operator on the target line exhibits a revenue elasticity to base fare variations of ca. -0.4 for base fare reductions and of ca. 0.5 for increases. In some areas of the base fare variations performed by operator1, revenue strongly depends on the decision of the competitor operator whether to follow or not. Furthermore, experiments within the artificial market of the model show that there are opportunities for increasing revenue that can be realised by re-thinking the role of a railcard, whereas a more radical step of introducing a personal level of discount appears to be disadvantageous. Nominal outcomes of a railcard removal combined with a base fare decrease strongly depend on the competitor's decision either to ignore the measure or to follow with its base fare level. As shown in a BehaviorSearch experiment, revenue can be significantly increased by an extension of the volume of seats allocated for special prices. This means that there is large potential for the focal TOC in optimising reduced fare allocation.

Activating special offers for trains with a low load factor within the framework of the current allocation rules significantly increases occupancy. However, additional demand-stimulating effects other than price are needed to keep the theoretical level of revenue superior to a situation without those specials. As experiments do not test the effects of a full switch to inventory-managed fares, it cannot be determined whether quantity-based RM is generally beneficial or not. There are situations in which classical RM increases revenue, but many in which average revenue slumps. Even through varying possible consumer preferences, there are no settings found in which the introduction of a semi-flexible fare leads to an increase of revenue compared to the base case.

Comparing the different scenarios amongst each other, all have in common that decisions of one operator significantly affect revenue and occupancy figures of the other. The experimental results advise managers of train operating companies to avoid fixed or purchase volume-dependent discounts and to closely observe intramodal competitors. The latter is due to the observation that effects of a controlled variation of the base fare level strongly depend on the rationale of intramodal competitors. Even though it is introduced alongside with railway-typical base fares, quantity-based RM can help to increase an incumbent TOC's revenue, but not necessarily does in all experimental cases.

6. Discussion

This thesis reconstructs the long-term development of passenger railway pricing in Europe from the perspective of path dependence theory. It identifies a rigidified pattern in the field of fare-setting among major European train operators – the standard railway tariff based on distance. Building on this finding, this work subsequently elaborates on possible efficient alternatives to an inert fare structure in the case of a specific train operator facing intramodal competition. For searching for a promising alternative to distance fares, a revenue simulation model including a broad scope of parameters is built. The model can be calibrated for differing market settings, making it a universal tool for performing "serious games" experiments in pricing, i. e., experiments for analysing the effects of pricing decisions made by transport operators or by external actors.

Similar to many qualitative studies made in the beginning of a research process, path constitution analysis is used in the present work to gain an understanding of the field and of the mechanisms that triggered the emergence of a commercial standard in passenger transportation by rail. This understanding is crucial for recognising a situation of path dependence and for developing a strategy to break that path. Hence, this methodological part of the study provides a general framework for the strategic analysis to be performed by any railway undertaking. In case managers find evidence for path dependence in their organisations, a strategic response to that situation requires to address the self-reinforcing mechanisms acting as drivers and stabilisers of that path.

The second methodological approach – a revenue simulation model that can be calibrated for a large set of purposes – represents a business intelligence tool needed for performing a detailed quantitative analysis of the extent of inefficiency caused by the lock-in situation. What makes that complementary method to path reconstruction indispensable is that the payoff of alternative options can be precisely quantified. Though the sheer set-up of a simulation tool is certainly not sufficient for implementing path-breaking change by an incumbent railway, it represents a necessary instrument for preparing a strategic move. It allows for calculating the effects of different options under investigation in an environment that comes close to real market processes. For this reason, the qualitative and the modelling part of this dissertation form a complementing pair of methods chosen with the aim of identifying a path and providing a basic toolset for path-breaking action.

6.1. Theoretical and practical implications of the findings

This work contributes to the theory of path dependence by underpinning it with a detailed description of a non-technical case. The history of railway fare policy sheds light on the details of self-reinforcing processes in place for a very long timeframe. Insights from that specific process can be used for further im-

© Springer Fachmedien Wiesbaden GmbH, part of Springer Nature 2014
N. Kellermann, *Searching for a path out of distance fares*, Edition KWV,
https://doi.org/10.1007/978-3-658-23112-5_6

provement of knowledge either on path creation (Garud et al. 2010; Garud & Karnøe 2001; Schreyögg et al. 2003) or path-breaking initiatives (cf. Karim & Mitchell 2000). As a methodological contribution for the analysis of self-reinforcing mechanisms, simulation modelling is used as a tool for explicitly representing adaptive expectations (cf. Arthur 1994a) in a market. At the same time, an efficient alternative to a situation of path dependence can be demonstrated by quasi-experimentation.

Furthermore, the thesis at hand adds an explicit modelling of social interaction and market dynamics to the existing framework of consumer choice theory. A fundamental theoretical concept in marketing – Prospect Theory – is operationalised and combined with a revenue management application. A model integrating artificial demand reaction to price and a classical RM inventory control can be used as an instrument for testing the outcome of different ways to coordinate pricing and RM activities (cf. Kocabiykoglu et al. 2011). The development of a RM model for railways extends mostly airline-oriented revenue management research to a broader area of price-setting. Finally, employing factor analysis instead of assuming that all measured effects can be fully attributed to a single pricing decision contributes to RM research methodology.

For practitioners, this thesis provides a concise review of European train operators' pricing through history, refuting the myth that there always was a natural way to charge passengers on the kilometre travelled. Knowledge about the historical development of fare policy and pricing attempts can generally be an inspiration for finding solutions to current challenges and help to avoid engaging in trajectories that turned out to be disadvantageous in the past.

Insights from the simulation experiments can be used as preliminary studies for practical pricing decisions or as a starting point for further modelling and market research. The agent-based method enables managers of train operating companies to gain a better understanding of the dynamics of the transportation market. It opens the view to intermodality, possible competitor "war gaming" scenarios and incorporates a truly grounded way of modelling demand. Thereby, the prototype simulation model outlined in this work is the base for a future application to be used for the revenue management of a railway network carrier. In line with the argument of Cleophas & Frank (2011), simulation results demonstrate managers that simply adding elements of revenue management to an existing fare structure can be beneficial, but not necessary increases revenue in all circumstances. Hence, RM applications are a useful path for railways to accede if they are combined with advanced analytics methods incorporating data mining, market research and "serious games" simulation experiments.

6.2. Limitations and outlook on further research

Within the present work, a path-dependent process is described and possible elements of a pricing structure that bear the potential of attaining a more efficient revenue situation for train operators are identified. As path dependence theory suggests an excessive organisational rigidity towards managerial action, future research could focus on ways to implement fare innovations experimentally found to be beneficial. In other words, further research is needed on promising management activities enabling a firm to reach the more efficient revenue level suggested by simulation modelling.

The historical development of fares has been studied based on data of selected train operators. Though being representative for Europe, the cases do not allow generalising that all railways were or are driven by path dependence in their pricing. From a perspective of path dependence theory, deviant cases in Europe, especially how the companies representing these cases escaped from self-reinforcement and lock-in are of specific interest. Following Puffert's (2002; 2009) studies on technical path dependence in different regions of the world, the results of the present study can also be compared with the development of passenger rail pricing in other continents.

Though the revenue simulation model set up in this work contains a broad parameter space, its use for one industry and one specific line prevails. Even within this limitation, only a subset of the possible parameter combinations could be explored. For increasing the external validity of the findings, they generally need to be replicated in different contexts. The measured elasticity is based on the assumption of independent demand for transportation in total. Though the model covers the potential for train operators to attain demand previously selecting other means of transport, it does not incorporate entirely new demand for mobility services, that may be, for instance, induced by very low prices. Thus, modelling a reactive market volume depending on all prices would substantially enrich the present model. Scholars interested in modelling dependent demand structures can make a draft on the recent work of Temath et al. (2013) and of Cizaire & Belobaba (2013).

The simulation model explicitly does not account for effects resulting from promotional activities, nor for general advertising and branding. Though reference price building is closely modelled, more emotional reactions to price are out of scope. If real-world outcomes of pricing decisions are to be estimated, these effects need to be accounted for separately. In what concerns experiments with railcard offers, the irrational consumer behaviour addressed by non-linear pricing could enrich the model. So far, consumer agents are not yet paying too much for their subscriptions while they are "happy about it" (Lambrecht & Skiera 2006). In principle, the simulation model is open for implementing possibly missing features with the help of additional parameters. Within the trade-off between clarity and complexity, marketing scholars are encouraged to implement additional features of behavioural pricing theory in an agent-based market model. Concentrating on the long-distance branch of a railway, fares implemented in this model do not represent the complex world of prices set by regional transport associations. A direction of further research to be followed by transportation scientists, operations research scholars or geographers could be to simulate pricing on regional transport markets. The following table summarises the factors that are covered by the simulation model developed and the ones that are exogenous.

Endogenous factors	Exogenous factors
Demand attained from competing operators & modes of transport	Induced demand for transport in general
Reference prices	Price fairness & satisfaction
Railway operator fares	Advertising & branding effects
	Non-linear pricing effects
	Fares managed by transport associations

Table 35: Factors within and without the model scope

In what concerns interaction effects, research is limited to the factor size analysis for a number of selected factors occurring together. More detailed insights may be found by systematically analysing and evaluating single manipulations or groups of manipulations together with their statistical interaction effects with other manipulations or groups of them. In line with that, it can be investigated whether the findings on revenue elasticity hold for other timeframes than the one-year period chosen. The agent-based method allows for investigating in more detail whether specific customer segments show other elasticity values. The prototype model presented in this work is ready for performing these more detailed experiments.

In a part of the experiments, Netlogo's BehaviorSearch extension is used for finding the highest fitness outcome across a large set of possible parameter combinations. Any search based on genetic algorithms bears the danger of finding local optima instead of an exact, truly optimal combination of parameters. Of course, also multiple equal peaks may exist. Therefore, results of the BehaviorSearch experiments have to be interpreted as preliminary. What is more, genetic algorithm search is extensively consuming computing capacity. With the current status of processor and memory performance, BehaviorSearch experiment replications remain limited in number and in the scope of parameters to be searched.

After all, it has to be emphasised that simulation results are not to be interpreted as accurate figures for a revenue prognosis. Cleophas et al. (2009: 332) state: "Complete knowledge of actual customer behavio[u]r can never be attained. Therefore, [...] the implications of revenue management decisions may be identified as rankings and general tendencies".

For future research on simulation modelling and pricing, there is an open agenda for introducing human psychology into economic models. Marketing and operations research scholars are encouraged to extent the present implementation of Prospect Theory with more elaborated forms of social interaction as well as other determinants of utility and their evolution in time. One possible direction for increasing complexity of social behaviour and decision rules is to implement adaptive expectations on the occupancy of a means of transport and a respective choice behaviour. Another direction is to introduce changing individual preferences that will shape market dynamics (cf. Janssen & Jager 2001).

From an OR perspective, a revenue simulation model calibrated for one line could be extended to more lines, and finally, to an entire network. This would allow for more elaborated experiments on individual choice and network effects. Scholars interested in a comparison between airline and railway pricing could explore the effects of a full switch between static fares and dynamic pricing (cf. Sato & Sawaki 2012; Elmaghraby & Keskinocak 2003). What is more, model validity could be increased by a true one-to-one reproduction of a transportation market. However, this future step requires abundant high-performance computing capacity. Generally, the type of simulation model presented can be used for any form of market studies beyond the transportation industry. Neighbouring fields of application are long distance bus services or studies on the dynamics on the petrol market. Also other perishable asset markets like food retailing are possible fields of extending the presented modelling approach. In the realm of grocery, a promising stream of research could be settled around reference price models developed in the 1980s and early 1990s relying on supermarket scanner panel data. The question is if and how these studies can be replicated with an agent-based model of the retailing market. Other future research opportunities arise in using the model for analysing the effects of promotional prices which are only available for a limited period of time. Again, an agent-based perspective on promotional pricing can substantially enrich prior research made in that area (cf. Greenleaf 1995). For conducting possible experiments on the timing of those promotional prices, more modelling, data mining and market research effort is needed to adequately model seasonal effects of demand.

6.3. Conclusions

A central insight from the analysis of pricing in the history of economic thought is that science is increasingly able to capture the emergence of market prices as well as the mechanisms of consumer choice. Moreover, the notion that the perception of prices is dynamic, or in other terms, that buying behaviour to a current price stimulus depends on prior transactions made, can progressively be implemented in marketing models. Agent-based simulation provides the adequate tool set for experimental research involving these fundamental marketing concepts and for effectively transferring them into business practice.

From the research on the historical development of railway fares, I con-clude that railway fares uniquely based on distance are not the original or tradi-tional way railways priced their services. In fact, the early days of railways showed a broad variety of fares and an unexpected openness of managers to-wards alternative tariff structures. However, European railways engaged in a path of static distance pricing and developed a broad variety of fares relating di-rectly or indirectly to the mile or kilometre travelled. As long as competing modes of transport were inexistent, a fixed charge per unit of distance was a highly efficient way of exploiting a railway network. This was predominantly due to the network effects of a commercial standard on the one hand and to simplic-ity in sales on the other. With the emergence of individual car and bus transport, disadvantages of this form of price-setting weakened the competitive position of railways. The immense growth of passenger transportation by car and by air can in part be explained with the inflexibility of railways to adapt their pricing and thus to react to the competitive situation on different routes.

Inefficiency of the path becoming manifest as a situation of a systemati-cally too low revenue level and market share attained by a train operating com-pany can be captured and quantified with the help of an agent-based simulation model. This type of model comes close to a representation of an empirical transportation market. Using such instrument for experimentally exploring on strategic options for determining fares is a promising way for railways to im-prove their pricing capability. Within the restrictions their own history entails on them, railways can use revenue simulation as a tool for regaining their origi-nal role as active players in the passenger transportation market.

The theory of organisational path dependence together with the notion of bounded rationality in consumer behaviour fundamentally changes the view on business processes from a mechanistic one to a perspective of dynamics, social interaction, and multiple equilibria. The simulation method adopted in this work can be used to identify inefficiency in an existing situation, but is generally appropriate for anticipating possible path-dependent trajectories beyond the case of pricing described. Thus, simulation can help to reduce the number of cases of "remediable inefficiency" (Liebowitz & Margolis 1995: 224) of which dis-tance fares are assumed to be one.

***

References

A., M. (1865), *The Imperial Railway of Great Britain, and Railway Reform.* Oxford and London: John Henry and James Parker.

Adam, Jean-Paul (1972), *Instauration de la politique des chemins de fer en France.* Paris: Presses universitaires de France.

Adamatti, Diana-Francisca, Dimuro Graçalis Pereira, and Helder Coelho, eds. (2014), *Interdisciplinary Applications of Agent-Based Social Simulation and Modeling:* Hershey.

Afuah, Allan (2013), "Are network effects really all about size? The role of structure and conduct," *Strategic Management Journal*, 34 (3), 257–273.

Alberty, M. (1911), *Der Übergang zum Staatsbahnsystem in Preußen. Seine Begründung, seine Durchführung und seine Folgen.* Jena: Gustav Fischer.

Allais, Maurice, Mario Del Viscovo, Louis D. de La Vinelle, Coenraad J. Ort, and Hellmuth S. Seidenfus (1965), *Options in transport tariff policy. Studies: Transport Series No. 1, 1965.*

Allenby, Greg M., Neeraj Arora, and James L. Ginter (1998), "On the Heterogeneity of Demand," *Journal of Marketing Research*, 35 (3), 384–389.

Allgœwer, Elisabeth (2009), "Eugen von Böhm-Bawerk (1851-1914)," in *Klassiker des ökonomischen Denkens. Band 2*, Heinz D. Kurz, ed. München: C.H. Beck, 48–64.

Ambrosius, Gerold, ed. (2013), *Trains across borders. Comparative studies on international cooperation in railway development. Integration von Infrastrukturen in Europa im historischen Vergleich*, Vol. 4. Baden-Baden: Nomos.

Anderson, Philip W., Kenneth J. Arrow, and David Pines, eds. (1988), *The Economy as an Evolving Complex System.* Reading, Massachusetts.: Addison-Wesley.

Andersson-Skog, Lena (2009), "Revisiting railway history: the case of institutional change and path dependence," in *The Evolution of Path Dependence. New Horizons in Institutional and Evolutionary Economics*, Lars Magnusson and Jan Ottosson, eds. Cheltenham: Edward Elgar, 70–86.

Antonelli, Cristiano (1997), "The economics of path-dependence in industrial organization," *International Journal of Industrial Organization*, 15 (6), 643–675.

Ariely, Dan, George Loewenstein, and Drazen Prelec (2003), ""Coherent Arbitrariness": Stable Demand Curves Without Stable Preferences," *The Quarterly Journal of Economics*, 118 (1), 73–106.

Armstrong, Alexander and Joern Meissner (2010), "Railway Revenue Management: Overview and Models. Working Paper," [available at http://www.meiss.com].

Armstrong, M. and R. Porter, eds. (2007), *Handbook of Industrial Organization:* Elsevier.

Arthur, W. Brian (1988), "Self-Reinforcing Mechanisms in Economics," in *The Economy as an Evolving Complex System*, Philip W. Anderson, Kenneth J. Arrow and David Pines, eds. Reading, Massachusetts.: Addison-Wesley, 9–31.
——— (1989), "Competing Technologies, Increasing Returns, and Lock-In by Historical Events.," *The Economic Journal* (99), 116–131.

© Springer Fachmedien Wiesbaden GmbH, part of Springer Nature 2014
N. Kellermann, *Searching for a path out of distance fares*, Edition KWV,
https://doi.org/10.1007/978-3-658-23112-5

——— (1990), "Positive Feedbacks in the Economy," *Scientific American*, 262 (2), 92–99.

——— (1992), "On Learning and Adaption in the Economy," Working paper of the Santa Fe Insititute, Santa Fe Institute.

——— (1994), "Competing Technologies, Increasing Returns, and Lock-In by Historical Small Events," in *Increasing returns and path dependence in the economy. Economics, cognition, and society*, W. Brian Arthur, ed. Ann Arbor: University of Michigan Press, 13–32.

——— (1994), *Increasing returns and path dependence in the economy. Economics, cognition, and society*. Ann Arbor: University of Michigan Press.

——— (1994a), "Inductive Reasoning and Bounded Rationality," *The American Economic Review*, 84 (2), 406–411.

——— (1999), "Complexity and the Economy," *Science*, 284 (5411), 107–109.

——— (2006), "Out-of-Equilibrium Economics and Agent-Based Modeling," in *Handbook of Computational Economics*, Leigh Tesfatsion and Kenneth L. Judd, eds.: Elsevier, 1551–1564.

Arx, Heinz v., ed. (2001), *Der Kluge reist im Zuge. Hundert Jahre SBB.* Zürich: AS-Verlag.

Aßländer, Michael S. and Hans G. Nutzinger (2008), "John Stuart Mill (1806-1873)," in *Klassiker des ökonomischen Denkens. Band 1*, Heinz D. Kurz, ed. München: C.H. Beck, 176–195.

Axelrod, Robert M. (1997), *The complexity of cooperation. Agent-based models of competition and collaboration.* Princeton, N.J: Princeton University Press.

Axtell, Robert L. and Joshua M. Epstein (1994), "Agent-Based Modelling: Undertanding Our Creations," *The Bulletin of the Santa Fe Institute*, 28–32.

Bagwell, Philip (1968), *The Railway Clearing House in the British Economy 1842-1922.* London: George Allen & Unwin Ltd.

Bailey, Elizabeth E. and Lawrence J. White (1974), "Reversals in Peak and Offpeak Prices," *The Bell Journal of Economics and Management Science*, 5 (1), 75–92.

Barnes, William, Myles Gartland, and Martin Stack (2004), "Old Habits Die Hard: Path Dependency and Behavioral Lock-In," *Journal of Economic Issues*, 38 (2), 371–377.

Bartelsheim, Ursula (2008), "Die Werbung bei der Deutschen Bundesbahn 1949-1989," in *Go easy - go Bahn. 200 Jahre Eisenbahn und Werbung*, Stefan Ebenfeld, ed. Nürnberg: DB-Museum, 150–189.

Barthelmeß, Hanns (1989 [1969]), ""Grünes Licht für rosa Zeiten". Betrachtungen zu den Sonderangeboten der DB. Reprint originating from 1969," in *40 Jahre Deutsche Bundesbahn, 1949-1989*, Horst Weigelt and Ulrich Langner, eds. Darmstadt: Hestra-Verlag, 314–315.

Becker, Karl-Heinz (1992), "Jede Leistung hat ihren Preis," in *Die Bundesbahn / Die Deutsche Bahn*, Deutsche Bundesbahn and Deutsche Reichsbahn, eds. Darmstadt: Hestra-Verlag, 499–500.

Belobaba, Peter (2009), "Fundamentals of Pricing and Revenue Management," in *The Global Airline Industry*, Peter Belobaba, Amedeo Odoni and Cynthia Barnhart, eds.: Wiley, 73–111.

Belobaba, Peter, Amedeo Odoni, and Cynthia Barnhart, eds. (2009), *The Global Airline Industry:* Wiley.

Ben-Akiva, Moshe E. and Steven R. Lerman (1985), *Discrete choice analysis. Theory and application to travel demand. MIT Press series in transportation studies*, Vol. 9. Cambridge, Massachusetts: MIT Press.

Ben-Akiva, Moshe E., Daniel McFadden, Makoto Abe, Ulf Böckenholt, Denis Bolduc, Dinesh Gopinath, Takayuki Morikawa, Venkatram Ramaswamy, Vithala Rao, David Revelt, and Dan Steinberg (1997), "Modeling Methods for Discrete Choice Analysis," *Marketing Letters*, 8 (3), 273-286.

Bergstrom, Ted and Jeffrey K. MacKie-Mason (1991), "Some Simple Analytics of Peak-Load Pricing," *The RAND Journal of Economics*, 22 (2), 241–249.

Bertherin, E. and T. Leimgruber (2002), "1902-2002! Hundert Jahre Internationales Eisenbahntransportkomitee. Hundert Jahre im Dienste der Bahnen," Berne.

Bett, W. H. (1945), *The Theory of Fare Collection on Railways and Tramways*. London: Railway World Ltd.

Bieberstein, Wulf F. M. von (1979), "Platzreservierung in der Expansion," in *Die Bundesbahn*, Deutsche Bundesbahn, ed. Darmstadt: Hestra-Verlag, 819–824.

Bitran, Gabriel and René Caldentey (2003), "An Overview of Pricing Models for Revenue Management," *Manufacturing & Service Operations Management*, 5 (3), 203–229.

Böhm-Bawerk, Eugen v. (1889), *Kapital und Kapitalzins. Zweite Abteilung: Positive Theorie des Kapitales*. Innsbruck: Wagner.

Boero, Riccardo and Flaminio Squazzoni (2005), "Does Empirical Embeddedness Matter? Methodological Issues on Agent-Based Models for Analytical Social Science," *Journal of Artificial Societies and Social Simulation*, 8 (4), 6.

Bofinger, Peter (2011), *Grundzüge der Volkswirtschaftslehre: eine Einführung in die Wissenschaft von Märkten*. München: Pearson.

Bonsall, Peter, Jeremy Shires, John Maule, Bryan Matthews, and Jo Beale (2007), "Responses to complex pricing signals: Theory, evidence and implications for road pricing," *Transportation Research*, 41 (7), 672–683.

Botimer, Theodore C. and Peter Belobaba (1999), "Airline pricing and fare product differentiation: A new theoretical framework," *Journal of the Operational Research Society*, 50, 1085–1097.

Brenck, Andreas (2003), "Neues Tarifsystem der Deutschen Bahn: Sinnvolle Preisgestaltung im öffentlichen Verkehr?," *ifo Schnelldienst*, 56 (16), 3–6.

Bridel, Pascal and Elisabeth Huck (2002), "Yet another look at Léon Walras's theory of tâtonnement," *European Journal of the History of Economic Thought*, 9 (4), 513–540.

Briesch, Richard A., Lakshman Krishnamurthi, Tridib Mazumdar, and S. P. Raj (1997), "A Comparative Analysis of Reference Price Models," *Journal of Consumer Research*, 24 (2), 202–214.

British Railways Board (1967/1968), "Passenger fares manual," not numbered, London.
——— (1974), "Selective Prices Manual," No. 15, London.

Bromberger, Laurent (1993), "Découvrez la nouvelle façon de prendre le train," *La vie du rail* (2379), 10–20.

Brunotte, Anna and Andreas Krämer (2003), "Das neue Preissystem der Bahn," in *Handbuch Preispolitik. Strategien - Planung - Organisation - Umsetzung*, Hermann Diller and Andreas Herrmann, eds. Wiesbaden: Gabler, 763–787.

Buttriss, Gary J. and Ian F. Wilkinson (2014), "Pinpointing the deeper structures, processes and mechanisms of change within interactional fields," *Australasian Marketing Journal*, 22 (1), 45–50.

Cantillon, Richard (1997 [1755]), *Essai sur la nature du commerce en général*. Paris: Éditions de l'Institut National d'Études Démographiques.

Carley, Kathleen M. (2002), "Computational organizational science and organizational engineering," *Organisational Processes*, 10 (5–7), 253–269.

Caspari, Volker (2008), "Alfred Marshall (1842-1922)," in *Klassiker des ökonomischen Denkens. Band 1*, Heinz D. Kurz, ed. München: C.H. Beck, 326–347.

Cassel, Gustav (1938 [1900]), "Grundsätze für die Bildung der Personentarife auf den Eisenbahnen," *Nordic Journal of Technical Economy*, 12 (2), 50–78.

Casson, Mark (2009), *The world's first railway system. Enterprise, competition, and regulation on the railway network in Victorian Britain*. Oxford, New York: Oxford University Press.

Chamberlin, Edward H. (1962), *The theory of monopolistic competition: A re-orientation of the theory of value*. Cambridge, Massachusetts: Harvard University Press.

Chandler, Alfred D. (1977), *The visible hand. The managerial revolution in American business*. Cambridge, Massachusetts: Belknap Press of Harvard University Press.

Chiang, Wen-Chyuan, Jason C. H. Chen, and Xiaojing Xu (2007), "An overview of research on revenue management: current issues and future research," *International Journal of Revenue Management*, 1 (1), 97–128.

Chlastacz, Michel (1981), "Un événement commercial. Entretien avec Jean Ravel, Directeur Commercial Voyageurs," *La vie du rail* (1810), 4–6.

Ciancimino, A., G. Inzerillo, S. Lucidi, and L. Palagi (1999), "A Mathematical Programming Approach for the Solution of the Railway Yield Management Problem," *Transportation Science*, 33 (2), 168–181.

CIT International Rail Transport Committee (2013), "The CIT's objectives," [available at www.cit-rail.org/en/objectives].
—— (2013a), "General Conditions of Carriage for Rail Passengers (GCC-CIV/PRR), [available at http://www.cit-rail.org/en/passenger-traffic/cit-documentation/].

Cizaire, Claire and Peter Belobaba (2013), "Joint optimization of airline pricing and fare class seat allocation," *Journal of Revenue and Pricing Management*, 12 (1), 83–93.

Cleophas, Catherine (2009), *Simulation-Based Analysis of Forecast Performance Evaluations for Airline Revenue Management*. Paderborn.
—— (2012), "Multi-agent modelling for revenue management," *Journal of Revenue and Pricing Management*, 11 (2), 240–242.
—— (2012a), "Assessing Multi-agent Simulations – Inspiration through Application," in *Highlights on Practical Applications of Agents and Multi-Agent Systems. Advances in Intelligent and Soft Computing*, Javier B. Pérez, Miguel A. Sánchez, Philippe Mathieu, Juan M. C. Rodríguez, Emmanuel Adam, Alfonso Ortega, María N. Moreno, Elena Navarro, Benjamin Hirsch, Henrique Lopes-Cardoso and Vicente Julián, eds.: Springer, 163-170.

Cleophas, Catherine and Philipp Bartke (2011), "Modeling strategic customers using simulations - with examples from airline revenue management. The State of the Art in the European Quantitative Oriented Transportation and Logistics Research – 14th Euro Working Group on Transportation & 26th Mini Euro Conference & 1st European Scientific Conference on Air Transport," *Procedia - Social and Behavioral Sciences*, 20 (0), 1060–1068.

Cleophas, Catherine and Michael Frank (2011), "Ten myths of revenue management - A practitioner's view," *Journal of Revenue and Pricing Management*, 10 (1), 26–31.

Cleophas, Catherine, Michael Frank, and Natalia Kliewer (2009), "Simulation-based key performance indicators for evaluating the quality of airline demand forecasting," *Journal of Revenue and Pricing Management*, 8 (4), 330–342.

Coase, Ronald H. (1937), "The Nature of the Firm," *Economica*, 4 (16), 386–405.

Cohen, Michael D., James G. March, and Johan P. Olsen (1972), "A Garbage Can Model of Organizational Choice," *Administrative Science Quarterly*, 17 (1), 1–25.

Copeland, Duncan G. and James L. McKenney (1988), "Airline Reservations Systems: Lessons from History," *MIS Quarterly*, 12 (3), 353–370.

Costet, Jean (1992), "Die Französischen Eisenbahnen SNCF," in *Die Bahnen Europas. Jahrbuch des Eisenbahnwesens*, Vol. 43, Heinz Dürr and Knut Reimers, eds. Darmstadt: Hestra-Verlag, 146–155.

Cournot, Antoine A. (1938 [1838]), *Recherches sur les principes mathématiques de la théorie des richesses. Collection des économistes et des réformateurs sociaux de la France*. Paris: Rivière.

Cowan, Robin (1990), "Nuclear Power Reactors: A Study in Technological Lock-in," *The Journal of Economic History*, 50 (03), 541–567.

Crelle, August L. (1840), *Ueber die Fahrpreise auf Eisenbahnen*. Berlin: G. Reimer.

Cross, Robert G. (1997), *Revenue Management. Hard-core tactics for market domination*. New York: Broadway Books.

Cusumano, Michael A., Yiorgos Mylonadis, and Richard S. Rosenbloom (1992), "Strategic Maneuvering and Mass-Market Dynamics: The Triumph of VHS over Beta," *Business History Review*, 66 (Special Issue 01), 51–94.

Cyert, Richard M. and James G. March (1963), *A Behavioral Theory of the Firm. Prentice-Hall behavioral sciences in business series*. Englewood Cliffs, New Jersey: Prentice-Hall.

D'Alessandro, Steven and Hume Winzar (2014), "Special issue on complex systems: Editor's forward," *Australasian Marketing Journal*, 22 (1), 2–3.

Dana, James D., Jr. (1998), "Advance-Purchase Discounts and Price Discrimination in Competitive Markets," *Journal of Political Economy*, 106 (2), 395–422.
——— (1999), "Using Yield Management to Shift Demand When the Peak Time is Unknown," *The RAND Journal of Economics*, 30 (3), 456–474.

David, Paul A. (1969), "Transport Innovation and Economic Growth: Professor Fogel on and off the Rails," *The Economic History Review*, 22 (3), 506–525.
——— (1975), *Technical choice, innovation, and economic growth. Essays on American and British experience in the nineteenth century*. London: Cambridge University Press.
——— (1985), "CLIO and the Economics of QWERTY," *American Economic Review*, 75 (2), 332–337.
——— (2001), "Path dependence, its critics, and the quest for 'historical economics'," in *Evolution and path dependence in economic ideas. Past and present*, Pierre Garrouste and Stavros Ioannides, eds. Cheltenham, UK; Northampton, Massachusetts, USA: Edward Elgar, 15–40.
——— (2007), "Path dependence: a foundational concept for historical social science," *Cliometrica*, 1 (2), 91–114.
——— (2012), *Doctoral colloquium May 14-15, 2012*. Personal communication. Berlin

David, Paul A. and Julie A. Bunn (1988), "The economics of gateway technologies and network evolution: Lessons from electricity supply history," *Information Economics and Policy*, 3 (2), 165–202.

Davis, Jason P., Kathleen Eisenhardt, and Christopher B. Bingham (2007), "Developing Theory Through Simulation Methods," *Academy of Management Review*, 32 (2), 480–499.

Decreton, Séverine (1995), "Le service public à l'épreuve de la tarification, l'exemple de la SNCF," *Revue administrative*, 48 (288), 639–645.

Degenhard, Maximilian (1993), "Jahresrückblick 1992 der Eisenbahnen. Französische Eisenbahnen (SNCF)," in *Die Deutsche Bahn*, Deutsche Bundesbahn and Deutsche Reichsbahn, eds. Darmstadt: Hestra-Verlag, 140–143.

den Hartigh, Erik and Fred Langerak (2001), "Managing increasing returns," *European Management Journal*, 19 (4), 370–378.

Desiraju, Ramarao and Steven M. Shugan (1999), "Strategic Service Pricing and Yield Management," *Journal of Marketing*, 63 (1), 44–56.

Deutsche Bundesbahn (1955), "Ratgeber für unsere Kunden. Personenverkehr Reisegepäck Expressgut," Frankfurt am Main.
——— (1979), "Bei der Bahn gibt's 7500 km Rabatt.," *Manager Magazin* (2).
——— (1979), *Die Bundesbahn.* Darmstadt: Hestra-Verlag.
——— (1987), "Fahr & Spar. Die neuen Preise der Bahn," Mainz.

Deutsche Bundesbahn and Deutsche Reichsbahn, eds. (1992), *Die Bundesbahn / Die Deutsche Bahn.* Darmstadt: Hestra-Verlag.
——— (1993), *Die Deutsche Bahn.* Darmstadt: Hestra-Verlag.

Deutsche Reichsbahn-Gesellschaft (1934), "Wegweiser für den Personenverkehr der Reichsbahn," Berlin.

Diaz, Rafael, ed. (2013), *Emerging M&S Applications in Industry and Academia Symposium and the Modeling and Humanities Symposium 2013. (EAIA and MatH 2013) : 2013 Spring Simulation Multi-Conference (SpringSim'13) : San Diego, California, USA, 7-10 April, 2013. Simulation series*, volume 45, number 5.

Diller, Hermann (2008), *Preispolitik.* Stuttgart: Kohlhammer.

Diller, Hermann and Andreas Herrmann, eds. (2003), *Handbuch Preispolitik. Strategien - Planung - Organisation - Umsetzung.* Wiesbaden: Gabler.

Dobbin, Frank (1994), *Forging Industrial Policy. The United States, Britain, and France in the Railway Age.* New York: Cambridge University Press.

Dobusch, Leonhard (2008), *Windows versus Linux. Markt - Organisation - Pfad.* Wiesbaden: VS Verlag für Sozialwissenschaften.

Donaghy, Thomas J. (1972), *Liverpool & Manchester Railway Operations 1831-1845.* Newton Abbot: David and Charles.

Dosi, Giovanni (1982), "Technological paradigms and technological trajectories: A suggested interpretation of the determinants and directions of technical change," *Research Policy*, 11 (3), 147–162.

Dranove, David and Neil Gandal (2003), "The Dvd-vs.-Divx Standard War: Empirical Evidence of Network Effects and Preannouncement Effects," *Journal of Economics & Management Strategy*, 12 (3), 363–386.

Dürr, Heinz (1992), "Die Deutschen Bahnen DB und DR," in *Die Bahnen Europas. Jahrbuch des Eisenbahnwesens*, Vol. 43, Heinz Dürr and Knut Reimers, eds. Darmstadt: Hestra-Verlag, 72–81.

Dürr, Heinz and Knut Reimers, eds. (1992), *Die Bahnen Europas. Jahrbuch des Eisenbahnwesens*, Vol. 43. Darmstadt: Hestra-Verlag.

Dutta, Goutam and Priyanko Ghosh (2012), "A passenger revenue management system (RMS) for a National Railway in an Emerging Asian Economy," *Journal of Revenue and Pricing Management*, 11 (5), 487–499.

Dutta, Shantanu, Mark Bergen, Daniel Levy, Mark Ritson, and Mark Zbaracki (2002), "Pricing as a Strategic Capability," *MIT Sloan Management Review*, 43 (3), 61–66.

Dutta, Shantanu, Mark Zbaracki, and Mark Bergen (2003), "Pricing Process as a Capability: A Resource-Based Perspective," *Strategic Management Journal* (24), 615–630.

Ebenfeld, Stefan, ed. (2008), *Go easy - go Bahn. 200 Jahre Eisenbahn und Werbung*. Nuremberg: DB-Museum.
——— (2008), "Verkehr als Ware und der Kunde als König - Die Deutsche Reichsbahn-Gesellschaft und ihre Werbung in den 1920er- und 1930er-Jahren," in *Go easy - go Bahn. 200 Jahre Eisenbahn und Werbung*, Stefan Ebenfeld, ed. Nürnberg: DB-Museum, 22–67.

Ebers, Mark and Wilfried Gotsch (2006), "Institutionenökonomische Theorien der Organisation," in *Organisationstheorien*, Alfred Kieser, ed. Stuttgart: Kohlhammer, 247–308.

Edmonds, Bruce and Ruth Meyer, eds. (2013), *Simulating Social Complexity. A handbook*. Berlin, Heidelberg.
——— (2013), "Introduction to the Handbook," in *Simulating Social Complexity. A handbook*, Bruce Edmonds and Ruth Meyer, eds. Berlin, Heidelberg, 3–11.

Ehret, Michael (2000): Innovative Kapitalnutzung. Die Entstehung neuer Business-to-Business-Märkte in der Internet-Ökonomie. Wiesbaden: Gabler; Deutscher Universitäts-Verlag.

Eichert, Wolfgang (2008), "François Quesnay (1694-1774)," in *Klassiker des ökonomischen Denkens. Band 1*, Heinz D. Kurz, ed. München: C.H. Beck, 57–67.

Eisenhardt, Kathleen (1989), "Building Theories from Case Study Research," *Academy of Management Review*, 14 (4), 532–550.
——— (1991), "Better Stories and Better Contructs: The Case for Rigor and Comparative Logic," *Academy of Management Review*, 16 (3), 620–627.

Elmaghraby, Wedad and Pınar Keskinocak (2003), "Dynamic Pricing in the Presence of Inventory Considerations: Research Overview, Current Practices, and Future Directions," *Management Science*, 49 (10), 1287–1309.

Emery, Fred (1970), "Some psychological aspects of price," *Pricing strategy*, 98–111.

Erickson, Gary M. and Johny K. Johansson (1985), "The Role of Price in Multi-Attribute Product Evaluations," *Journal of Consumer Research*, 12 (2), 195–199.

Eurail Group (2012), *InterRail Passes – 40 Years on Track. 40th anniversary of InterRail Passes*. Utrecht.

Eurobarometer (2012), "Rail Competition Report. Special Eurobarometer 388"

European Commission (1996), "White Paper. A Strategy for Revitalising the Community's Railways," COM(96)421, Brussels.

—— (2013), "Proposal for a Directive of the European Parliament and of the Council. amending Directive 2012/34/EU of the European Parliament and of the Council of 21 November 2012 establishing a single European railway area, as regards the opening of the market for domestic passenger transport services by rail and the governance of the railway infrastructure," COM(2013) 29/2, Brussels.

—— (2013a), *European Railways at a junction: the Commission adopts proposals for a Fourth Railway Package.* Brussels.

European Court of Justice (1985) *EURlex,* 1556–1603.

Farrell, Joseph and Paul Klemperer (2007), "Coordination and Lock-In: Competition with Switching Costs and Network Effects," in *Handbook of Industrial Organization,* M. Armstrong and R. Porter, eds.: Elsevier, 1967–2072.

Farrell, Joseph and Garth Saloner (1985), "Standardization, Compatibility, and Innovation," *The RAND Journal of Economics,* 16 (1), 70–83.

Faugère, Mireille (2010), "High-speed transportation as flagship for rail - history of the TGV," in *Railway Transformation,* Martin Streichfuss, ed. Hamburg: DVV Media Group GmbH | Eurailpress, 61–69.

Favin-Lévêque, Jean-Claude (2009), *Concurrence ferroviaire. La France peut-elle gagner?* Paris: Éditions Lignes de Repères.

Favre, Thierry (2011), *Railway posters.* Woodbridge, Suffolk: Antique Collectors' Club.

Feldbaum, Bettina (2008), "Das englische Eisenbahnplakat - Ein kurzer historischer Überblick," in *Go easy - go Bahn. 200 Jahre Eisenbahn und Werbung,* Stefan Ebenfeld, ed. Nürnberg: DB-Museum, 262–273.

Fink, Carole (1984), *The Genoa Conference. European diplomacy, 1921-1922.* Chapel Hill: University of North Carolina Press.

Forrester, Jay W. (1961), *Industry dynamics.* Cambridge, Massachusetts: MIT Press.

—— (1969), *Urban dynamics.* Cambridge, Massachusetts: MIT Press.

—— (1971), *World dynamics.* Cambridge, Massachusetts: Wright-Allen Press.

Frank, Michael, Martin Friedemann, and Anika Schröder (2008), "Principles for simulations in revenue management," *Journal of Revenue and Pricing Management,* 7 (1), 7–16.

Frank, Ulrich, ed. (2004), *Wissenschaftstheorie in Ökonomie und Wirtschaftsinformatik. Theoriebildung und -bewertung, Ontologien, Wissensmanagement.* Wiesbaden: Deutscher Universitäts-Verlag.

Funk, Ulrich (1992), "70 Jahre Internationaler Eisenbahnverband UIC," in *Die Bundesbahn / Die Deutsche Bahn,* Deutsche Bundesbahn and Deutsche Reichsbahn, eds. Darmstadt: Hestra-Verlag, 1344–1345.

Furubotn, Eirik G. and Svetozar Pejovich (1972), "Property Rights and Economic Theory: A Survey of Recent Literature," *Journal of Economic Literature,* 10 (4), 1137–1162.

Gall, Lothar (1999), "Eisenbahn in Deutschland: Von den Anfängen bis zum Ersten Weltkrieg," in *Die Eisenbahn in Deutschland. Von den Anfängen bis zur Gegenwart,* Lothar Gall and Manfred Pohl, eds. München: Verlag C. H. Beck, 13–70.

Gall, Lothar and Manfred Pohl, eds. (1999), *Die Eisenbahn in Deutschland. Von den Anfängen bis zur Gegenwart.* München: Verlag C. H. Beck.

REFERENCES

Galt, William (1865), *Railway Reform: its Importance and Practicability considered as affecting the Nation, the Shareholders, and the Government.* London: Longman, Green, Longman, Roberts & Green.

Garber, Thorsten (2012), "Kundenversteher und Nachwuchsschmied. Porträt von Prof. Christian Homburg," *Die Absatzwirtschaft* (6), 26–28.

Gardner, Martin (1970), "The game of life," *Scientific American*, 223 (4), 120–123.

Garrouste, Pierre and Stavros Ioannides, eds. (2001), *Evolution and path dependence in economic ideas. Past and present.* Cheltenham, UK; Northampton, Massachusetts, USA: Edward Elgar.

Garud, Raghu and Peter Karnøe, eds. (2001), *Path dependence and creation*, Vol. 138.
——— (2001), "Path dependence as a process of mindful deviation," in *Path dependence and creation*, Vol. 138, Raghu Garud and Peter Karnøe, eds., 1–40.

Garud, Raghu, Arun Kumaraswamy, and Peter Karnøe (2010), "Path Dependence or Path Creation?," *Journal of Management Studies*, 47 (4), 760–774.

Ghorbani, Amineh (2013), *Structuring Socio-technical Complexity - Modelling Agent Systems Using Institutional Analysis:* Delft University of Technology.

Gilbert, Nigel (2008), *Agent-based models.* Los Angeles: Sage.
——— (2010), *Computational Social Science. Sage benchmarks in social research methods.* London: Sage.

Gilbert, Nigel and Klaus G. Troitzsch (2005), *Simulation for the social scientist.* Maidenhead: Open University Press.

Gläser, Jochen and Grit Laudel (2010), *Experteninterviews und qualitative Inhaltsanalyse als Instrumente rekonstruierender Untersuchungen.* Wiesbaden: VS Verlag für Sozialwissenschaften.

Gopalakrishnan, Raja and Narayan Rangaraj (2010), "Capacity Management on Long-Distance Passenger Trains of Indian Railways," *Interfaces*, 40 (4), 291–302.

Gossen, Hermann H. (1854), *Entwickelung der Gesetze des menschlichen Verkehrs, und der daraus fließenden Regeln für menschliches Handeln.* Braunschweig: Friedrich Vieweg und Sohn.

Gourvish, Terry (1986), *British Railways, 1948-73. A business history.* Cambridge, New York: Cambridge University Press.
——— (2002), *British Rail 1974–1997: From Integration to Privatisation.* Oxford: Oxford University Press.

Gray, Thomas (1825), *Observations on a General Iron Rail-Way or Land-Steam Conveyance.* London: Baldwin, Cradock, and Joy.

Greenleaf, Eric A. (1995), "The Impact of Reference Price Effects on the Profitability of Price Promotions," *Marketing Science*, 14 (1), 82–104.

Greve, Henrich R. and Marc-David L. Seidel (2014), "The Thin Red Line between Success and Failure: Path Dependence in the Diffusion of Innovative Production Technologies," *Strategic Management Journal*, forthcoming.

Grimm, Volker, Uta Berger, Finn Bastiansen, Sigrunn Eliassen, Vincent Ginot, Jarl Giske, John Goss-Custard, Tamara Grand, Simone K. Heinz, Geir Huse, Andreas Huth, Jane U. Jepsen, Christian Jørgensen, Wolf M. Mooij, Birgit Müller, Guy Pe'er, Cyril Piou, Steven F. Railsback, Andrew M. Robbins, Martha M. Robbins, Eva Rossmanith, Nadja Rüger, Espen Strand, Sami Souissi, Richard A. Stillman, Rune

Vabø, Ute Visser, and Donald L. DeAngelis (2006), "A standard protocol for describing individual-based and agent-based models," *Ecological Modelling*, 198 (1–2), 115–126.

Grimm, Volker, Uta Berger, Donald L. DeAngelis, J. G. Polhill, Jarl Giske, and Steven F. Railsback (2010), "The ODD protocol: A review and first update," *Ecological Modelling*, 221 (23), 2760–2768.

Grimm, Volker and Steven F. Railsback (2005), *Individual-based modeling and ecology. Princeton series in theoretical and computational biology.* Princeton: Princeton University Press.

Gutenberg, Erich (1955), *Der Absatz. Grundlagen der Betriebswirtschaftslehre*, Vol. 2. Berlin, Heidelberg, New York: Springer.
—————(1958), *Einführung in die Betriebswirtschaftslehre.* Wiesbaden: Gabler.
—————(1984), *Der Absatz. Grundlagen der Betriebswirtschaftslehre*, Vol. 2. Berlin, Heidelberg, New York: Springer.

Hannan, Michael T. and John Freeman (1984), "Structural Inertia and Organizational Change," *American Sociological Review*, 49 (2), 149–164.

Hanstein, Reinhard (2011), "Privatisierung und Verstaatlichung - „Grundtakt" der Eisenbahngeschichte?," *Eisenbahn-Revue International* (2), 100–102.

Harrison, Richard J., Lin Zhiang, Glenn R. Carroll, and Kathleen M. Carley (2007), "Simulation Modeling in Organizational and Management Research," *Academy of Management Review*, 32 (4), 1229–1245.

Harti, Maria, Hans-Joachim Luhm, and Andreas Schwilling (2010), "Revenue management as a facilitator of performance improvement," in *Railway Transformation*, Martin Streichfuss, ed. Hamburg: DVV Media Group GmbH | Eurailpress, 82–96.

Hawke, G. R. (1969), "Pricing Policy of Railways in England and Wales before 1881," in *Railways in the Victorian economy: studies in finance and economic growth*, Malcolm C. Reed, ed.: David and Charles, 76–110.

Hayek, Friedrich A. (1928), "Das intertemporale Gleichgewichtssystem der Preise und die Bewegungen des Geldwertes," *Weltwirtschaftliches Archiv*, 2, 33–76.
—————(1945), "The Use of Knowledge in Society," *The American Economic Review*, 35 (4), 519–530.

Held, Fabian P., Ian F. Wilkinson, Robert E. Marks, and Louise Young (2014), "Agent-based Modelling, a new kind of research," *Australasian Marketing Journal*, 22 (1), 4–14.

Helson, Harry (1964), *Adaptation-Level Theory. An Experimental and Systematic Approach to Behavior* New York: Harper & Row.

Holtmann, Jan P. (2008), *Pfadabhängigkeit strategischer Entscheidungen. Eine Fallstudie am Beispiel des Bertelsmann-Buchclubs Deutschland.* Köln: Kölner Wissenschaftsverlag.

Hossain, Tanjim and John Morgan (2009), "The Quest for QWERTY," *The American Economic Review*, 99 (2), 435–440.

Hoyer, Wayne D. and Deborah J. MacInnis (2007), *Consumer behavior.* Boston: Houghton Mifflin.

Ihrig, Martin and Klaus G. Troitzsch (2013), "An Extended Research Framework for the Simulation Era," in *Emerging M&S Applications in Industry and Academia Symposium and the Modeling and Humanities Symposium 2013. (EAIA and MatH 2013): 2013 Spring Simulation Multi-Conference (SpringSim '13): San Diego, California, USA, 7-10 April, 2013. Simulation series*, volume 45, number 5, Rafael Diaz, ed., 99–106.

Intergovernmental Organisation for International Carriage by Rail (OTIF) (1980), "COTIF. Convention concerning International Carriage by Rail of 9 May 1980,"
——— (1980a), CIV. Uniform Rules concerning the Contract for International Carriage of Passengers and Luggage by Rail"
——— (2013), "General information"

Jaffé, William (1967), "Walras' Theory of Tatonnement: A Critique of Recent Interpretations," *Journal of Political Economy*, 75 (1), 1–19.

James, Edmund J. (1891), "Reform in Railroad Passenger Fares," *The Quarterly Journal of Economics*, 5 (2), 165–192.

Janssen, Marco A. and Wander Jager (2001), "Fashions, habits and changing preferences: Simulation of psychological factors affecting market dynamics," *Journal of Economic Psychology*, 22 (6), 745–772.

Janssen, Marco A. and Elinor Ostrom (2006), "Empirically based, agent-based models," *Ecology and Society*, 11 (2), 37.

Jarzabkowski, Paula (2008), "Shaping Strategy as a Structuration Process," *Academy of Management Journal*, 51 (4), 621–650.

Jevons, William S. (1871), *The Theory of Political Economy*. London: Macmillan.

Kahneman, Daniel, Jack L. Knetsch, and Richard H. Thaler (1991), "Anomalies: The Endowment Effect, Loss Aversion, and Status Quo Bias," *The Journal of Economic Perspectives*, 5 (1), 193–206.

Kahneman, Daniel and Amos Tversky (1979), "Prospect Theory: An Analysis of Decision under Risk," *Econometrica*, 47 (2), 263–291.
——— (1984), "Choices, values, and frames," *American Psychologist*, 39 (4), 341–350.

Kalmbach, Peter (2008), "Thomas Robert Malthus (1766-1834)," in *Klassiker des ökonomischen Denkens. Band 1*, Heinz D. Kurz, ed. München: C.H. Beck, 89–104.

Kalwani, Manohar U. and Chi K. Yim (1992), "Consumer Price and Promotion Expectations: An Experimental Study," *Journal of Marketing Research*, 29 (1), 90–100.

Kalwani, Manohar U., Chi K. Yim, Heikki J. Rinne, and Yoshi Sugita (1990), "A Price Expectations Model of Customer Brand Choice," *Journal of Marketing Research*, 27 (3), 251–262.

Kalyanaram, Gurumurthy and John D. C. Little (1994), "An Empirical Analysis of Latitude of Price Acceptance in Consumer Package Goods," *Journal of Consumer Research*, 21 (3), 408–418.

Kalyanaram, Gurumurthy and Russell S. Winer (1995), "Empirical Generalizations from Reference Price Research," *Marketing Science*, 14 (3), G161-G169.

Kamakura, Wagner A., Byung-Do Kim, and Jonathan Lee (1996), "Modeling Preference and Structural Heterogeneity in Consumer Choice," *Marketing Science*, 15 (2), 152–172.

Karim, Samina and Will Mitchell (2000), "Path-Dependent and Path-Breaking Change: Reconfiguring Business Resources Following Acquisitions in the U.S. Medical Sector, 1978-1995," *Strategic Management Journal*, 21 (10/11), 1061–1081.

Katz, Michael L. and Carl Shapiro (1985), "Network Externalities, Competition, and Compatibility," *The American Economic Review*, 75 (3), 424–440.

Kay, Neil M. (2013), "Rerun the tape of history and QWERTY always wins," *Research Policy*, 42 (6–7), 1175–1185.

Kieser, Alfred, ed. (2006), *Organisationstheorien*. Stuttgart: Kohlhammer.

Kirsch, David A. (1996), *The Electric Car and the Burden of History: Studies in Automotive Systems Rivalry in America, 1890-1996*. Ph.D. dissertation, Stanford University, UMI 97-14137.

Kirzner, Israel M. (1994), *Classics in Austrian economics: A Sampling in the History of a Tradition. Volume I: The Founding Era*. London: William Pickering.
—— (1994), *Classics in Austrian economics: A Sampling in the History of a Tradition. Volume II: The interwar period*. London: William Pickering.
—— (1994), *Classics in Austrian economics: A Sampling in the History of a Tradition. Volume III: The Age of Mises and Hayek*. London: William Pickering.

Klein, Hemjö (1993), "Jahresrückblick 1992 der Deutschen Bahnen. Personenverkehr," in *Die Deutsche Bahn*, Deutsche Bundesbahn and Deutsche Reichsbahn, eds. Darmstadt: Hestra-Verlag, 32–40.

Knoop, Douglas (1923), *Outlines of Railway Economics*. London: Macmillan.

Kocabiykoglu, Ayse, Ioana Popescu, and Catalina Stefanescu (2011), *Pricing and Revenue Management: The Value of Coordination*.

Koch, Jochen, Martin Eisend, and Arne Petermann (2009), "Path Dependence in Decision-Making Processes: Exploring the Impact of Complexity under Increasing Returns," *BuR Business Research Journal*, 2 (1).

Koski, Heli and Tobias Kretschmer (2005), "Entry, Standards and Competition: Firm Strategies and the Diffusion of Mobile Telephony," *Review of Industrial Organization*, 26 (1), 89-113.

Kraft, Edwin R., Bellur N. Srikar, and Robert L. Phillips (2000), "Revenue Management in Railroad Applications," *Transportation Quarterly*, 54 (1), 157–176.

Krishnamurthi, Lakshman, Tridib Mazumdar, and S. P. Raj (1992), "Asymmetric Response to Price in Consumer Brand Choice and Purchase Quantity Decisions," *Journal of Consumer Research*, 19 (3), 387–400.

Krüger, Rainer and Michael Rößler (1989 [1981]), "Rabatte, Sonderangebote, Kundenwünsche. Reprint originating from 1981," in *40 Jahre Deutsche Bundesbahn, 1949-1989*, Horst Weigelt and Ulrich Langner, eds. Darmstadt: Hestra-Verlag, 504–505.

Kuhn, Thomas S. (1996 [1962]), *The structure of scientific revolutions*. Chicago: University of Chicago Press.

Kurz, Heinz D. (2008), "David Ricardo (1772-1823)," in *Klassiker des ökonomischen Denkens. Band 1*, Heinz D. Kurz, ed. München: C.H. Beck, 120–139.
—— (2008a), "Hermann Heinrich Gossen (1810-1858)," in *Klassiker des ökonomischen Denkens. Band 1*, Heinz D. Kurz, ed. München: C.H. Beck, 196–216.
—— (2008b), "William Petty (1623-1687)," in *Klassiker des ökonomischen Denkens. Band 1*, Heinz D. Kurz, ed. München: C.H. Beck, 9–45.
—— (2008), *Klassiker des ökonomischen Denkens. Band 1*. München: C.H. Beck.
—— (2009), *Klassiker des ökonomischen Denkens. Band 2*. München: C.H. Beck.

Kuß, Alfred (2011), *Marketing-Theorie. Eine Einführung*. Wiesbaden: Gabler.

Küttner, Michael (1981), "Theorie unter dem Non-Statement View und der Kuhnsche Wissenschaftler," *Zeitschrift für allgemeine Wissenschaftstheorie*, 12 (1), 163-177.

Lakatos, Imre (1970), "Falsification and the Methodology of Scientific Research Programmes," in *Criticism and the Growth of Knowledge*, Imre Lakatos and Musgrave, eds. Cambridge: Cambridge University Press, 91–196.
———— (1976), *Proofs and refutations. The logic of math. discovery. Ed. by John Worrall and Elie Zahar.* Cambridge: Cambridge University Press.
———— (1978), *Mathematics, science and epistemology. Philosophical Papers Volume 2.* Cambridge: Cambridge University Press.

Lakatos, Imre and Musgrave, eds. (1970), *Criticism and the Growth of Knowledge.* Cambridge: Cambridge University Press.

Lambrecht, Anja and Bernd Skiera (2006), "Paying Too Much and Being Happy about It: Existence, Causes, and Consequences of Tariff-Choice Biases," *Journal of Marketing Research*, 43 (2), 212–223.

Lampe-Helbig, Konrad (1989 [1966]), "Die neuen Personentarife bei der Deutschen Bundesbahn und ihre historische Entwicklung. Reprint originating from 1966," in *40 Jahre Deutsche Bundesbahn, 1949-1989*, Horst Weigelt and Ulrich Langner, eds. Darmstadt: Hestra-Verlag, 267–268.

Lancaster, John (2003), "The financial risk of airline revenue management," *Journal of Revenue and Pricing Management*, 2 (2), 158–165.

Langley, Ann (1999), "Strategies for Theorizing from Process Data," *The Academy of Management Review*, 24 (4), 691–710.

Laundy, J. H. (1949), "The problem of railway passenger fares and train services. A suggested plan for equalising passenger travel over both rail and road services," Reprinted from the Railway Gazette of January 28, 1949.

Law, Averill M. (2007), *Simulation modeling and analysis. McGraw-Hill series in industrial engineering and management science.* Boston: McGraw-Hill.

Leonard-Barton, Dorothy (1992), "Core capabilities and core rigidities: A paradox in managing new product development," *Strategic Management Journal*, 13 (S1), 111–125.

Levitt, Theodore (1960), "Marketing Myopia," *Harvard business review*, 38 (4), 24–47.

Liebowitz, Stan J. and Stephen E. Margolis (1990), "The Fable of the Keys," *Journal of Law and Economics*, 33 (1), 1–25.
———— (1994), "Network Externality: An Uncommon Tragedy," *The Journal of Economic Perspectives*, 8 (2), 133–150.
———— (1995), "Path Dependence, Lock-in, and History," *Journal of Law, Economics, & Organization*, 11 (1), 205–226.
———— (2013), "The Troubled Path of the Lock-in Movement," *Journal of Competition Law and Economics*, 9 (1), 125–152.

Link, Heike (2004), "PEP - A Yield-Management Scheme for Rail Passenger Fares in Germany," *Japan Railway & Transport Review*, 38, 50–55.

List, Friedrich (1833), *Über ein sächsisches Eisenbahn-System als Grundlage eines allgemeinen deutschen Eisenbahn-Systems und insbesondere die Anlegung einer Eisenbahn von Leipzig nach Dresden.* Leipzig: Liebeskind.

Locklin, D. P. (1933), "The Literature on Railway Rate Theory," *The Quarterly Journal of Economics*, 47 (2), 167–230.

Lodge, Martin (2002), *On different tracks. Designing railway regulation in Britain and Germany.* Westport: Praeger.

Lorscheid, Iris, Bernd-Oliver Heine, and Matthias Meyer (2012), "Opening the 'black box' of simulations: increased transparency and effective communication through the systematic design of experiments," *Computational and Mathematical Organization Theory*, 18 (1), 22-62.

Lucas, Robert E. (1976), "Econometric policy evaluation: A critique," *Carnegie-Rochester Conference Series on Public Policy*, 1 (0), 19–46.

Luhmann, Niklas (1995 [1984]), *Social systems. Writing science.* Stanford, California: Stanford University Press.

Magnusson, Lars and Jan Ottosson, eds. (2009), *The Evolution of Path Dependence. New Horizons in Institutional and Evolutionary Economics.* Cheltenham: Edward Elgar.

Mahoney, James (2000), "Path Dependence in Historical Sociology," *Theory and Society*, 29 (4), 507–548.

Malthus, Thomas R. (1820), *Principles of political economy.* London: John Murray.

Marks, Robert E. (2007), "Validating Simulation Models: A General Framework and Four Applied Examples," *Computational Economics*, 30 (3), 265-290.

Marshall, Alfred (1959 [1890]), *Principles of economics.* London: Macmillan.

Martin, Ron and Peter Sunley (2006), "Path dependence and regional economic evolution," *Journal of Economic Geography*, 6 (4), 395–437.

Massow, Michael von and Elkafi Hassini (2013), "Pricing strategy in the presence of reference prices with thresholds," *Journal of Revenue and Pricing Management*, 12 (4), 339–359.

Mayhew, Glenn E. and Russell S. Winer (1992), "An Empirical Analysis of Internal and External Reference Prices Using Scanner Data," *Journal of Consumer Research*, 19 (1), 62–70.

Mazumdar, Tridib, S. P. Raj, and Indrajit Sinha (2005), "Reference Price Research: Review and Propositions," *Journal of Marketing*, 69 (4), 84–102.

McCarthy, E. J. (1960), *Basic marketing: a managerial approach.* Homewood, Illinois: Irwin

McFadden, Daniel (1986), "The Choice Theory Approach to Market Research," *Marketing Science*, 5 (4), 275–297.

Menger, Carl (1871), *Grundsätze der Volkswirthschaftslehre.* Vienna: W. Braumüller.
——— (1883), *Untersuchungen über die Methode der Socialwissenschaften und der Politischen Oekonomie insbesondere.* Leipzig: Duncker & Humblot.

Meunier, Jacob (2001), *On the fast track: French Railway Modernization and the Origins of the TGV 1944-1983.* Westport, Conneticut: Praeger.

Meyer, Tobias G. (2012), *Path dependence in two-sided markets. A simulation study on technological path dependence with an application to platform competition in the smartphone industry*. Dissertation Freie Universität Berlin.

Meyer, Tobias G. and Michael Kleinaltenkamp (2011), "Does quality win? A Simulation Study on Technological Path Dependence in Two-sided Markets with an Application to Platform Competition in the Smartphone Industry," *Proceedings of the Conference of the Australian and New Zealand Marketing Academy*.

Midgley, David, Robert E. Marks, and Dinesh Kunchamwar (2007), "Building and assurance of agent-based models: An example and challenge to the field," *Complexities in Markets Special Issue*, 60 (8), 884–893.

Milford, Karl (2008), "Carl Menger (1840-1921)," in *Klassiker des ökonomischen Denkens. Band 1*, Heinz D. Kurz, ed. München: C.H. Beck, 306–325.

Mill, John S. (1857 [1848]), *Principles of Political Economy With Some of Their Applications to Social Philosophy*. Manchester: Routledge & Sons.

Miller, John H. (1998), "Active Nonlinear Tests (ANTs) of Complex Simulation Models," *Management Science*, 44 (6), 820–830.

Miller, John H. and Scott E. Page (2007), *Complex adaptive systems. An introduction to computational models of social life*. Princeton, N.J: Princeton University Press.

Mitchell, B. R. (1964), "The Coming of the Railway and United Kingdom Economic Growth," *The Journal of Economic History*, 24 (3), 315–336.

Mitev, Nathalie N. (1996), "More than a failure? The computerized reservation systems at French Railways," *Information Technology & People*, 9 (4), 8–19.

Monroe, Kent B. (1973), "Buyers' Subjective Perceptions of Price," *Journal of Marketing Research*, 10 (1), 70–80.

Nagle, Thomas T. and Reed K. Holden (2002), *The strategy and tactics of pricing. A guide to profitable decision making*. Upper Saddle River, New Jersey: Prentice-Hall.

Nance, Richard E. and Robert G. Sargent (2002), "Perspectives on the Evolution of Simulation," *Operations Research*, 50 (1), 161–172.

Nasiry, Javad and Ioana Popescu (2011), "Dynamic Pricing with Loss-Averse Consumers and Peak-End Anchoring," *Operations Research*, 59 (6), 1361–1368.

Nerlove, Marc (1958), "Adaptive Expectations and Cobweb Phenomena," *The Quarterly Journal of Economics*, 72 (2), 227–240.

Newman, Peter (1960), "The Erosion of Marshall's Theory of Value," *The Quarterly Journal of Economics*, 74 (4), 587–599.

Nitzsch, Rüdiger von (1998), "Prospect Theory und Käuferverhalten," *DBW Die Betriebswirtschaft*, 58 (5), 622–634.

North, Douglass C. (1990), *Institutions, Institutional Change and Economic Performance. Political Economy of Institutions and Decisions*. New York: Cambridge University Press.

North, Michael J. and Charles M. Macal (2007), *Managing business complexity. Discovering strategic solutions with agent-based modeling and simulation.* Oxford: Oxford University Press.

Olaru, Doina and Sharon Purchase (2014), "Rethinking validation: Efficient search of the space of parameters for an agent-based model," *Australasian Marketing Journal,* 22 (1), 60–68.

Orcutt, Guy H. (1957), "A New Type of Socio-Economic System," *The Review of Economics and Statistics,* 39 (2), 116–123.

Osterwalder, Alexander and Yves Pigneur (2010), *Business model generation. A handbook for visionaries, game changers, and challengers.* Hoboken, New Jersey: Wiley.

Ostrom, Thomas M. (1988), "Computer simulation: The third symbol system," *Journal of Experimental Social Psychology,* 24 (5), 381–392.

OTIF, see Intergovernmental Organisation for International Carriage by Rail

Oum, Tae H. and Chunyan Yu (1994), "Economic Efficiency of Railways and Implications for Public Policy: A Comparative Study of the OECD Countries' Railways," *Journal of Transport Economics and Policy,* 28 (2), 121–138.

Page, Scott E. (2006), "Path Dependence," *Quarterly Journal of Political Science,* 1 (1), 87–115.

Pajunen, Kalle (2008), "The Nature of Organizational Mechanisms," *Organization Studies,* 29 (11), 1449–1468.

Parducci, Allen (1965), "Category judgment: A range-frequency model," *Psychological Review,* 72 (6), 407–418.

Paukner, Gerd (1992), "Jahresrückblick 1991 der europäischen Eisenbahnen. Spanische Staatsbahnen (RENFE)," in *Die Bundesbahn / Die Deutsche Bahn,* Deutsche Bundesbahn and Deutsche Reichsbahn, eds. Darmstadt: Hestra-Verlag, 198–201.

Penz, Reinhard and Birger Priddat (2009), "Thorstein B. Veblen (1857-1929)," in *Klassiker des ökonomischen Denkens. Band 2,* Heinz D. Kurz, ed. München: C.H. Beck, 83–101.

Pérez, Javier B., Miguel A. Sánchez, Philippe Mathieu, Juan M. C. Rodríguez, Emmanuel Adam, Alfonso Ortega, María N. Moreno, Elena Navarro, Benjamin Hirsch, Henrique Lopes-Cardoso, and Vicente Julián, eds. (2012), *Highlights on Practical Applications of Agents and Multi-Agent Systems. Advances in Intelligent and Soft Computing:* Springer.

Perrot, Franz (1870), *Die deutschen Eisenbahnen. Beiträge zur Kenntniß und zur Reform des deutschen Eisenbahnwesens.* Rostock: Ernst Kuhn's Verlag.

Pettigrew, A. M. (1990), "Longitudinal Field Research on Change: Theory and Practice," *Organization Science,* 1 (3), 267–292.

Petty, William (1662), "A treatise of taxes & contributions," London: Brooke. Full text available at http://socserv.mcmaster.ca/econ/ugcm/3ll3/petty/taxes.txt

Pierson, Paul (2000), "The Limits of Design: Explaining Institutional Origins and Change," *Governance,* 13 (4), 475–499.

Pigou, Arthur C. (1999 [1920]), *Economics of welfare.* Basingstoke: Macmillan.

Pölt, Stefan (2011), "The rise and fall of RM," *Journal of Revenue and Pricing Management*, 10 (1), 23–25.

Popescu, Ioana and Yaozhong Wu (2007), "Dynamic Pricing Strategies with Reference Effects," *Operations Research*, 55 (3), 413–429.

Popper, Karl R. (2002 [1945]), *The open society and its enemies*. London: Routledge.

Postrel, Steven R. (1990), "Competing Networks and Proprietary Standards: The Case of Quadraphonic Sound," *The Journal of Industrial Economics*, 39 (2), 169–185.

Prescott, Edward C. (1975), "Efficiency of the Natural Rate," *Journal of Political Economy*, 83 (6), 1229–1236.

Puffert, Douglas J. (2002), "Path Dependence in Spatial Networks: The Standardization of Railway Track Gauge," *Explorations in Economic History*, 39 (3), 282–314.
—— (2009), *Tracks Across Continents. Paths Through History. The Economic Dynamics of Standardization in Railway Gauge*. Chicago: The University of Chicago Press.

Quesnay, François (1758), *Tableau Économique avec son explication, ou extrait des économies royales de Sully*. Paris.

Ragin, Charles C. (1987), *The comparative method. Moving beyond qualitative and quantitative strategies*. Berkeley, California: University of California Press.

Ragin, Charles C. and Howard S. Becker (1992), *What is a case? Exploring the foundations of social inquiry*. Cambridge, New York: Cambridge University Press.

Railsback, Steven F., Steven L. Lytinen, and Stephen K. Jackson (2006), "Agent-based Simulation Platforms: Review and Development Recommendations," *Simulation*, 82 (9), 609–623.

Rand, William and Roland T. Rust (2011), "Agent-based modeling in marketing: Guidelines for rigor," *International Journal of Research in Marketing*, 28 (3), 181–193.

Rank, Emil (1895), *Das Eisenbahntarifwesen in seiner Beziehung zu Volkswirtschaft und Verwaltung*. Vienna: A. Hölder.

Rao, Vithala R. (1984), "Pricing Research in Marketing: The State of the Art," *The Journal of Business*, 57 (1), S39.

Reed, Malcolm C., ed. (1969), *Railways in the Victorian economy: studies in finance and economic growth*. Newton Abbot: David and Charles.

Ricardo, David (1817), *Principles of Political Economy and Taxation*. London: John Murray.

Rittershausen, H. (1989 [1950]), "Bundesbahn im Wettbewerb. Reprint originating from 1950," in *40 Jahre Deutsche Bundesbahn, 1949-1989*, Horst Weigelt and Ulrich Langner, eds. Darmstadt: Hestra-Verlag, 28–33.

Robinson, Stewart (2007), *Simulation. The Practice of Model Development and Use*. Hoboken, New Jersey: Wiley.

Rogers, Everett M. (1962), *Diffusion of innovations*. New York: Free Press.

Rohrer, John and Muzafer Sherif, eds. (1951), *Social psychology at the crossroads. the University of Oklahoma lectures in social psychology*. Oxford: Harper.

Sarter, Adolf (1927), *Verkehrswerbung bei den Eisenbahnen.* Berlin: Verlag der verkehrswissenschaftlichen Lehrmittelgesellschaft.

Sato, Kimitoshi and Katsushige Sawaki (2012), "Dynamic pricing of high-speed rail with transport competition," *Journal of Revenue and Pricing Management*, 11 (5), 548–559.

Say, Jean-Baptiste (2006 [1803]), *Oeuvres complètes. I Traité d'Économie Politique ou simple exposition de la manière dont se forment, se distribuent et se consomment les richesses.* Paris: Economica.

Schelling, Thomas C. (1971), "Dynamic models of segregation," *The Journal of Mathematical Sociology*, 1 (2), 143–186.

Schiefelbusch, Martin and Sonja Ziemer (2013), ""Seamless travel" - international rover tickets for rail travel in Europe," in *Trains across borders. Comparative studies on international cooperation in railway development. Integration von Infrastrukturen in Europa im historischen Vergleich*, Vol. 4, Gerold Ambrosius, ed. Baden-Baden: Nomos, 217–283.

Schivelbusch, Wolfgang (2011 [1977]), *Geschichte der Eisenbahnreise. Zur Industrialisierung von Raum und Zeit im 19. Jahrhundert.* Frankfurt am Main: Fischer-Taschenbuch-Verlag.

Schnell, Peter and Karl O. Paganetti (1989 [1986]), "Europäische Reisezugfahrplankonferenz. Geschichte und Entwicklung. Reprint originating from 1986," in *40 Jahre Deutsche Bundesbahn, 1949-1989*, Horst Weigelt and Ulrich Langner, eds. Darmstadt: Hestra-Verlag, 617–619.

Scholl, Michael and Dirk Totzek (2011), "Die Preispolitik professionalisieren," *Harvard Business Manager Edition* (4), 34–40.

Schreyögg, Georg and Jörg Sydow, eds. (2003), *Strategische Prozesse und Pfade. Managementforschung*, Vol. 13. Wiesbaden: Gabler.
———— (2011), "Organizational Path Dependence: A Process View," *Organization Studies*, 32 (3), 321–335.

Schreyögg, Georg, Jörg Sydow, and Jan P. Holtmann (2011), "How history matters in organisations: The case of path dependence," *Management & Organizational History*, 6 (1), 81–100.

Schreyögg, Georg, Jörg Sydow, and Jochen Koch (2003), "Organisatorische Pfade - Von der Pfadabhängigkeit zur Pfadkreation?," in *Strategische Prozesse und Pfade. Managementforschung*, Vol. 13, Georg Schreyögg and Jörg Sydow, eds. Wiesbaden: Gabler, 257–294.

Schwalbe, Ulrich (2008), "Léon Walras (1834-1910)," in *Klassiker des ökonomischen Denkens. Band 1*, Heinz D. Kurz, ed. München: C.H. Beck, 242–266.

Scott, Peter (2001), "Path Dependence and Britain's "Coal Wagon Problem"," *Explorations in Economic History*, 38, 366–385.

Seawright, Jason and John Gerring (2008), "Case Selection Techniques in Case Study Research. A Menu of Qualitative and Quantitative Options," *Political Research Quarterly*, 61 (2), 294–308.

Serra, Antonio (1982 [1613]), "Breve trattato delle cause che possono fare abbondare li Regni d'oro e d'argento dove non sono miniere con applicazione al Regno di Napoli, Napoli, 1613," *Scrittori classici italiani di economia politica. Parte antica.*

Sherif, Muzafer, Daniel Taub, and Carl I. Hovland (1958), "Assimilation and contrast effects of anchoring stimuli on judgments," *Journal of Experimental Psychology*, 55 (2), 150–155.

Siggelkow, Nicolaj (2007), "Persuasion With Case Studies," *Academy of Management Journal*, 50 (1), 20–24.

Simon, Hermann and Martin Fassnacht (2009), *Preismanagement. Strategie - Analyse - Entscheidung - Umsetzung*. Wiesbaden: Gabler.

Smith, Adam (1776), *An Inquiry into the Nature and Causes of the Wealth of Nations*. London: Strahan and Cadell.

Smith, Barry C., John F. Leimkuhler, and Ross M. Darrow (1992), "Yield Management at American Airlines," *Interfaces*, 22 (1), 8–31.

SNCF (1968-1971), *Le nuancement tarifaire*. Archives historiques dossier 26LM0465
——— (2013), "Les tarifs voyageurs. Conditions générales de vente," VO 0131.
——— (2013a), "Le train en France depuis 1827," [available at http://www.sncf.com/fr/portrait-du-groupe/histoire-sncf?date=1827#].

Sneed, Joseph D. (1971), *The logical structure of mathematical physics. Synthese library*. Dordrecht: Reidel.

Speck, Georg (2011), "Der öffentliche Gebrauch der Eisenbahnen," *Eisenbahn-Revue International* (1), 42–45.

Stegmüller, Wolfgang (1973), *Theorie und Erfahrung: Zweiter Halbband. Theorienstrukturen und Theoriendynamik. Probleme und Resultate der Wissenschaftstheorie und Analytischen Philosophie*, 2, 2. Halbband: Springer.

Strasser, Sandra (1996), "The Effect of Yield Management on Railroads," *Transportation Quarterly*, 50 (2), 47–55.

Streichfuss, Martin, ed. (2010), *Railway Transformation*. Hamburg: DVV Media Group GmbH | Eurailpress.

Strobel, Manfred (1977), "Marktorientierte Preisgestaltung - scharfe Kalkulationen," in *Jahrbuch des Eisenbahnwesens 1977*, Wolfgang Vaerst and Heinrich Lehmann, eds. Darmstadt: Hestra-Verlag, 30–34.

Strohmaier, Rita (2008), "Richard Cantillon (1680-1734)," in *Klassiker des ökonomischen Denkens. Band 1*, Heinz D. Kurz, ed. München: C.H. Beck, 46–56.

Sturn, Richard (2008), "Adam Smith (1723-1790)," in *Klassiker des ökonomischen Denkens. Band 1*, Heinz D. Kurz, ed. München: C.H. Beck, 68–88.

Sumberg, Theodore A. (1991), "Antonio Serra: A Neglected Herald of the Acquisitive System," *American Journal of Economics and Sociology*, 50 (3), 365–373.

Sydow, Jörg, Georg Schreyögg, and Jochen Koch (2009), "Organizational Path Dependence: Opening the Black Box," *Academy of Management Review*, 34 (4), 689–709.

Sydow, Jörg, Arnold Windeler, Gordon Müller-Seitz, and Knut Lange (2012), "Path Constitution Analysis: A Methodology for Understanding Path Dependence and Path Creation," *BuR Business Research Journal*, 5 (2), 1–22.

Talluri, Kalyan T. and Garrett van Ryzin (2005), *The theory and practice of revenue management. International series in operations research & management science*, Vol. 68. New York: Springer.

Tellis, Gerard J. (1986), "Beyond the Many Faces of Price: An Integration of Pricing Strategies," *Journal of Marketing*, 50 (4), 146–160.

Temath, Christian, Michael Frank, Stefan Polt, and Leena Suhl (2013), "Modelling dependent demand structures in a network-based revenue opportunity model," *Journal of Revenue and Pricing Management*, 12 (2), 162–176.

Tesfatsion, Leigh and Kenneth L. Judd, eds. (2006), *Handbook of Computational Economics:* Elsevier.

Thaler, Richard H. (1980), "Toward a positive theory of consumer choice," *Journal of Economic Behavior & Organization*, 1 (1), 39–60.
——— (1985), "Mental Accounting and Consumer Choice," *Marketing Science*, 4 (3), 199–214.

Tisue, Seth and Uri Wilensky (2004), "NetLogo: A Simple Environment for Modeling Complexity," Presented at the International Conference on Complex Systems, Boston, May 16–21, 2004. Available at http://ccl.sesp.northwestern.edu/papers/netlogo-iccs2004.pdf.

Troitzsch, Klaus G. (2013), "Historical introduction," in *Simulating Social Complexity. A handbook*, Bruce Edmonds and Ruth Meyer, eds. Berlin, Heidelberg, 13–22.
——— (2014), "Analysing Simulation Results Statistically: Does Significance Matter?," in *Interdisciplinary Applications of Agent-Based Social Simulation and Modeling*, Diana-Francisca Adamatti, Dimuro Graçalis Pereira and Helder Coelho, eds.: Hershey, (submitted version).

Tversky, Amos and Daniel Kahneman (1991), "Loss Aversion in Riskless Choice: A Reference-Dependent Model," *The Quarterly Journal of Economics*, 106 (4), 1039–1061.

UIC [International Union of Railways] (2006), Leaflet 106. *Standard International Passenger Tariff (TCV)*. Paris: UIC.
——— (2008), Leaflet 130. *Commercial framework for the international distribution of rail products*. Paris: UIC.

Vaerst, Wolfgang and Heinrich Lehmann, eds. (1977), *Jahrbuch des Eisenbahnwesens 1977*. Darmstadt: Hestra-Verlag.

van Suntum, Ulrich (2008), "William Stanley Jevons (1835-1882)," in *Klassiker des ökonomischen Denkens. Band 1*, Heinz D. Kurz, ed. München: C.H. Beck, 267–286.

van Waterschoot, Walter and Christophe van den Bulte (1992), "The 4P Classification of the Marketing Mix Revisited," *Journal of Marketing*, 56 (4), 83–93.

Vargo, Stephen L. and Robert F. Lusch (2004), "Evolving to a New Dominant Logic for Marketing," *Journal of Marketing*, 68 (1), 1–17.

Vaughn, Karen I. (1994), *Austrian economics in America. The migration of a tradition. Historical perspectives on modern economics*. Cambridge, New York: Cambridge University Press.
——— (1999), "Hayek's Implicit Economics: Rules and the Problem of Order," *The Review of Austrian Economics*, 11 (1-2), 129-144.

Veblen, Thorstein (1915), *Imperial Germany and the industrial revolution*. New York; London: Macmillan.

Vergne, Jean-Philippe (2013), "QWERTY Is Dead, Long Live Path Dependence!," Forthcoming in *Research Policy*, Available at SSRN: http://ssrn.com/abstract=2254964.

Vergne, Jean-Philippe and Rodolphe Durand (2010), "The Missing Link Between the Theory and Empirics of Path Dependence: Conceptual Clarification, Testability Issue, and Methodological Implications," *Journal of Management Studies*, 47 (4), 736–759.

Volkmann, John (1951), "Scales of judgment and their implications for social psychology," in *Social psychology at the crossroads. The University of Oklahoma lectures in social psychology*, John Rohrer and Muzafer Sherif, eds. Oxford: Harper, 273–298.

VÖV Verband öffentlicher Verkehr [Swiss Association of Public Transport] (undated), "Geschichte des Generalabonnements,"
——— (2007), "Manual Direkter Verkehr," Berne.

Waldrop, M. M. (1992), *Complexity. The emerging science and the edge of order and chaos*. New York: Simon & Schuster.

Walras, Léon (1988 [1874-1926]), *Éléments d'économie politique pure ou théorie de la richesse sociale. Édition comparée des éditions de 1874, 1889, 1896, 1900 et 1926. Auguste et Léon Walras. Oeuvres économiques complètes.* Paris: Economica.

Walz, Werner (1971), *Die schönen Plakate der Deutschen Bundesbahn:* Boldt.

Weatherford, Lawrence R. and Samuel E. Bodily (1992), "A Taxonomy and Research Overview of Perishable-Asset Revenue Management: Yield Management, Overbooking, and Pricing," *Operations Research*, 40 (5), 831–844.

Weber, Karsten (2004), "Der wissenschaftstheoretische Status von Simulationen," in *Wissenschaftstheorie in Ökonomie und Wirtschaftsinformatik. Theoriebildung und -bewertung, Ontologien, Wissensmanagement*, Ulrich Frank, ed. Wiesbaden: Deutscher Universitäts-Verlag, 191–210.

Weigelt, Horst and Ulrich Langner, eds. (1989), *40 Jahre Deutsche Bundesbahn, 1949-1989.* Darmstadt: Hestra-Verlag.

Wilensky, Uri and Mitchel Resnick (1999), "Thinking in Levels: A Dynamic Systems Approach to Making Sense of the World," *Journal of Science Education and Technology*, 8 (1), 3–19.

Williamson, Oliver E. (1985), *The economic institutions of capitalism. Firms, markets, relational contracting.* New York: Free Press.

Winer, Russell S. (1986), "A Reference Price Model of Brand Choice for Frequently Purchased Products," *Journal of Consumer Research*, 13 (2), 250–256.
——— (1989), "A multi-stage model of choice incorporating reference prices," *Marketing Letters*, 1 (1), 27-36.

Wolkowitsch, Maurice (2004), "Chapitre XII - La politique tarifaire des compagnies de chemins de fer secondaires," *Revue d'histoire des chemins de fer* (30), 421–464.

Wu, Chien-Fu and Michael Hamada (2009), *Experiments. Planning, analysis, and optimization.* Hoboken, New Jersey: Wiley.

Yeoman, Ian (2013), "To discount or not, that is the question," *Journal of Revenue and Pricing Management*, 12 (3), 205–206.
——— (2013a), "The importance of consumer behavior," *Journal of Revenue and Pricing Management*, 12 (5), 383–384.

Yin, Robert K. (1981), "The Case Study Crisis: Some Answers," *Administrative Science Quarterly*, 26 (1), 58–65.

——— (2009), Case study research. Design and methods. Applied social research methods series, Vol. 5. Los Angeles, California: Sage.

Ziegler, Dieter (1996), *Eisenbahnen und Staat im Zeitalter der Industrialisierung. Die Eisenbahnpolitik der deutschen Staaten im Vergleich.* Stuttgart: F. Steiner.

Zimmermann, Benedikt, Catherine Cleophas, and Michael Frank (2011), "Universeller Simulator für Revenue Management," *Internationales Verkehrswesen*, 63 (3), 76–80.

Appendix A Source code

This appendix contains a simplified version of the original source code of the revenue simulation model implemented in Netlogo 5.0.3. Where appropriate for a better understanding of the functions used in the revenue simulation model, I use additional explicating text and pseudo-code instead of representing the original Netlogo code. The central functions of the model can also be found in the conceptual protocol as a part of the dissertation text.

For an initial understanding of the code representing the market process modelled, the relations between the model functions are displayed on the following page. The overview also puts the different functions into their logical sequence within the model setup as well as the model steps.

After the setup of the model, in which schedules are imported and basic characteristics of consumers are set, the flow of a tick begins. First, prices are set according to the rules train operators follow and through observer intervention. Subsequently, consumers affected with mobility requirements search for transport offers available. In most cases, they have multiple options and thus need to perform a utility comparision to decide which offer to choose. Reporter functions are activated if necessary. They are mostly used for calculating the transport firm's price response to an individual request and to calculate the reference values emerging out of individual price experience.

© Springer Fachmedien Wiesbaden GmbH, part of Springer Nature 2014
N. Kellermann, *Searching for a path out of distance fares*, Edition KWV,
https://doi.org/10.1007/978-3-658-23112-5

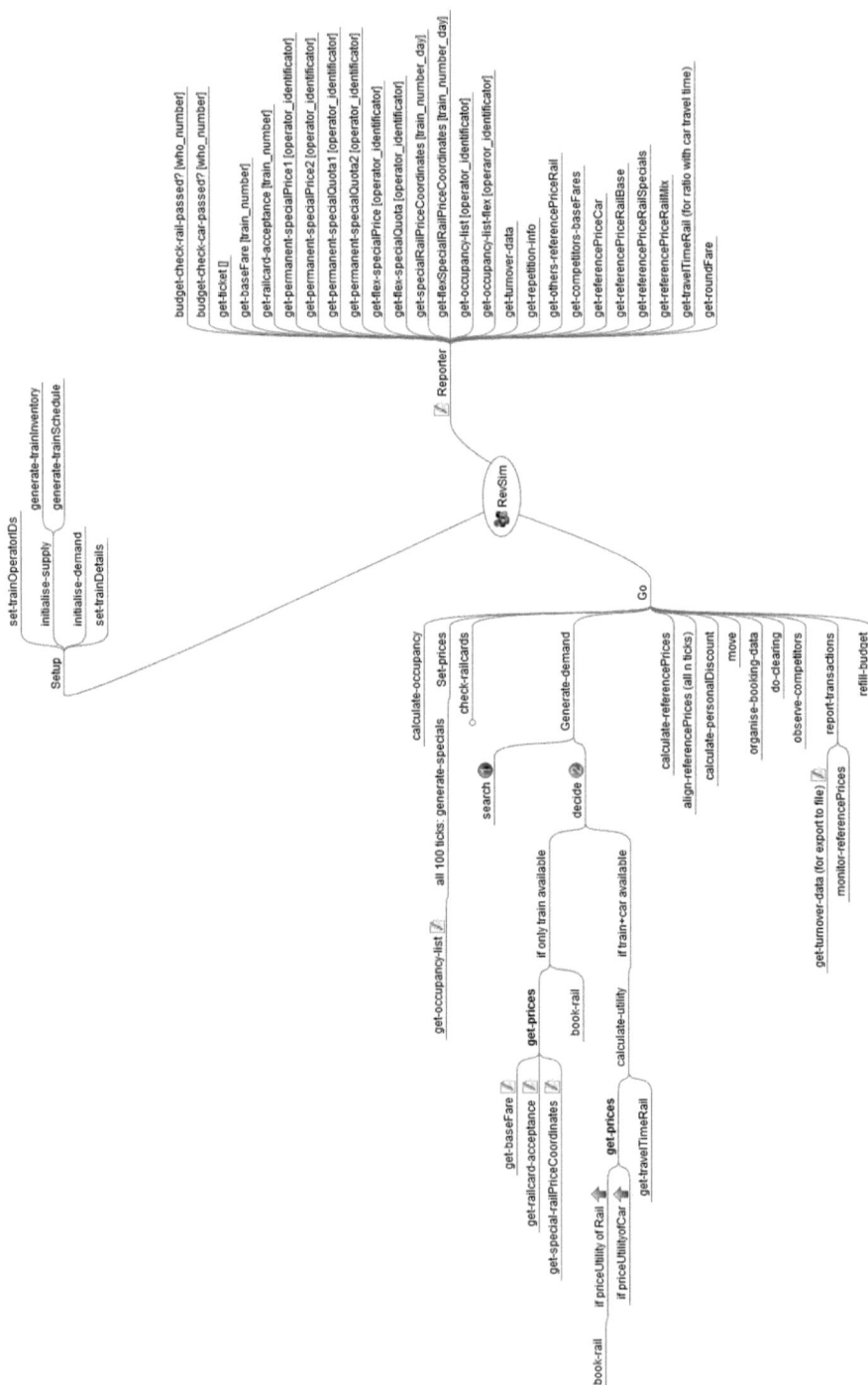

Source code

```
extensions [ table matrix profiler ]
globals
[
```

global variables are primarily used for model observation and reporting

```
]

breed [ trainOperators trainOperator ]
breed [ trainsets trainset ] ;rolling stock
breed [ trains train ] ;scheduled trains
breed [ passengers passenger ]

trainOperators-own
[
   RM ;applies quantity-based RM (y/n)
   my_id
   my_trainsets
   my_runs
   my_trains ;contains simple 1-item-list of all trains run by an operator
   my_schedule
   my_turnover ;temporary sum used in clearing
   my_tickTurnover
   my_totalTurnover ;turnover aggregated for all runs
   my_revenueShare
   my_revenueShareRecord
   my_permanentSpecialPrice1
   my_permanentSpecialPrice2
   my_flexSpecialPrice
   my_flexSpecialQuota
   my_bookingsList ;contains (train ID) (number of seats booked on this train)
   my_priceStrategy
   my_competitorsBaseFareMemory1 ;if available, prices of one of the competitors
   my_competitorsBaseFareMemory2 ;if available, prices of the other of the two competitors
   my_competitorsSpecialsMemory1
   my_competitorsSpecialsMemory2
]

trainsets-own [ my_operator ]

trains-own
[
   my_operator ;can be 1, 2, or 3
   my_number
   my_departureTime
   my_capacity
   my_baseFare
   my_priceInventoryMatrix
   my_currentOccupancy
   my_occupancyRecord ;lists all entries of t-1 that are currently stored in the priceInventoryMatrix
   my_averageOccupancy
   my_category
   my_travelTime
   permanentSpecialsAvailable ;boolean
   flexSpecialsAvailable ;boolean
   my_specialsBooked
   railcardAllowed
```

```
]

selectedTrains-own
[
  my_averageOccupancy
  my_number
]

Passengers-own ; links to other individuals are representing friends & family
[
  my_car
  my_publicTransportAccess
  my_age
  my_degreeOfFlexibility ; reflects the passenger's capability to take an earlier/later transport offer
  my_preferenceForFlexibility ; reflects the passenger's attitude to restrictions
  my_railcard ; boolean
  my_rc ; 0=no railcard, 1=railcard
  my_socioGroup
  my_lossAversion
  my_railcardValidity ; integer in days from 365 to 0
  my_railcardInUse
  my_budget
  my_demand ; containing list (t1) (t2) t1=time till mobility demand; t2=clocktime
  my_predecision ; determines whether a price calculation has to be made for rail prices (needed for
processor time saving)
  my_demandMatrix ; contains demand (day & time) for forecast period
  my_availability
  my_chosenTrain
  my_transactionsRail ; contains rail base prices including railcard fares paid until forgotten
  my_transactionsRailLoyalty ; contains the amount paid of a loyalty transaction
  my_transactionsRailLoyaltyTime ; contains the rest validity of the transaction valid for loyalty
  my_transactionsRailSpecials ; contains special prices paid until they are forgotten
  my_transactionsCar
  my_referencePriceRailBase
  my_referencePriceRailSpecials
  my_referencePriceRailMix
  my_referencePriceCar
  my_currentRailPrice
  my_specialCoordinates
  my_personalDiscount
  railUtility
  carUtility
]

;--------------------------------------------------------------------------------
to setup

  clear-all

  set initialFuelPrice FUELPRICE
  set initialRailcardPrice RAILCARDPRICE
  set preferenceForFlexibilityThreshold1 [value] ; controls the consumers' switching be-
haviour from standard fare to flex specials
  set preferenceForFlexibilityThreshold2 [value] ; controls the consumers' switching from
standard fare or flex specials to restrictive specials
  set globalReferencePriceCar 0
  set globalReferencePriceRailBase 0
  set globalReferencePriceRailSpecials 0
  set globalReferencePriceRailMix 0
```

```
    create-trainOperators NUMBER_trainOperators [set my_bookingsList []]
    let i 0
    foreach sort trainOperators
    [
      ask ?
      [
        setxy 15 (15 - i)
        set shape "wheel"
        set color random 100 set size 0.5
      ]
      set i i + 1
    ]
    set-trainOperatorIDs
    foreach sort trainOperators
    [
      ask ?
      [
        if my_id = 1 [set RM true]
        if my_id = 2 [set RM false]
        if my_id = 3 [set RM false]
        set my_competitorsBaseFareMemory1 []
        set my_competitorsBaseFareMemory2 []
        set my_competitorsSpecialsMemory1 []
        set my_competitorsSpecialsMemory2 []
      ]
    ]

  set listTicketChar [ "A" "B" "C" "D" "E" "F" "G" "H" "I" "J" "K" "L" "M" "N" "O"
"P" "Q" "R" "S" "T" "U" "V" "W" "X" "Y" "Z" "1" "2" "3" "4" "5" "6" "7" "8" "9" ]
  set ticketList []
  set car_performance 0
  set rail_performance 0
  set clearingRail []
  set averageRailUtilityData []
  set averageCarUtilityData []
  set specialsList []
  ask patch -10 0 [set pcolor red set plabel "City A"]
  ask patch 10 0 [set pcolor red set plabel "City B" ]
  initialise-supply
  initialise-demand
  set-trainDetails  ;e. g., individual travel time
  reset-ticks
end

;--------------------------------------------------------------------------------
to profile
```

This function is needed to observe processor time used by the core functions of the model.

```
    profiler:start         ;start profiling
    repeat 465 [ go ]
    profiler:stop          ;stop profiling
    print profiler:report  ;view the results
    profiler:reset         ;clear the data

end
```

```
;---------------------------------------------------------------------
to go

    set railcardsSoldTick 0
    if NUMBER_TRAINOPERATORS > 1 [set PERSONALDISCOUNT false] ;feature not implemented
for more than 1 operator
    if PERSONALDISCOUNT = true [set RAILCARD false] ;implemented in order to make sure
that these scenarios are treated separately

    if ticks > 10 [calculate-occupancy]
    set-prices
    check-railcards
    generate-demand ;generate demand for the specific tick

    calculate-referencePrices
    if ticks > 25 AND ticks mod 14 = 0 [align-referencePrices] ;align reference prices
with interlinked passengers, e. g., once every 14 ticks
```

This setting can be manipulated by the observer. Caution: number of n ticks must be updated in align-referencePrices with the railcard validity considered.

```
    if PERSONALDISCOUNT = true [calculate-personalDiscount]
    move
    do-clearing
    observe-competitors
    report-transactions
    refill-budget
    set clearingRail []
    tick
end

;---------------------------------------------------------------------
to set-trainOperatorIDs

    let i 1
    foreach sort trainOperators ;set ID numbers for each individual train operator
      [
        ask ?
        [
            set my_id i
            set i i + 1
        ]
      ]

end

;---------------------------------------------------------------------
to-report get-ticket []

    let ticket ""
    while [ticket = ""]
    [
        repeat 6 [set ticket word ticket (one-of listTicketChar)]
        if length ticketList > 0 [  if member? ticket ticketList [ set ticket "" ]]
;make sure that no double ticket is generated
    ]

    set ticketList lput ticket ticketList
    report ticket
end
```

```
;-------------------------------------------------------------------------------
to initialise-supply

    generate-train_inventory
    generate-train_schedule

end


;-------------------------------------------------------------------------------
to generate-train_inventory
```

The function generates the trainsets and the seat configuration for each train operator. Those are loaded from an external file representing the necessity to import inventory and schedule data from other information systems of the firm.

```
foreach sort trainOperators
    [
      ask ?
      [

        file-open "trainsets.txt"
        while [ not file-at-end? ]
        [
          set trainsetData list file-read file-read
          if item 0 trainsetData = my_id
          [
            set my_trainsets my_trainsets + item 1 trainsetData
            set total_trainsets total_trainsets + my_trainsets
            hatch-trainsets my_trainsets [setxy 10 0 set my_operator word "operator"
? ]
            ;user-message "Trainsets for one operator loaded!"

          ]

        ]
        file-close
      ]
    ]
end


;-------------------------------------------------------------------------------
to generate-train_schedule
```

Represents daily runs of trains in time in each direction.

```
set trainList []
set simplifiedTrainList []
foreach sort trainOperators
    [
      ask ?
      [
      set my_runs 0
      set my_schedule table:make
      set globalTrainSchedule table:make
      set my_trains []
      file-open "schedule.txt"
      while [ not file-at-end? ]
      [
          set scheduleData (list (file-read) (file-read) (file-read) ) ;contains (ID)
(trainpairs) (frequency)
```

```
if item 0 scheduleData = my_id
[
    set my_runs item 1 scheduleData
```

If the first number = ID, following number is the number of train pairs running between A and B during the tick.

```
set total_runningTrainPairs total_runningTrainPairs + my_runs

;creation of a simple operator schedule

let frequency item 2 scheduleData ;frequency in which the trains run during the day,
```
e. g. a train every 2 hours
```
    let timeBuffer 24 - (my_runs * frequency)
    if timeBuffer < 0 [ user-message "Data error - incorrect train frequency."
]
    let startTime int random-normal (timeBuffer / 2) 1
    if startTime > timeBuffer [set startTime timeBuffer print "Start time has
been reset."]
    let i 0
    let operator_id my_id
    repeat my_runs ;trains from A to B
        [

        let ticket get-ticket ;get a single identifier for any train running

        let time startTime + i * frequency
        let infoList ["origin A" "destination B" "DepartureTime:"]
        set infoList lput time infoList

        set my_trains lput ticket my_trains
        hatch-trains 1
        [
          set my_operator operator_id
          set my_number ticket
          set my_capacity [number of seats]
          set my_category "unknown"
          set my_travelTime "unknown"
          set my_departureTime time
          set permanentSpecialsAvailable false
          set flexSpecialsAvailable false
          set my_occupancyRecord []
        ]
        table:put my_schedule ticket infoList
        set simplifiedTrainList fput list my_id ticket simplifiedTrainList
        set trainList lput list ticket time trainList
        set i i + 1
        ]
    set i 0
    repeat my_runs ;trains from B to A
        [
        let ticket get-ticket

        let time startTime + i * frequency
        let infoList ["origin B" "destination A" "DepartureTime:"]
        set infoList lput time infoList

        set my_trains lput ticket my_trains
        hatch-trains 1
```

Set the basic characteristics of the trains.

```
                [
                    set my_operator operator_id
                    set my_number ticket
                    set my_capacity [number of seats]
                    set my_category "unknown"
                    set my_travelTime "unknown"
                    set my_departureTime time
                    set permanentSpecialsAvailable false
                    set flexSpecialsAvailable false
                    set my_occupancyRecord []
                ]
                table:put my_schedule ticket infoList
                set simplifiedTrainList fput list my_id ticket simplifiedTrainList
                set trainList lput list ticket time trainList ;ID for the train & time
                set i i + 1
                ]
            table:put globalTrainSchedule my_id my_schedule
        ]
    ]
    ]
    file-close


    ask trains with [my_operator = 1 ] [ set railCardAllowed true ]
    ask trains with [my_operator = 2 ] [ set my_capacity [number of seats] ]
    set trainList shuffle trainList
  ]

end

;-------------------------------------------------------------------------------
to initialise-demand

 set numberPassengers [number]
 set selectedPassengers [number]
 create-passengers numberPassengers [set size 0.2] ;passengers in Cities A and B
```

Here, the basic characteristics of consumer agents are set.

```
ask passengers
  [
    set my_socioGroup ""
    set my_lossAversion 1 + random-float 1
    setxy 10 0
    fd (0.75 + random-float 2 )
    set my_transactionsRail []
    set my_transactionsRailSpecials []
    set my_transactionsCar []
    set my_railcard false
    set my_railcardInUse false
    set my_specialCoordinates "void"
    set my_age random-normal 40 20
    set my_degreeOfFlexibility precision (random 100 / 100) 2 ;sets the individual ability
to choose other trains than the exact fit to the demand time
    set my_preferenceForFlexibility precision (random 100 / 100) 2 ;Reflects the con-
sumer's attitude to restrictions in ticket use
    if my_age > 95 [set my_age 95]
```

```
    set my_budget random-normal [number A] [number B] ;initial monthly mobility budget
```
according to market research data
```
    set my_car false   ;supply passengers with individual cars
    let i random-float 1
    if i > [empirical figure derived from official statistics] ;x% of the passengers own a car
      [
        set my_car true
        set shape "car"
      ]

]
```

This part of code distributes inhabitants of the grid to a position according to empirical figures.

```
ask n-of selectedPassengers passengers
    [
      setxy -10 0
      fd (0.75 + random-float 1)
    ]

 let loop_counter 1
 let number_of_loops 10

 repeat number_of_loops ;randomly set links to other passengers.
 [
    let percentage int (loop_counter / number_of_loops * 100)
    ;if loop_counter = 1 [print word "Time started: " date-and-time]
    ask n-of int (numberPassengers * 0.1) passengers [create-link-with one-of other
passengers]

    ;print (word "Set-up of links " percentage "% completed.")
    ;if loop_counter = number_of_loops [print word "Time ended: " date-and-time]
    set loop_counter loop_counter + 1
 ]
 ask links [hide-link]
```

If market research data is available, consumers can be divided into different segments with different preferences.

```
ask n-of (count passengers * [market research result]) passengers with [my_socioGroup =
"" AND my_car = true]
    [
      set my_socioGroup "carAddicted"
    ]
ask n-of (count passengers * [market research result]) passengers with [my_socioGroup =
"" AND my_car = true]
    [
      set my_socioGroup "traditionalist"
    ]
ask n-of (count passengers * [market research result]) passengers with [my_socioGroup =
"" AND my_age < [market research result]]
    [
      set my_socioGroup "calculatingYoung"
    ]
ask n-of (count passengers * [market research result]) passengers with [my_socioGroup =
""]
    [
      set my_socioGroup "commuter"
    ]
```

```
ask n-of (count passengers * [market research result]) passengers with [my_socioGroup =
""]
  [
    set my_socioGroup "situativeDecisionMaker"
  ]
ask n-of (count passengers * [market research result]) passengers with [my_socioGroup =
""]
  [
    set my_socioGroup "networkMobilists"
  ]
ask passengers with [my_socioGroup = ""]
  [
    set my_socioGroup "undefined"
  ]
```

This command supplies passengers with public transport access.
```
 ask n-of (count passengers * [number]) passengers
  [
    set my_publicTransportAccess true
  ]
```

```
ask passengers with [my_socioGroup != "carAddicted"]
  [
```
This supplies consumers with railcards. If who mod 8 = 0 ; 1/8 of the population initially have got a railcard.
```
if who mod x = 0
      [
        set my_railcard true
        set my_railcardValidity random 365
        set railcardCounter railcardCounter + 1
      ]
  ]
end
```

```
;--------------------------------------------------------------------------------
to generate-demand
```

This element prepares the model for a possible extension of dependent demand, but is not used for the
experiments described:
```
  ;ask n-of ( [number] - ([number] * CumulatedRailPriceChange% / 3 / 100 )) passen-
gers
```

```
  ask n-of selectedPassengers passengers
  [
    set my_demand []
    set my_availability []
    set my_currentRailPrice 0
    set my_railcardInUse false
    set my_specialCoordinates "void"
    set my_chosenTrain "none"
    set my_predecision "nothing"
```

This function lets consumer agents forget transactions made longer ago, it also involves the optional
observer activation of a random forgetting feature.

```
    let memoryLength 10
    ;car

    if length my_transactionsCar > memoryLength
    [
```

```
    while [length my_transactionsCar > memoryLength]
    [
      if RANDOM_FORGETTING = true
      [
        let n random (memoryLength + 1)
        set my_transactionsCar remove-item n my_transactionsCar
        set my_transactionsCar but-first my_transactionsCar
        ;print (word who ": I forgot item no. " n " of my car transactions")
      ]
      if RANDOM_FORGETTING = false [set my_transactionsCar but-first
my_transactionsCar] ;print "I forgot the first paid price saved in
my_transactionsCar"]
    ]
  ]
  ;rail base fare

  if length my_transactionsRail > memoryLength
  [

    while [length my_transactionsRail > memoryLength]
    [
      if RANDOM_FORGETTING = true
      [
        let n random (memoryLength + 1)
        set my_transactionsRail remove-item n my_transactionsRail
        set my_transactionsRail but-first my_transactionsRail
        ;print (word who ": I forgot item no. " n " of my rail transactions")
      ]
      if RANDOM_FORGETTING = false [set my_transactionsRail but-first
my_transactionsRail] ;print "I forgot the first paid price saved in
my_transactionsRail" ]
    ]
  ]
  ;rail specials

  if length my_transactionsRailSpecials > memoryLength
  [
    while [length my_transactionsRailSpecials > memoryLength]
    [
      set my_transactionsRailSpecials but-first my_transactionsRailSpecials
;print "I forgot the first paid price saved in my_transactionsRail"]
    ]
  ]
  if RANDOM_FORGETTING = true
    [
      let chance random-float 1
      if chance > 0.7 ;30% probability of forgetting one item
      [
        let n random length my_transactionsRailSpecials
        if length my_transactionsRailSpecials > 0 [set
my_transactionsRailSpecials remove-item n my_transactionsRailSpecials]
        ;set my_transactionsRailSpecials but-first my_transactionsRailSpecials
        ;print (word "I forgot item no. " n " of my rail specials transac-
tions")
      ]
    ]
```

The simulation model incorporates a simplified booking horizon of 10 days.

```
    let t1 random 10
```

```
    let t2 int (random-normal 6 3 + random-normal 6 3 )  ;set demand time for the specific
day. Demand is only for route A to B and v.v..
    set t2 t2 + (random 2 * 0.5)
    ;let t2 (random 24 + (random 2 * 0.5))  ;alternative simplified way of creating mobility
demand
    if t2 > 24 [set t2 24]
    set my_demand list t1 t2
    search
    decide

  ]
end
```

;--

```
to search
```

In this function, passengers with demand are searching for transport offers.

```
;get available trains
set trainList shuffle trainList
let selectedTrain "none"
let i 0
while [i < length trainList]  ;trainList contains list of train ID and departure time
[
  let helpVariable (item i trainList)
  if item 1 helpVariable = item 1 my_demand
  [
    set selectedTrain item 0 helpVariable
    set i 999  ;implemented for reasons of processor time saving
  ]
  set i i + 1
]
```

First, passengers search for trains scheduled next to their time of mobility need.

```
if selectedTrain = "none"  ;search for approximate fit - transport offer fitting the request within
1/2h
[

  set trainList shuffle trainList
  set i 0
  let r random 2

  if r = 1  ;random order of search to avoid that consumers always take the first train on the list
  [
    while [i < length trainList]
    [
      let helpVariable item i trainList

      ;print word "My demand time is: (+/- 1h is OK" item 1 my_demand
      ;print word "The item i of trainList I currently see: " item 1 item i train-
List

      if item 1 helpVariable = (item 1 my_demand - 0.5)
      [
        set selectedTrain item 0 helpVariable
        set i 999
      ]
      if item 1 helpVariable = (item 1 my_demand + 0.5)
      [
        set selectedTrain item 0 helpVariable
```

```
      set i 999
    ]

    set i i + 1
  ]

]

if r = 0
[
  while [i < length trainList]
  [
    let helpVariable item i trainList

    if item 1 helpVariable = (item 1 my_demand + 0.5)
    [
      set selectedTrain item 0 helpVariable
      set i 999

      ;  set selectedTrain "none"
      ;  set trialCounter trialCounter + 1
      ;]

    ]

    if item 1 helpVariable = (item 1 my_demand - 0.5)
    [
      set selectedTrain item 0 helpVariable
      set i 999
    ]
    set i i + 1
  ]

  ]
]

if selectedTrain = "none" ;  search for approximate fit - a transport offer fitting the request with-
in 1 hour
[
  set trainList shuffle trainList
  set i 0
  let r random 2

  if r = 1 ;random order of search to avoid consumers always take the first train on the list
  [
    while [i < length trainList]
    [
      let helpVariable item i trainList

      ;print word "My demand time is: (+/- 1h is OK" item 1 my_demand
      ;print word "The item i of trainList I currently see: " item 1 item i train-
List

      if item 1 helpVariable = (item 1 my_demand - 1)
      [
        set selectedTrain item 0 helpVariable
        set i 999
      ]

      if item 1 helpVariable = (item 1 my_demand + 1)
```

```
    [
      set selectedTrain item 0 helpVariable
      set i 999
    ]

    set i i + 1
  ]

]

if r = 0
[
  while [i < length trainList]
  [
    let helpVariable item i trainList

    if item 1 helpVariable = (item 1 my_demand + 1)
    [
      set selectedTrain item 0 helpVariable
      set i 999
    ]

    if item 1 helpVariable = (item 1 my_demand - 1)
    [
      set selectedTrain item 0 helpVariable
      set i 999
    set i i + 1
  ]

]

]
```

Consumers can also look for additional public transport alternatives and choose the one with the lowest price. Technically, this implies the same search procedure described above.

```
let alternative_train1 "none"
let alternative_train2 "none"

;set trialCounter 0
if selectedTrain != "none"
[
  set i 0
  set trainList shuffle trainList
  let r random 2

  if r = 1
  [

    while [i < length trainList]
    [

      let helpList item i trainList ;contains (train_ID) (time of departure)
      if item 1 helpList = (item 1 my_demand - 1) OR item 1 helpList = (item 1
my_demand - 0.5)
      [
        if selectedTrain != item 0 helpList [ set alternative_train1 item 0 help-
List set i 999]
      ]
```

```
      if item 1 helpList = (item 1 my_demand + 1) OR item 1 helpList = (item 1
my_demand + 0.5)
      [
        if selectedTrain != item 0 helpList [ set alternative_train2 item 0 help-
List set i 999]
      ]

      set i i + 1
    ]
  ]

  if r = 0
  [

    while [i < length trainList]
    [

      let helpList item i trainList ;contains (train_ID) (time of departure)
        if item 1 helpList = (item 1 my_demand + 1) OR item 1 helpList = (item 1
my_demand + 0.5)
        [
          if selectedTrain != item 0 helpList [ set alternative_train1 item 0
helpList set i 999]
        ]

        if item 1 helpList = (item 1 my_demand - 1) OR item 1 helpList = (item 1
my_demand - 0.5)
        [
          if selectedTrain != item 0 helpList [ set alternative_train2 item 0
helpList set i 999]
        ]
        set i i + 1


    ]
  ]

]
```

For processor speed reasons, alternatives can be eliminated here if needed.
```
;set alternative_train1 "none"
;set alternative_train2 "none"
```

```
set my_availability (list ( my_car ) ( selectedTrain ) (alternative_train1) (al-
ternative_train2)); car available (true/false) and string ID of selected train, if
no selected train: string "none".
;print word "My_availability: " my_availability
```

If the consumer has a link wih a car-owner & this owner is ready to borrow it, car availability is set true.
This is based on the global variable "carBorrowingProbability".

```
repeat 2 ;sets how many trials a passenger attempts to find an available car
  [
    if item 0 my_availability = false
    [
      ;show "I have no car available. Searching for a family/friend who has a
car..."
```

```
    let input false
    let a random 100



    if count my-links > 0
    [
      let theFriend [other-end] of one-of my-links
      let friendsCarExisting false
      set friendsCarExisting [my_car] of theFriend
      if friendsCarExisting = true
      [
        if a < CARBORROWINGPROBABILITY [ set input true ]
      ]
      set my_availability but-first my_availability
      set my_availability fput input my_availability
    ]
  ]
]

end
```

```
;--------------------------------------------------------------------------------
to get-prices
```

This function can be called both by decide and calculate-utility.

The different means of transport are consecutively checked for their fares beginning with car transportation.

```
    set carPrice precision ([distance] / 100 * [fuel consumption] * FUELPRICE / [em-
pirical car load factor] ) 2 ;average load factor of a car, alternatively 1 + random-float 1
      ;print word "carPrice: " carPrice



if item 1 my_availability != "none" ;if there is a train available
[

  ;rail 1st alternative

  ;check the baseFare
    set my_currentRailPrice 0
    let train_number item 1 my_availability
    ;if train_number = "none" [];print "No train available, thus railPrice of 0 cal-
culated."]
```

There can be a railPrice of 0 if the consumer has found no train fitting her/his transport request, however, this is not a problem because it only occurs in cases where just the car price is needed.

```
    set my_chosenTrain train_number
    ;print word "(1) My chosen train: " my_chosenTrain


    let railPrice get-baseFare train_number
    ;print word "Initial railprice found: " railprice
    if personalDiscount = true
    [
```

```
    set railprice precision (railprice - (railprice * my_personalDiscount / 100))
2
    print (word "Railprice after including a personal discount of "
my_personalDiscount " %: " railprice)
  ]
```

```
;check if a railcard is accepted on the train chosen
  let railCardAcceptance false
  set railCardAcceptance get-railcard-acceptance train_number
  if RAILCARD = true
  [
    if my_railcard = true AND my_railcardValidity > 0
    [
      if railcardAcceptance = true
      [
        set railprice (railprice * 0.5)
        let input_fare railprice
        set railprice get-roundFare input_fare
        set my_railcardInUse true
      ]
    ]
  ]
  set my_currentRailPrice railPrice
  ;print word "(1.1) Standard fare calculated: " railprice
```

```
;check for flexSpecials (if applicable) on the train chosen

  let column item 0 my_demand ;=day of demand
  let train_number_day list (train_number) (column) ;train_number is in item 1
my_availability, day of demand in item o my_demand
  let specialRailPriceCoordinates get-flexSpecialRailPriceCoordinates
train_number_day ;includes check of quota

  let flexSpecialRailPrice item 0 specialRailPriceCoordinates
  ;print word "(1.2) Flex fare calculated: " flexSpecialRailPrice
  let row item 1 specialRailPriceCoordinates
  set column item 2 specialRailPriceCoordinates

  if is-string? item 0 specialRailPriceCoordinates ;if it contains the string "unavailable"
  [
    ;print "(1.2) No flex specials available."
  ]

  if not is-string? item 0 specialRailPriceCoordinates
  [
    if railprice <= flexSpecialRailPrice
    [
      ;print "(1.2) There is a flex special but it's not cheaper than regular
fare."
    ]

    if railprice > flexSpecialRailPrice
    [
```

In the case above, the special is the best price to be considered in utility calculation, however, the consumer agent can still choose to ignore that special.

```
      ifelse my_preferenceForFlexibility < preferenceForFlexibilityThreshold1 ;the
threshold to switch from standard fare to flex special fare
      [
        set my_currentRailPrice flexSpecialRailPrice
```

```
      set my_specialCoordinates list (row) (column)
      ;print "(1.2) A flex special will be booked in book-rail if utility of
rail is superior..."
      ;print word "My_specialCoordinates (row=8!, column):"
my_specialCoordinates
    ]
    [
      ;print "(1.2) There is cheaper flex special, but I prefer the flexibility
of a standard ticket"
      ;print "(1.2) A flex special was ignored for preference reasons."
    ]
  ]
]
```

;check for restrictive permanent specials on the train chosen

```
  set column item 0 my_demand  ;=day of demand
  set train_number_day list (train_number) (column)  ;train_number is in item 1
my_availability
  set specialRailPriceCoordinates get-specialRailPriceCoordinates train_number_day
;includes check of quota

  let specialRailPrice item 0 specialRailPriceCoordinates
  ;print word "(1.3) Restrictive special fare calculated: " specialRailPrice
  set row item 1 specialRailPriceCoordinates
  set column item 2 specialRailPriceCoordinates

  if specialRailPrice = "unavailable" [];print "I checked for a special on that
train, no special available"]
  if specialRailPrice = 0 [print "Error. Check specials procedure & matrix!"]
  if specialRailPrice != 0 AND specialRailPrice != "unavailable" [];print word
"Special found on my chosen train, price: " specialRailPrice]
```

;result for restictive specials

```
  if is-string? item 0 specialRailPriceCoordinates [];set my_currentRailPrice
railprice]  ;if it contains the string "unavailable"
  if not is-string? item 0 specialRailPriceCoordinates
  [
    if railprice <= specialRailPrice
    [
      ;print "(1.3) There is a restrictive special but it's not cheaper than regu-
lar fare."
    ]

    if railprice > specialRailPrice [if not is-string? flexSpecialRailPrice [if
flexSpecialRailPrice < specialRailPrice [print "There is a restrictive special,
but it's not cheaper than the flex special."]]]

    if not is-string? flexSpecialRailPrice
    [
      if railprice > specialRailPrice AND flexSpecialRailPrice > specialRailPrice
      [
```

The restrictive special is the best price to be considered in utility calculation, however, consumer agents could still choose to ignore the special.

```
        ifelse my_preferenceForFlexibility < preferenceForFlexibilityThreshold2
        [
          set my_currentRailPrice specialRailPrice
```

```
        set my_specialCoordinates list (row) (column)
      ]
      [
        ;print "There is cheaper special, but I prefer the flexibility of a
standard ticket"
        ;print "(1.3) A restrictive special was ignored for preference reasons."
      ]
    ]
  ]
    if is-string? flexSpecialRailPrice ;no comparison needed because there is no flex spe-
cial available
    [
      if railprice > specialRailPrice
      [
```

The restrictive special is the best price to be considered in utility calculation, however, the consumer agent can still choose to ignore that special.

```
        ifelse my_preferenceForFlexibility < preferenceForFlexibilityThreshold2
        [
          set my_currentRailPrice specialRailPrice
          set my_specialCoordinates list (row) (column)
        ]
        [
          ;print "(1.3) There is cheaper restrictive special, but I prefer the
flexibility of a standard ticket or flex special ticket."
          ;print "(1.3) A restrictive special was ignored for preference reasons."

        ]
      ]
    ]
  ]
```

In the following, the same procedure is repeated for alternative offers available for the consumer agent. At this point, future modelling effort could provide a more sophisticated decisionmaking process on the question when a consumer decides to extent the search. For instance, this could be realised with an El-Farol algorithm or based on existing reference prices.

```
]
  ;rail 2nd alternative


  if item 2 my_availability != "none"
  [
    let degreeOfFlexibility my_degreeOfFlexibility
    let searchAgain get-repetition-info degreeOfFlexibility
    let train_number item 2 my_availability

    if searchAgain = true
    [
      ;print "I decided to search for another train for cheaper prices..."

      let railPrice2 get-baseFare train_number
      if personalDiscount = true [set railprice2 precision (railprice2 - (rail-
price2 * my_personalDiscount / 100)) 2]

      let railCardAcceptance false
      set railCardAcceptance get-railcard-acceptance train_number
      if RAILCARD = true [ if my_railcard = true AND my_railcardValidity > 0 [ if
railcardAcceptance = true [set railprice2 (railprice2 * 0.5) let input_fare rail-
price2 set railprice2 get-roundFare input_fare ]]]
```

```
      ;print word "(2.1) Base fare calculated: " railprice2

      if railprice2 < my_currentRailPrice
      [
         set my_currentRailPrice railprice2
         ;print "(2.1) There is a cheaper base fare in option2 than
my_currentRailPrice."
         ;print word "My chosen train before: " my_chosenTrain
         set my_chosenTrain train_number
         set my_specialCoordinates "void"
         ;print word "My chosen train afterwards: " my_chosenTrain
      ]
      ;check for flex specials on the train

      let column item 0 my_demand  ;=day of demand
      let train_number_day list (train_number) (column)
      let specialRailPriceCoordinates2 get-flexSpecialRailPriceCoordinates
train_number_day

      let flexSpecialRailPrice2 item 0 specialRailPriceCoordinates2
      let row item 1 specialRailPriceCoordinates2
      set column item 2 specialRailPriceCoordinates2

      if is-string? item 0 specialRailPriceCoordinates2  ;if it contains the string "una-
vailable"
      [
         ;print "(2.2) No flexSpecial available."
      ]

      if not is-string? item 0 specialRailPriceCoordinates2
      [
        if railprice2 <= flexSpecialRailPrice2
        [
           ;print "(2.2) There is a flex special but it's not cheaper than regular
fare."
        ]
        if railprice2 > flexSpecialRailPrice2
        [
           ;special is the best price to be considered in utility calculation

           if flexSpecialRailPrice2 < my_currentRailPrice
           [
             ifelse my_preferenceForFlexibility < preferenceForFlexibilityThresh-
old1  ;the threshold to switch from standard fare to flex special fare
             [
                ;print "(2.2) I found a better price for me (flex special of 2nd
option)."
                set my_currentRailPrice flexSpecialRailPrice2
                set my_specialCoordinates list (row) (column)
                set my_chosenTrain train_number
             ]
             [
                ;print "(2.2) There is cheaper flex special, but I prefer the flexi-
bility of a standard ticket"
                ;print "(2.2) A flex special was ignored for preference reasons (2nd
train alternative)."
             ]
           ]
        ]
      ]
```

```
      set train_number_day list (train_number) (column)
      set specialRailPriceCoordinates2 get-specialRailPriceCoordinates
train_number_day

      let specialRailPrice2 item 0 specialRailPriceCoordinates2
      ;print word "(2.3) Restrictive special price calculated: " specialRailPrice2
      set row item 1 specialRailPriceCoordinates2
      set column item 2 specialRailPriceCoordinates2

      if specialRailPrice2 = "unavailable" [];print "I checked for a special on
that train, no special available"]
      if specialRailPrice2 = 0 [print "Error. Check specials procedure & matrix!"]
      ;if specialRailPrice2 != 0 AND specialRailPrice != "unavailable" [];print
word "Special found on my chosen 2nd train, price: " specialRailPrice2]

      ;result
      if is-string? item 0 specialRailPriceCoordinates2
      [
        ;print "(2.3.) No restrictive special available."
      ]
      if not is-string? item 0 specialRailPriceCoordinates2
      [
        if railprice2 <= specialRailPrice2
        [
          ;print "(2.3) There is a restrictive special but it's not cheaper than
regular fare of 2nd option."
        ]

        if railprice2 > specialRailPrice2
        [
          ;special is the best price to be considered in utility calculation


          if specialRailPrice2 < my_currentRailPrice
          [
            ifelse my_preferenceForFlexibility < preferenceForFlexibilityThresh-
old2
            [
              ;print "(2.3) I found a better price for me (special of 2nd op-
tion)."
              set my_currentRailPrice specialRailPrice2
              set my_specialCoordinates list (row) (column)
              ;print word "My_specialCoordinates: " my_specialCoordinates
              ;print word "My chosen train before: " my_chosenTrain
              set my_chosenTrain train_number
              ;print word "My chosen train afterwards: " my_chosenTrain
            ]
            [
              ;print "(2.3) There is cheaper restrictive special, but I prefer the
flexibility of either a flex special or a standard ticket"
              ;print "(2.3) A restrictive special was ignored for preference rea-
sons (2nd train alternative)."

            ]
          ]
        ]
      ]
    ]
  ]
```

```
;rail 3rd alternative


if item 3 my_availability != "none"
[
   let degreeOfFlexibility my_degreeOfFlexibility
   let searchAgain get-repetition-info degreeOfFlexibility ;plus influence of distance
to reference price and El-Farol-algorithm possible
   let train_number item 3 my_availability

   if searchAgain = true
   [
      ;print "I decided to search for yet another train for cheaper prices..."

      let railPrice3 get-baseFare train_number
      if personalDiscount = true [set railprice3 precision (railprice3 - (rail-
price3 * my_personalDiscount / 100)) 2]

      ;check if railcard is accepted on the train chosen
      let railCardAcceptance false
      set railCardAcceptance get-railcard-acceptance train_number
      if RAILCARD = true [ if my_railcard = true AND my_railcardValidity > 0 [ if
railcardAcceptance = true [set railprice3 (railprice3 * 0.5) let input_fare rail-
price3 set railprice3 get-roundFare input_fare]]]

      ;print word "(3.1) Base fare calculated: " railPrice3
      if railprice3 < my_currentRailPrice
         [
            ;print "(3.1.) There is a cheaper base fare in option 3 than
my_currentRailPrice."
            set my_currentRailPrice railprice3
            ;print word "My chosen train before: " my_chosenTrain
            set my_chosenTrain train_number
            set my_specialCoordinates "void"
            ;print word "My chosen train afterwards: " my_chosenTrain
         ]

      let column item 0 my_demand ;=day of demand
      let train_number_day list (train_number) (column) ;train_number is in item 1
my_availability, day of demand in item o my_demand
      let specialRailPriceCoordinates3 get-flexSpecialRailPriceCoordinates
train_number_day ;includes check of quota

      let flexSpecialRailPrice3 item 0 specialRailPriceCoordinates3
      let row item 1 specialRailPriceCoordinates3
      set column item 2 specialRailPriceCoordinates3

      ;result for flexSpecials

      if is-string? item 0 specialRailPriceCoordinates3 ;if it contains the string "una-
vailable"
         [
         ;print "(3.2) No flex special available."
         ]

      if not is-string? item 0 specialRailPriceCoordinates3
         [
            if railprice3 <= flexSpecialRailPrice3
            [
```

```
              ;print "(3.2) There is a flex special but it's not cheaper than regular
fare."
         ]

         if railprice3 > flexSpecialRailPrice3
         [

            if flexSpecialRailPrice3 < my_currentRailPrice
            [
               ifelse my_preferenceForFlexibility < preferenceForFlexibilityThresh-
old1 ;the threshold to switch from standard fare to flex special fare
               [
                  ;print "(3.2) I found a better price for me (flex special of 3rd
option)."
                  set my_currentRailPrice flexSpecialRailPrice3
                  set my_specialCoordinates list (row) (column)
                  ;print word "My_specialCoordinates: " my_specialCoordinates
                  ;print word "My chosen train before: " my_chosenTrain
                  set my_chosenTrain train_number
                  ;print word "My chosen train afterwards: " my_chosenTrain
               ]
               [
                  ;print "(3.2) There is cheaper flex special, but I prefer the flexi-
bility of a standard ticket."
                  ;print "(3.2) A flex special was ignored for preference reasons (3rd
train alternative)."
               ]
            ]
         ]

      set train_number_day list (train_number) (column)
      set specialRailPriceCoordinates3 get-specialRailPriceCoordinates
train_number_day

      let specialRailPrice3 item 0 specialRailPriceCoordinates3
      ;print word "(3.3) Restrictive special price calculated: " specialRailPrice3
      set row item 1 specialRailPriceCoordinates3
      set column item 2 specialRailPriceCoordinates3

      if specialRailPrice3 = "unavailable" [];print "I checked for a special on
that train, no special available"]
      if specialRailPrice3 = 0 [print "Error. Check specials procedure & matrix!"]
      ;if specialRailPrice3 != 0 AND specialRailPrice != "unavailable" [];print
word "Special found on my chosen 2nd train, price: " specialRailPrice3]

      ;result for restrictive specials
      if is-string? item 0 specialRailPriceCoordinates3
      []

      if not is-string? item 0 specialRailPriceCoordinates3
      [
        if railprice3 <= specialRailPrice3
        [
           ;print "(3.3.) There is a restrictive special but it's not cheaper than
regular fare of 3rd option."
        ]

        if railprice3 > specialRailPrice3
        [
```

The special is the best price to be considered in utility calculation.

```
if specialRailPrice3 < my_currentRailPrice
[
   ifelse my_preferenceForFlexibility < preferenceForFlexibilityThresh-
```
old2 ;the threshold to switch from flex to restrictive specials
```
   [
     ;print "I found yet a better price for me (special of 3rd option)."
     set my_currentRailPrice specialRailPrice3
     set my_specialCoordinates list (row) (column)
     set my_chosenTrain train_number
   ]
   [
      ;print "(3.3) There is cheaper restrictive special, but I prefer the
```
flexibility of a either a flex special or a standard ticket"
```
      ;print "(3.3) A restrictive special was ignored for preference rea-
```
sons (3rd train alternative)."
```
   ]
  ]
 ]
 ]
 ]
```

end


```
;-----------------------------------------------------------------------------
to decide
```

This function is designed for consumer agents to choose the means of transport having the highest value of utility for them.

```
if my_socioGroup = "carAddicted"
[
  let who_number who
  let passed budget-check-car-passed? who_number

  ifelse passed = true
  [
     get-prices
```
This is necessary for renewing car price after a fuel price change derived from observer intervention or experimental design.
```
     set my_transactionsCar lput carPrice my_transactionsCar
     ;print "I always take my car"
  ]
  [
     set idleDemandCounter idleDemandCounter + 1
     ;print "I always use my car but had not enough budget to use it today."
  ]
]


if my_socioGroup != "carAddicted"
[

   if item 0 my_availability = true AND item 1 my_availability = "none"
```
Contains if car available, 1st selected train. Consequently, other trains in my_availability are ignored.
```
   [
     let who_number who
```

```
    let passed budget-check-car-passed? who_number

    ifelse passed = true
    [
      get-prices ;necessary for renewing car price after a fuel price change
      set my_transactionsCar lput carPrice my_transactionsCar
      ;print "I didn't find a train offer and took my car"
    ]
    [
      set idleDemandCounter idleDemandCounter + 1
      ;print "I did't find a train offer, but had not enough budget to use my
car"
    ]

  ]


  if item 0 my_availability = false AND item 1 my_availability != "none"
  [
    ;print "I don't have a car and had to take the train"
```

The function book-rail includes all statistics & budget check.

```
    get-prices
    book-rail
  ]
```

The following code applies in a situation in which utility calculation is necessary. The calculation also includes & calls get-prices.

```
  if item 0 my_availability = true AND item 1 my_availability != "none"
  [


    calculate-utility


    if railUtility > carUtility
    [
      ;print "I found a train and selected rail because it's more useful for me"
      book-rail
    ]

    if carUtility >= railUtility
    [
      let who_number who
      let passed budget-check-car-passed? who_number

      ifelse passed = true
      [
        set my_transactionsCar lput carPrice my_transactionsCar
        ;print "I found a train but took the car because it's more useful for
me"
      ]
      [
        set idleDemandCounter idleDemandCounter + 1
      ]
    ]
  ]
```

```
  ; residual message
  if item 0 my_availability = false AND item 1 my_availability = "none"
  [
    set idleDemandCounter idleDemandCounter + 1
    ;print "No car available, no train found --> mobility demand not fulfilled"
  ]
]
```

```
end
```

```
;---------------------------------------------------------------------------
to set-prices
```

Here, any distance between place A and place B is set in kilometres. A possible extension is to enter different distances for rail and car.

```
  let kmDistance [distance]
```

This renew of the current prices supposes that special prices and quotas are amended dynamically.

```
  ask trainOperators with [RM = true]
    [
      set my_permanentSpecialPrice1 specialPrice1_input
      set my_permanentSpecialPrice2 specialPrice2_input
      set my_flexSpecialPrice flexSpecialPrice_input
    ]


  if ticks = 0 ;initial price-setting generating baseFares for each train
  [

   ask trainOperators with [RM = false]
     [
       set my_permanentSpecialPrice1 "void"
       set my_permanentSpecialPrice2 "void"

       set my_flexSpecialPrice "void"
       set my_flexSpecialQuota "void"
     ]


    ;set base fares for operator 1
    ;---------------------------
    
    let operator1_baseFare [empirical value]
    let input_fare operator1_baseFare
    set operator1_baseFare get-roundFare input_fare
    ;print word "Base fare after rounding in tick 0:" operator1_baseFare

    ;show count trainOperators with [RM = true]

    ask trains with [my_operator = 1]
    [
      set my_baseFare operator1_baseFare
      let train_number my_number
      let operator_identificator my_operator

      let permanentSpecialPrice1 get-permanentSpecialPrice1 operator_identificator
```

```
    let permanentSpecialPrice2 get-permanentSpecialPrice2 operator_identificator
    let permanentSpecialQuota1 0
    let permanentSpecialQuota2 0
    let flexSpecialPrice get-flexSpecialPrice operator_identificator
    let flexSpecialQuota 0
```

This builds a 10-day forecast price-inventory-matrix.
```
    ;print matrix:pretty-print-text my_priceInventoryMatrix


  ]


  ;set base fares for operator 2
  ;----------------------------

  if NUMBER_TRAINOPERATORS = 2
  [

    let operator2_baseFare int ((operator2_railPrice * kmDistance * [empirical
rate]) + kmDistance * [empirical rate]) ;in cents
    set input_fare ( operator2_baseFare / 100 )
    set operator2_baseFare get-roundFare input_fare

    ask trains with [my_operator = 2]
    [
      set my_baseFare operator2_baseFare
      let operator_identificator my_operator
      let train_number my_number
      let permanentSpecialPrice1 get-permanentSpecialPrice1 opera-
tor_identificator
      let permanentSpecialPrice2 get-permanentSpecialPrice2 opera-
tor_identificator
      let permanentSpecialQuota1 0
      let permanentSpecialQuota2 0
      let flexSpecialPrice get-flexSpecialPrice operator_identificator
      let flexSpecialQuota 0
```

This builds a 10-day forecast price-inventory matrix.

```
    ]
  ]

  ;set base fares for operator 3
  ;----------------------------

  if NUMBER_TRAINOPERATORS = 3
  [

    let operator2_baseFare int ((operator2_railPrice * kmDistance * [empirical
rate]) + kmDistance * [empirical rate]) ;in cents
    set input_fare ( operator2_baseFare / 100 )
    set operator2_baseFare get-roundFare input_fare


    ask trains with [my_operator = 2]
    [
      set my_baseFare operator2_baseFare
      let operator_identificator my_operator
      let train_number my_number
```

```
        let permanentSpecialPrice1 get-permanentSpecialPrice1 opera-
tor_identificator
        let permanentSpecialPrice2 get-permanentSpecialPrice2 opera-
tor_identificator
        let permanentSpecialQuota1 0
        let permanentSpecialQuota2 0
        let flexSpecialPrice get-flexSpecialPrice operator_identificator
        let flexSpecialQuota 0
```

This builds a 10-day forecast price-inventory matrix.

```
        ;print matrix:pretty-print-text my_priceInventoryMatrix
        ;if RM applied, changes in book-rail required!
      ]

    let operator3_baseFare [empirical rate] + [empirical rate] * opera-
tor3_railPrice / 100
    set input_fare operator3_baseFare
    set operator3_baseFare get-roundFare input_fare

    ask trains with [my_operator = 3]
    [
      set my_baseFare operator3_baseFare
      let operator_identificator my_operator
      let train_number my_number
      let permanentSpecialPrice1 get-permanentSpecialPrice1 opera-
tor_identificator
      let permanentSpecialPrice2 get-permanentSpecialPrice2 opera-
tor_identificator
      let permanentSpecialQuota1 0
      let permanentSpecialQuota2 0
      let flexSpecialPrice get-flexSpecialPrice operator_identificator
      let flexSpecialQuota 0
```

This builds a 10-day forecast price inventory matrix.

```
    ]
  ]

  ask trains with [my_baseFare = 0] [print who user-message "some trains still
do not have a base fare..." ]
  ]
```

Here, permanent special prices are activated, or made available for under-utilised trains. The time limit can be amended at this position.

```
  if ticks > 99 AND ticks mod 10 = 0 [generate-specials]

  if ticks > 0 ;continuous price-setting

  [
```

Here, the price-inventory-matrix of each train is continuously amended with potentially new prices and quotas.

```
    ask trains with [my_operator = 1]
    [

      let operator_identificator my_operator
      let train_number my_number

      let permanentSpecialPrice1 get-permanentSpecialPrice1 operator_identificator
```

```
let permanentSpecialPrice2 get-permanentSpecialPrice2 operator_identificator
let permanentSpecialQuota1 get-permanentSpecialQuota1 train_number
let permanentSpecialQuota2 get-permanentSpecialQuota2 train_number
let flexSpecialPrice get-flexSpecialPrice operator_identificator
let flexSpecialQuota get-flexSpecialQuota train_number


;saving data of the first column of the matrix before it gets removed
if ticks > 10
[
    let occupancy precision ((1 - (matrix:get my_priceInventoryMatrix 6 0 ) /
my_capacity) * 100) 1 ;(1 - free seats / capacity)
    set my_currentOccupancy occupancy
    ;print word "Current Occupancy identified: " occupancy
    set my_occupancyRecord lput occupancy my_occupancyRecord
]


;amend fares for operator 1
;-------------------------


let operator1_baseFare int [empirical rate] ;in cents
;print word "operator1_baseFare: " operator1_baseFare

;print word "(ticks>1) operator1_baseFare before rounding: " opera-
tor1_baseFare
let input_fare ( operator1_baseFare / 100 )
set operator1_baseFare get-roundFare input_fare
;print word "(ticks>1) operator1_baseFare after rounding: " opera-
tor1_baseFare

set my_baseFare operator1_baseFare

;increment data stored in the priceInventoryMatrix for the next day
let output_part1 matrix:get-row my_priceInventoryMatrix 0
let input_part1 output_part1 ;identical because the forecast period doesn't change

let output_part2 matrix:get-row my_priceInventoryMatrix 1
let input_part2 but-first output_part2
set input_part2 lput my_baseFare input_part2

let output_part3 matrix:get-row my_priceInventoryMatrix 2
let input_part3 but-first output_part3
set input_part3 lput permanentSpecialPrice1 input_part3 ;special of e. g., x₁€

let output_part4 matrix:get-row my_priceInventoryMatrix 3
let input_part4 but-first output_part4
set input_part4 lput permanentSpecialQuota1 input_part4 ; quota of e. g., 2 seats

let output_part5 matrix:get-row my_priceInventoryMatrix 4
let input_part5 but-first output_part5
set input_part5 lput permanentSpecialPrice2 input_part5 ;special of e. g., x₂€

let output_part6 matrix:get-row my_priceInventoryMatrix 5
let input_part6 but-first output_part6
set input_part6 lput permanentSpecialQuota2 input_part6 ; quota of e. g., 2 seats

let output_part7 matrix:get-row my_priceInventoryMatrix 6
let input_part7 but-first output_part7
```

```
      set input_part7 lput my_capacity input_part7

      let output_part8 matrix:get-row my_priceInventoryMatrix 7
      let input_part8 but-first output_part8
      set input_part8 lput flexSpecialPrice input_part8

      let output_part9 matrix:get-row my_priceInventoryMatrix 8
      let input_part9 but-first output_part9
      set input_part9 lput flexSpecialQuota input_part9

      set my_priceInventoryMatrix matrix:from-row-list (list (input_part1) (in-
put_part2) (input_part3) (input_part4) (input_part5) (input_part6) (input_part7)
(input_part8) (input_part9))

    ]

    if NUMBER_trainOperators = 2
    [

      ;amend fares for operator 2
      ;--------------------------

      let operator2_baseFare int ((operator2_railPrice * kmDistance * [empirical
rate]) + kmDistance * [empirical rate]) ;in cents
      let input_fare ( operator2_baseFare / 100 )
      set operator2_baseFare get-roundFare input_fare
      ;print word "Operator2 baseFare: " operator2_baseFare

      ask trains with [my_operator = 2]
      [
        let operator_identificator my_operator
        let train_number my_number
        let permanentSpecialPrice1 get-permanentSpecialPrice1 opera-
tor_identificator
        let permanentSpecialPrice2 get-permanentSpecialPrice2 opera-
tor_identificator
        let permanentSpecialQuota1 get-permanentSpecialQuota1 train_number
        let permanentSpecialQuota2 get-permanentSpecialQuota2 train_number
        let flexSpecialPrice get-flexSpecialPrice operator_identificator
        let flexSpecialQuota get-flexSpecialQuota train_number


      ;saving data of the first column of the matrix before it gets removed
        if ticks > 10
          [
            let occupancy precision ((1 - (matrix:get my_priceInventoryMatrix 6 0
) / my_capacity) * 100) 1 ;(1 - free seats / capacity)
            set my_currentOccupancy occupancy
            ;print word "Current Occupancy identified for a train of operator 2: "
occupancy
            set my_occupancyRecord lput occupancy my_occupancyRecord
          ]

        set my_baseFare operator2_baseFare

      ;increment data stored in the priceInventoryMatrix for the next day
          let output_part1 matrix:get-row my_priceInventoryMatrix 0
          let input_part1 output_part1 ;identical because the forecast period doesn't change

          let output_part2 matrix:get-row my_priceInventoryMatrix 1
```

```
        let input_part2 but-first output_part2
        set input_part2 lput my_baseFare input_part2

        let output_part3 matrix:get-row my_priceInventoryMatrix 2
        let input_part3 but-first output_part3
        set input_part3 lput permanentSpecialPrice1 input_part3 ;special of e. g., x₁€

        let output_part4 matrix:get-row my_priceInventoryMatrix 3
        let input_part4 but-first output_part4
        set input_part4 lput permanentSpecialQuota1 input_part4

        let output_part5 matrix:get-row my_priceInventoryMatrix 4
        let input_part5 but-first output_part5
        set input_part5 lput permanentSpecialPrice2 input_part5 ;special of e. g., x₂€

        let output_part6 matrix:get-row my_priceInventoryMatrix 5
        let input_part6 but-first output_part6
        set input_part6 lput permanentSpecialQuota2 input_part6

        let output_part7 matrix:get-row my_priceInventoryMatrix 6
        let input_part7 but-first output_part7
        set input_part7 lput my_capacity input_part7

        let output_part8 matrix:get-row my_priceInventoryMatrix 7
        let input_part8 but-first output_part8
        set input_part8 lput flexSpecialPrice input_part8

        let output_part9 matrix:get-row my_priceInventoryMatrix 8
        let input_part9 but-first output_part9
        set input_part9 lput flexSpecialQuota input_part9

      set my_priceInventoryMatrix matrix:from-row-list (list (input_part1)
(input_part2) (input_part3) (input_part4) (input_part5) (input_part6) (in-
put_part7) (input_part8) (input_part9))


      ]
    ]

    ;amend base fares for operator 2 and 3
    ;-------------------------------------
    if NUMBER_trainOperators = 3
    [
      let operator2_baseFare int ((operator2_railPrice * kmDistance * [empirical
rate]) + kmDistance * [empirical rate])   ;in cents
      let input_fare ( operator2_baseFare / 100 )
      set operator2_baseFare get-roundFare input_fare

      ask trains with [my_operator = 2]
      [
        let operator_identificator my_operator
        let train_number my_number
        let permanentSpecialPrice1 get-permanentSpecialPrice1 opera-
tor_identificator
        let permanentSpecialPrice2 get-permanentSpecialPrice2 opera-
tor_identificator
        let permanentSpecialQuota1 get-permanentSpecialQuota1 train_number
        let permanentSpecialQuota2 get-permanentSpecialQuota2 train_number
        let flexSpecialPrice get-flexSpecialPrice operator_identificator
        let flexSpecialQuota get-flexSpecialQuota train_number
```

```
;saving data of the first column of the matrix before it gets removed
if ticks > 10
[
    let occupancy precision ((1 - (matrix:get my_priceInventoryMatrix 6 0 )
/ my_capacity) * 100) 1 ;(1 - free seats / capacity)
    set my_currentOccupancy occupancy
    ;print word "Current Occupancy identified: " occupancy
    set my_occupancyRecord lput occupancy my_occupancyRecord
]

set my_baseFare operator2_baseFare

;increment data stored in the priceInventoryMatrix for the next day
let output_part1 matrix:get-row my_priceInventoryMatrix 0
let input_part1 output_part1 ;identical because the forecast period doesn't change

let output_part2 matrix:get-row my_priceInventoryMatrix 1
let input_part2 but-first output_part2
set input_part2 lput my_baseFare input_part2

let output_part3 matrix:get-row my_priceInventoryMatrix 2
let input_part3 but-first output_part3
set input_part3 lput permanentSpecialPrice1 input_part3 ;special of e.g., x₁€

let output_part4 matrix:get-row my_priceInventoryMatrix 3
let input_part4 but-first output_part4
set input_part4 lput permanentSpecialQuota1 input_part4

let output_part5 matrix:get-row my_priceInventoryMatrix 4
let input_part5 but-first output_part5
set input_part5 lput permanentSpecialPrice2 input_part5 ;special of e.g., x₂€

let output_part6 matrix:get-row my_priceInventoryMatrix 5
let input_part6 but-first output_part6
set input_part6 lput permanentSpecialQuota2 input_part6

let output_part7 matrix:get-row my_priceInventoryMatrix 6
let input_part7 but-first output_part7
set input_part7 lput my_capacity input_part7

let output_part8 matrix:get-row my_priceInventoryMatrix 7
let input_part8 but-first output_part8
set input_part8 lput flexSpecialPrice input_part8

let output_part9 matrix:get-row my_priceInventoryMatrix 8
let input_part9 but-first output_part9
set input_part9 lput flexSpecialQuota input_part9

set my_priceInventoryMatrix matrix:from-row-list (list (input_part1) (in-
put_part2) (input_part3) (input_part4) (input_part5) (input_part6) (input_part7)
(input_part8) (input_part9))
]

let operator3_baseFare [empirical rate] + [empirical rate] * opera-
tor3_railPrice / 100

set input_fare operator3_baseFare
set operator3_baseFare get-roundFare input_fare
```

```
    ask trains with [my_operator = 3]
    [
        let operator_identificator my_operator
        let train_number my_number
```

    Import the current prices and quotas for specials
```
        let permanentSpecialPrice1 get-permanentSpecialPrice1 operator_identificator
        let permanentSpecialPrice2 get-permanentSpecialPrice2 opera-
tor_identificator
            let permanentSpecialQuota1 get-permanentSpecialQuota1 train_number
            let permanentSpecialQuota2 get-permanentSpecialQuota2 train_number
            let flexSpecialPrice get-flexSpecialPrice operator_identificator
            let flexSpecialQuota get-flexSpecialQuota train_number
```

    ;saving data of the first column of the matrix before it gets removed
```
        if ticks > 10
        [
            let occupancy precision ((1 - (matrix:get my_priceInventoryMatrix 6 0 )
/ my_capacity) * 100) 1 ;(1 - free seats / capacity)
                set my_currentOccupancy occupancy
                ;print word "Current Occupancy identified: " occupancy
                set my_occupancyRecord lput occupancy my_occupancyRecord
        ]
```

```
        set my_baseFare operator3_baseFare
```

    ;increment data stored in the priceInventoryMatrix for the next day

```
        let output_part1 matrix:get-row my_priceInventoryMatrix 0
        let input_part1 output_part1 ;identical because the forecast period doesn't change

        let output_part2 matrix:get-row my_priceInventoryMatrix 1
        let input_part2 but-first output_part2
        set input_part2 lput my_baseFare input_part2

        let output_part3 matrix:get-row my_priceInventoryMatrix 2
        let input_part3 but-first output_part3
        set input_part3 lput permanentSpecialPrice1 input_part3 ; special of e. g., x₁ €

        let output_part4 matrix:get-row my_priceInventoryMatrix 3
        let input_part4 but-first output_part4
        set input_part4 lput permanentSpecialQuota1 input_part4

        let output_part5 matrix:get-row my_priceInventoryMatrix 4
        let input_part5 but-first output_part5
        set input_part5 lput permanentSpecialPrice2 input_part5 ; special of e. g., x₂ €

        let output_part6 matrix:get-row my_priceInventoryMatrix 5
        let input_part6 but-first output_part6
        set input_part6 lput permanentSpecialQuota2 input_part6

        let output_part7 matrix:get-row my_priceInventoryMatrix 6
        let input_part7 but-first output_part7
        set input_part7 lput my_capacity input_part7

        let output_part8 matrix:get-row my_priceInventoryMatrix 7
        let input_part8 but-first output_part8
        set input_part8 lput flexSpecialPrice input_part8

        let output_part9 matrix:get-row my_priceInventoryMatrix 8
```

```
        let input_part9 but-first output_part9
        set input_part9 lput flexSpecialQuota input_part9

        set my_priceInventoryMatrix matrix:from-row-list (list (input_part1) (in-
put_part2) (input_part3) (input_part4) (input_part5) (input_part6) (input_part7)
(input_part8) (input_part9))


        ]
    ]
    ask trains with [my_baseFare = 0] [print who user-message "Some trains still
do not have a base fare..." ]


    ]

end

;-----------------------------------------------------------------------------
to-report get-flexSpecialPrice [operator_identificator]

let flexSpecialPrice 0 ;decided by train_operators
ask one-of trainOperators with [my_ID = operator_identificator]
[
   set flexSpecialPrice my_flexSpecialPrice
]

report flexSpecialPrice

end
;-----------------------------------------------------------------------------
to-report get-flexSpecialQuota [train_number];
```

This reporter sets three different quotas depending on the occupancy of the respective train.

```
let flexSpecialQuota "void"


ask one-of trains with [my_number = train_number]
   [
     set flexSpecialQuota matrix:get my_priceInventoryMatrix 8 9

     if my_operator = 1 AND FLEXSPECIAL = true AND ticks mod 5 = 0 AND ticks > 99
```

The train "auto-observes" its occupancy and amends its quota every 5 ticks.

```
     [
       print "Flex Special Quota ---"
       print (word "Train " my_number "Average occupancy: " my_averageOccupancy "My
capacity: " my_capacity)

       if my_averageOccupancy > flexSpecialOccupancyThreshold1 [set flexSpecialQuo-
ta int (my_capacity * flexSpecialSmallQuota / 100)]

       if my_averageOccupancy > flexSpecialOccupancyThreshold2 AND
my_averageOccupancy <= flexSpecialOccupancyThreshold1 [set flexSpecialQuota int
(my_capacity * flexSpecialMediumQuota / 100)]
       if my_averageOccupancy <= flexSpecialOccupancyThreshold2 [set flexSpe-
cialQuota int (my_capacity * flexSpecialLargeQuota / 100)]
       print (word "Train: " my_number " of operator" my_operator " has calculated
a flexSpecialQuota of " flexSpecialQuota)

     ]
```

```
      ]
```

if flexSpecialQuota = "void" [user-message "Error. A selected train was not
identified for flexible specials"]
   ;print word "reported value FLXSP quota: " flexSpecialQuota

report flexSpecialQuota

end

```
;-------------------------------------------------------------------------------
to-report get-permanentSpecialPrice1 [operator_identificator]
```

A possible extension to this reporter is the detailed price management of single trains (train_numbers).

let permanentSpecialPrice1 0 ;the price of permanent specials is subject to the decision of
train_operators
  ask one-of trainOperators with [my_ID = operator_identificator]
  [
    set permanentSpecialPrice1 my_permanentSpecialPrice1
  ]

  report permanentSpecialPrice1

end

```
;-------------------------------------------------------------------------------
to-report get-permanentSpecialPrice2 [operator_identificator]

  let permanentSpecialPrice2 0
  ask one-of trainOperators with [my_ID = operator_identificator]
  [
    set permanentSpecialPrice2 my_permanentSpecialPrice2
  ]

  report permanentSpecialPrice2

end

;-------------------------------------------------------------------------------
to-report get-permanentSpecialQuota1 [train_number]

  let permanentSpecialQuota1 "void"

  ask one-of trains with [my_number = train_number]
  [
    set permanentSpecialQuota1 matrix:get my_priceInventoryMatrix 3 9

    if my_operator = 1 AND PERMANENTSPECIAL = true AND ticks mod 5 = 0 AND ticks >
99
```
The train "auto-observes" its occupancy and amends quota every 5 ticks.
```
    [
      ;print "PMSP Quota #1---"
      ;print (word "Train " my_number "Average occupancy: " my_averageOccupancy
"My capacity: " my_capacity)

      if my_averageOccupancy > ( permanentSpecialOccupancyThreshold1 ) [set perma-
nentSpecialQuota1 0]
```

```
        if my_averageOccupancy > ( permanentSpecialOccupancyThreshold2 ) AND
my_averageOccupancy <= ( permanentSpecialOccupancyThreshold1 ) [set permanentSpe-
cialQuota1 int (my_capacity * permanentSpecialSmallQuota1 / 100)]
        if my_averageOccupancy <= ( permanentSpecialOccupancyThreshold2 ) [set per-
manentSpecialQuota1 int (my_capacity * permanentSpecialLargeQuota1 / 100)]
      ;print (word "Train: " my_number " of operator" my_operator " has calculated
a permanentSpecialQuota1 of " permanentSpecialQuota1)


    ]
  ]

  if permanentSpecialQuota1 = "void" [user-message "Error. A selected train was
not identified for permanent Specials"]
    ;print word "reported value PMSP quota1: " permanentSpecialQuota1

  report permanentSpecialQuota1

end

;--------------------------------------------------------------------------------
to-report get-permanentSpecialQuota2 [train_number]

  let permanentSpecialQuota2 "void"

  ask one-of trains with [my_number = train_number]
  [
    set permanentSpecialQuota2 matrix:get my_priceInventoryMatrix 5 9

    if my_operator = 1 AND PERMANENTSPECIAL = true AND ticks mod 5 = 0 AND ticks >
99
```

The train "auto-observes" its occupancy and amends the quota every 5 ticks.

```
    [
      ;print "PMSP Quota #2---"
      ;print (word "Train " my_number "Average occupancy: " my_averageOccupancy
"My capacity: " my_capacity)


      if my_averageOccupancy > (permanentSpecialOccupancyThreshold1 ) [set perma-
nentSpecialQuota2 0]
      if my_averageOccupancy > (permanentSpecialOccupancyThreshold2 ) AND
my_averageOccupancy <= (permanentSpecialOccupancyThreshold1) [set permanentSpe-
cialQuota2 int (my_capacity * permanentSpecialSmallQuota2 / 100)]
      if my_averageOccupancy <= (permanentSpecialOccupancyThreshold2 ) [set perma-
nentSpecialQuota2 int (my_capacity * permanentSpecialLargeQuota2 / 100)]
      ;print (word "Train: " my_number " of operator" my_operator " has calculated
a permanentSpecialQuota2 of " permanentSpecialQuota2)


    ]
  ]

  if permanentSpecialQuota2 = "void" [user-message "Error. A selected train was
not identified for permanent Specials"]
    ;print word "reported value PMSP quota2: " permanentSpecialQuota2

  report permanentSpecialQuota2

end
```

```
;------------------------------------------------------------------------
to-report get-baseFare [train_number]

let railPrice 0
ask one-of trains with [my_number = train_number]
  [
    set railPrice my_baseFare
    ;print "train_number found and railPrice indicated"
    if railprice = 0 [user-message "A base fare of 0 was calculated."]
  ]
report railPrice
end


;------------------------------------------------------------------------
to-report get-specialRailPriceCoordinates [train_number_day]
```

This and the following reporter functions are key for implementing a model of a real-world reservation system for quantity-based RM, it checks in the price-inventory-matrix whether there is a free seat available.

```
  let train_number item 0 train_number_day

  let row 0
  let column item 1 train_number_day

  let specialRailPrice "unavailable"
  let freeQuota 0
  let freeQuota2 0
  ;let column item 0 my_demand

  ask one-of trains with [my_number = train_number]
  [
    if PERMANENTSPECIAL = true AND permanentSpecialsAvailable = true
    [


      ;print (word "In get-specialRailPriceCoordinates. Checking if a specials
quota is available for " train_number "...")

      set freeQuota matrix:get my_priceInventoryMatrix 3 column
      ;print (word "Free quota row 3 for train no. " train_number ": " freeQuota)
      if freeQuota >= 1
      [
        ;print word freeQuota " seats @ best price available!"
        set specialRailPrice matrix:get my_priceInventoryMatrix 2 column
        set row 2
      ]

      if freeQuota < 1
      [
        ;print "Unfortunately no free seat available for best price"
        set freeQuota2 matrix:get my_priceInventoryMatrix 5 column

        ;print (word "Free quota row 5 for train no. " train_number ": " free-
Quota2)
        if freeQuota2 = 0 [];print "Unfortunately even no free seat available for
2nd best price"]
        if freeQuota2 >= 1
        [
```

```
          ;print word freeQuota2 " seats @ 2nd best price available"
          set specialRailPrice matrix:get my_priceInventoryMatrix 4 column
          set row 4
      ]
    ]
```

This procedure can be continued with more price-steps.

```
    ]
  ]

  let specialRailPriceCoordinates (list (specialRailPrice) (row) (column))
  report specialRailPriceCoordinates ; list containing (specialRailPrice) (row)
(column)
end

;------------------------------------------------------------------------------
to-report get-flexSpecialRailPriceCoordinates [train_number_day]


  let train_number item 0 train_number_day

  let row 0
  let column item 1 train_number_day

  let flexSpecialRailPrice "unavailable"
  let freeQuota 0

  ;let column item 0 my_demand

  ask one-of trains with [my_number = train_number]
  [
    if FLEXSPECIAL = true AND flexSpecialsAvailable = true
    [
      ;print (word "In get-flexSpecialRailPriceCoordinates. Checking if a flex
specials quota is available for " train_number "...")

      set freeQuota matrix:get my_priceInventoryMatrix 8 column
      ;print (word "Free quota row 8 for train no. " train_number ": " freeQuota)

      if freeQuota >= 1
      [
        ;print word freeQuota " seat(s) for a flex special available!"
        set flexSpecialRailPrice matrix:get my_priceInventoryMatrix 7 column
        set row 7
      ]
    ]

  ]

  let specialRailPriceCoordinates (list (flexSpecialRailPrice) (row) (column))
  ;print word "SpecialRailPrice coordinates for flex fares to be reported: " spe-
cialRailPriceCoordinates
  report specialRailPriceCoordinates ;list containing (specialRailPrice)(row)(column)
end
;------------------------------------------------------------------------------
to-report get-railcard-acceptance [train_number]

  let railCardAcceptance false
```

```
    if train_number != "none"
    [
      ask one-of trains with [my_number = train_number]
      [
        if (my_number = train_number) [ if railCardAllowed = true [set railCardAc-
ceptance true ]]
      ]
    ]
    report railCardAcceptance
end
```

```
;--------------------------------------------------------------------------------
to calculate-utility
```

This function calculates utility according to Kahneman's & Tversky's Prospect Theory. It also includes other factors for decision: Public transport access, comparable travel time on the line, sociodemographic preferences, and a comparison between car and rail nominal prices (price distance).

```
  get-prices
```

```
set railUtility 0
set carUtility 0
```

Actual prices and expected prices are compared as described in the dissertation ODD protocol. All actual perceived prices are compared to the mixed reference price consumer agents develop. This calculation is represented in pseudo-code.

```
Repeat for car and rail transportation
[
Identify whether a price is lower or higer than expected
Calculate the utility value according to the operationalisation of Prospect Theory
]
Enrich the values for car and rail transportation with specific bonuses and malus-
es derived from other factors influencing the decision for a means of transport
```

```
set averageRailUtilityData lput railUtility averageRailUtilityData
set averageCarUtilityData lput carUtility averageCarUtilityData
end
```

```
;--------------------------------------------------------------------------------
to-report budget-check-rail-passed? [who_number]

  let passed false
    ifelse my_budget > my_currentRailPrice
    [
      set passed true
      set my_budget my_budget - my_currentRailPrice
      set rail_performance rail_performance + [distance]
    ]
    [set idleDemandCounter idleDemandCounter + 1]

  report passed
end
```

```
;--------------------------------------------------------------------------------
to-report budget-check-car-passed? [who_number]

  let passed false
    ifelse my_budget > carPrice
    [
```

```
      set passed true
      set my_budget my_budget - carPrice
      set car_performance car_performance + [distance]
    ]
      [set idleDemandCounter idleDemandCounter + 1]

  report passed
end
```

;---
```
to book-rail
```

In this function, the actual economic transaction takes place.

```
let who_number who
let passed budget-check-rail-passed? who_number ;boolean

if passed = true
[
   let helpList list my_chosenTrain my_currentRailPrice ;train_no and price paid right
now

   ifelse clearingRail = [] [set clearingRail fput helpList clearingRail ] [ set
clearingRail lput helpList clearingRail ]
```

Seat inventory update & transactions memory
```
   let train_number my_chosenTrain
   let day item 0 my_demand

 ;print word "my_specialCoordinates: " my_specialCoordinates

   if my_specialCoordinates = "void" ;the price booked is a base fare
   [

     set my_transactionsRail lput my_currentRailPrice my_transactionsRail
     ;set my_transactionsRailTime
     if my_railcardInUse - true [set railcardFareTickTurnover railcardFareTickTurn-
over + my_currentRailPrice] ;for plotting operator 1 revenue mix

     ask one-of trains with [my_number = train_number ] ;AND my_operator = 1]
     [
       let freeSeats matrix:get my_priceInventoryMatrix 6 day
       if freeSeats < 1 [];output-print "Over-utilisation. Negative number of free
seats."] ;This situation can – to some extent – be acceptable in a railway context.
       set freeSeats freeSeats - 1
       matrix:set my_priceInventoryMatrix 6 day freeSeats
     ]
   ]

   if is-list? my_specialCoordinates   ;if a special is sold and specialCoordinates != "void", "un-
available"
   [
     let row (item 0 my_specialCoordinates + 1 ) ;in order to adress the seat capacity related
to the special price
     ;print word "Row: " row
     let column item 1 my_specialCoordinates
     ;print word "column: " column
     ;print (word "Booking a row no." row " special for train " train_number "...")
```

;Different options of individual memorisation of this price following Mental accounting theory (Thaler 1985)

```
      set my_transactionsRailSpecials lput my_currentRailPrice
my_transactionsRailSpecials
      set specialsTickTurnover specialsTickTurnover + my_currentRailPrice

      ask one-of trains with [ my_number = train_number ]
      [
        let freeQuota 0
        set freeQuota matrix:get my_priceInventoryMatrix row column ;
```
the fact that there is at least 1 free seat has been confirmed before in the function get-specialRailPriceCoordinates

```
        ;print word "Free quota before booking: " freeQuota
        if freeQuota = 0 [user-message "Error. Free quota of 0 calculated, but
my_specialCoordinates is a list containing (specialPrice) (row) (column"]
        if freeQuota < 0 [user-message "Error. Negative number of specials quota" ]

        if freeQuota > 0
        [
          set freeQuota freeQuota - 1
          matrix:set my_priceInventoryMatrix row column freeQuota
          ;print word "free quota after booking: " freeQuota
          if row != 8 [set specialsSoldCounter specialsSoldCounter + 1 ]
          if row = 8 [set flexSpecialsSoldCounter flexSpecialsSoldCounter + 1 ]
          let freeSeats matrix:get my_priceInventoryMatrix 6 day
          set freeSeats freeSeats - 1
          matrix:set my_priceInventoryMatrix 6 day freeSeats
        ]
      ]
    ]
  set my_specialCoordinates "void"
  ]
end

;-------------------------------------------------------------------------
to organise-booking-data

foreach sort trainOperators with [RM = true]    ;calls all operators applying RM
[
  ask ?
  [
    let i 0
    let j 0

    while [i < length clearingRail] ;
```
increment no. of seats booked if train_ID is on the list, or add a new train_ID to the list

```
    [
      set j 0
      let doublesIdentified false
      let booked_train item 0 (item i clearingRail) ;
```
clearing rail: List of (train ID) (price paid)

```
      ;print word "booked train: " booked_train
      let checkVariable list my_id booked_train   ;
```
checking if trainID belongs to the operator the function is currently dealing with

```
      ;print word "Check variable: " checkVariable

      if member? checkVariable simplifiedTrainList
      [
        ;print "OK. This booked train belongs to the operator currently asked..."
```

```
          ifelse empty? my_bookingsList
          [
            let helpList list (booked_train) ( 1 )
            set my_bookingslist fput helpList my_bookingsList
            ;print word "My_bookingsList was empty, now it contains an entry: "
my_bookingsList
            set helplist []
          ]
          [
            ;print "my_bookingsList is not empty, checking for doubles"
            while [j < length my_bookingsList]
            [
            if member? booked_train item j my_bookingsList
              [
                set doublesIdentified true
                let numberOfBookedSeats item 1 item j my_bookingsList + 1
                let helpList list (booked_train) (numberOfBookedSeats)

                set my_bookingsList replace-item j my_bookingsList helpList
                ;print "Another booking on an existing train added"
                ;print my_bookingsList
                set helpList []
              ]
            set j j + 1
            ]
            if doublesIdentified = false
            [
              ;print "This train is not yet part of the bookings list, entry gets
added with 1 reserved seat..."
              let helpList list (booked_train) (1)
              set my_bookingsList lput helpList my_bookingsList
              set helpList []
            ]
          ]
        ]

   set i i + 1

    ]
   ;print word "My Bookings list after iteration: " my_bookingslist
   ]
]
end

;------------------------------------------------------------------------------
to do-clearing

ask trainOperators
[
    set my_turnover 0
    set my_tickTurnover 0
    let keylist table:keys my_schedule
    let i 0
    let key ""
    while [i < length clearingRail]
    [
      set key item 0 (item i clearingRail)
      if member? key keylist = true
      [
        set my_turnover my_turnover + item 1 (item i clearingRail)
        ;print "my turnover"
```

```
      ;print my_turnover
      ;user-message "train identified, paid amount cleared to operator"
      ]
      set key ""
      set my_tickTurnover my_tickTurnover + my_turnover
      set my_turnover 0
      set i i + 1
    ]
    if my_id = 1  ;in case other operators accept the railcard or apply specials, revenue clearing must
be amended
      [
        set my_tickTurnover my_tickTurnover + railcardTickTurnover  ;all railcard turno-
ver cleared to operator 1
        ;print word "Revenue generated by operator 1 including railcardTurnover: "
int my_tickturnover
        set totalRailcardTurnover totalRailCardTurnover + railcardTickTurnover

        let standardFareTickTurnover (my_tickTurnover - railcardFareTickTurnover -
specialsTickTurnover - railcardTickTurnover)
        set-current-plot "Operator1_RevenueMix"
        set-current-plot-pen "StandardFare" plot standardFareTickTurnover
        set-current-plot-pen "RailcardFare" plot railcardFareTickTurnover
        set-current-plot-pen "Specials" plot specialsTickTurnover
        set-current-plot-pen "Railcard_fee" plot railcardTickTurnover
        set railcardFareTickTurnover 0
        set specialsTickTurnover 0
        set railcardTickTurnover 0
      ]
    set railTickTurnover railTickTurnover + my_tickTurnover
    set totalRailTurnover totalRailTurnover + my_tickTurnover  ;total for all operators
    set my_totalTurnover my_totalTurnover + my_tickTurnover
  ]

  if ticks = 0 [ set averageRailTurnover totalRailTurnover ]
  if ticks > 0 [ set averageRailTurnover totalRailTurnover / ticks ]
end

;--------------------------------------------------------------------------------
to report-transactions

monitor-referencePrices
let marketVolumeKm rail_performance + car_performance  ;calculate market volume in pas-
senger kilometres
set market_share_rail rail_performance / marketVolumeKm
set market_share_car car_performance / marketVolumeKm
set railcardHolders count passengers with [my_railcard = true]
let i 1
while [i <= NUMBER_trainOperators]
[
  ask trainOperators with [my_id = i]
  [
    let plotPen word "pen" i
    if railTickTurnover != 0 [set my_revenueShare my_tickTurnover / railTickTurno-
ver * 100]
    if railTickTurnover = 0 [set my_revenueShare ( my_revenueShareRecord / ticks )
]  ;reason: smoothing of the plot
    if ticks > 0 [set my_RevenueShareRecord my_RevenueShareRecord +
my_revenueShare ]
    set-current-plot "Revenue_Share_per_tick"
    if ticks > 0 [set-current-plot-pen plotPen plot my_revenueShare]
```

```
    ;report nominal revenue this tick
    if my_id = 1 [set operator1_revenue int my_tickTurnover]
    if my_id = 2 [set operator2_revenue int my_tickTurnover]
    if my_id = 3 [set operator3_revenue int my_tickTurnover]
  ]

set i i + 1
]
set-current-plot "Rail_Turnover_per_tick"
if ticks > 0 [set-current-plot-pen "pen1" plot railTickTurnover ]
set railTickTurnover 0
set rail_performance 1
set car_performance 1

;report utility data aggregated for all passengers per tick
let helpSum 0
set i 0
while [i < length averageRailUtilityData]
[
  set helpSum helpSum + item i averageRailUtilityData
  set i i + 1
]
set averageRailUtilityTick helpSum / i
set helpSum 0
set i 0
while [i < length averageCarUtilityData]
[
  set helpSum helpSum + item i averageCarUtilityData
  set i i + 1
]
set averageCarUtilityTick helpSum / i
set averageRailUtilityData []
set averageCarUtilityData []

;calculate global & operatorwise occupancy of trains
let globalOccupancySum 0
let operator1_occupancySum 0
let operator2_occupancySum 0
let operator3_occupancySum 0
let numberOfTrains count trains
let operator1_numberOfTrains count trains with [my_operator = 1]
let operator2_numberOfTrains count trains with [my_operator = 2]
let operator3_numberOfTrains count trains with [my_operator = 3]

ask trains
[
  ;print word "my_currentOccupancy" my_currentOccupancy
  set globalOccupancySum globalOccupancySum + my_currentOccupancy

  if my_operator = 1 [set operator1_occupancySum operator1_occupancySum +
(my_currentOccupancy + x [if necessary, a fixed value derived from transactions that are out of scope
of the model]) ]
  if my_operator = 2 [set operator2_occupancySum operator2_occupancySum +
(my_currentOccupancy + x [if necessary, a fixed value derived from transactions that are out of scope
of the model]) ]
  if my_operator = 3 [set operator3_occupancySum operator3_occupancySum +
my_currentOccupancy ]

]
```

```
set globalTrainOccupancy globalOccupancySum / numberOfTrains
;print word "Occupancy sum: " occupancySum
;print word "Average occupancy of trains calculated for this tick: " global-
TrainOccupancy

set operator1_occupancy operator1_occupancySum / operator1_numberOfTrains
if operator2_numberOfTrains != 0 [set operator2_occupancy operator2_occupancySum /
operator2_numberOfTrains]
if operator3_numberOfTrains != 0 [set operator3_occupancy operator3_occupancySum /
operator3_numberOfTrains]
end

;-------------------------------------------------------------------------
to-report get-turnover-data []
```

This reporter can be used for exporting generated data in a sorted way into a file.

```
    let fileEntry []
    set fileEntry fput ";" fileEntry
    set fileEntry lput word ticks " ticks;" fileEntry

    foreach sort trainOperators
    [
      ask ?
      [
        set fileEntry lput word my_ID ";" fileEntry
        set fileEntry lput word precision (my_totalTurnover) 2 ";" fileEntry
      ]
    ]
    set fileEntry lput "Total rail turnover;" fileEntry
    set fileEntry lput word precision (totalRailTurnover) 2 ";" fileEntry
    report fileEntry ; contains sorted list of trainOperator_ID my_totalTurnover

end

;-------------------------------------------------------------------------
to move
```

This function is for graphical illustration only.

```
ask trainsets
[
  if (patch-here = patch 10 0) [ facexy -10 0 ]
  if (patch-here = patch -10 0) [ facexy 10 0 ]
  if (who mod 2) = 0 [ fd 0.2 ]
  fd 1
]
end

;-------------------------------------------------------------------------
to refill-budget

ask passengers
[
   if ticks mod 30 = 0 AND ticks > 0 [set my_budget int (my_budget + random-normal
[value A] [value B])]
   ;statistical amount of money spent on car usage per month: [empirical value]
]
end
```

```
;---------------------------------------------------------------------------
to check-railcards
```

This function represents the empirical fact that a certain share of railcard owners do not renew their card once it has expired. At the same time, through calling non-railcard-owners to buy one, it keeps the total number of railcards roughly stable. The motivation for this is that not enough market research data is available yet for a more detailed modelling of railcard buying behaviour.

```
  let expiredCounter1 0 ;consumers with an expired railcard
  let expiredCounter2 0 ;consumers who do not renew their card
  let expiredCounter3 0
  let repurchaseThreshold [value] ;[value] % renew their railcard
  ;print word "repurchaseThreshold: " repurchaseThreshold

  let railcardPriceDifference (int (100 * RAILCARDPRICE / initialRailcardPrice ))
- 100
  ;print word "Railcard Price Difference: " railcardPriceDifference
  ask passengers with [my_railcard = true]
  [
    if my_railcardValidity >= 1 [set my_railcardValidity my_railcardValidity - 1]
    if my_railcardValidity = 0 ;decide whether to buy a new one
    [
      set expiredCounter1 expiredCounter1 + 1
      let i random 100
      ifelse i > repurchaseThreshold ;[empirical value]% don't buy a new one
      [
        set my_railcard false
        set my_railcardValidity 0
        set expiredCounter2 expiredCounter2 + 1
      ]
      [
        buy-railcard
      ]
    ]
  ]

  if ticks > 0 AND ticks < 1000 AND RAILCARD = true
  [
    let numberOfRailcardBuyers int (0.25 + ((expiredCounter1 * [non-renewal rate])
+ railcardPriceDifference * [value])) ;assuming a [value] elasticity of demand and [empirical
value]% of expired railcards to be replaced
    ;print word "numberOfRailcardBuyers: " numberOfRailcardBuyers

    ask n-of numberOfRailcardBuyers passengers with [my_railcard = false AND
my_socioGroup != "carAddicted" ] [ buy-railcard ]
  ]

  if ticks > [timeframe] [consider-railcard]
end

;---------------------------------------------------------------------------
to consider-railcard
```

This function is prepared for modelling a more detailed way consumers decide whether to buy a new railcard or not. It is not used for the experiments outlined above.

```
  if RAILCARD = true
  [
    ask passengers with [my_railCard = false and my_socioGroup != "carAddicted"]
    [
```

```
    let my_railExpenses 0
    if length my_transactionsRail > 5
    [
      let i 0
      while [ i < length my_transactionsRail ]
      [
        ;print word "My initial rail expenses: " my_railExpenses
        set my_railExpenses my_railExpenses + item i my_transactionsRail
        ;print word "Item in my_transactionsRail: " my_transactionsRail
        ;print word "My incremented rail expenses: " my_railExpenses
        set i i + 1
      ]
      if my_railExpenses > [threshold value] [buy-railcard]
    ]
  ]
]
end

;--------------------------------------------------------------------------------
to buy-railcard
```

This function processes the railcard buying transaction.

```
  let currentRailcardPrice RAILCARDPRICE

  if RAILCARD = true
  [
    if my_budget > currentRailcardPrice
    [
      set my_budget my_budget - currentRailcardPrice
      set my_railCard true
      set my_railCardValidity 365
      set railcardTickTurnover railcardTickTurnover + currentRailcardPrice
      set railcardsSoldTick railcardsSoldTick + 1
    ]
    if my_budget < currentRailcardPrice [] ;print "Budget constraint. I can't af-
ford a railcard now."]
  ]
end

;--------------------------------------------------------------------------------
to-report get-repetition-info [degreeOfFlexibility]
```

This reporter uses the consumer's flexibility to switch to another train to generate a decision whether to search for another train or not.

```
  let searchAgain false

  let a random-float 1
  if degreeOfFlexibility >= a [set searchAgain true]

  report searchAgain

end


;--------------------------------------------------------------------------------
to generate-specials
```

Special offers can only be booked if they are activated by this function.

```
  ask trainOperators with [ RM = true ]
  [
    let operator_identificator my_id
    ask trains with [my_operator = operator_identificator]
    [
      if PERMANENTSPECIAL = true [set permanentSpecialsAvailable true]
    ]
  ]
  ask trainOperators with [ RM = true ]
  [
    let operator_identificator my_id
    ask trains with [my_operator = operator_identificator]
    [
      if FLEXSPECIAL = true [set flexSpecialsAvailable true]
    ]
  ]
end

;--------------------------------------------------------------------------------
to observe-competitors
```

Train operators can observe the prices published by their competitors and react to pricing decisions made by them. The rules of behaviour implemented in the present model are limited to an ignoring or a follower strategy, however, other options of reaction are prepared for future extensions of the model.

```
  let i 0
  while [i <= NUMBER_TRAINOPERATORS]
  [
    if i = 1 [ask trainOperators with [my_ID = 1] [ set my_priceStrategy opera-
tor1_priceStrategy ] ]
    if i = 2 [ask trainOperators with [my_ID = 2] [ set my_priceStrategy opera-
tor2_priceStrategy ] ]
    if i = 3 [ask trainOperators with [my_ID = 3] [ set my_priceStrategy opera-
tor3_priceStrategy ] ]

    set i i + 1
  ]
 ;memorise competitor prices
  ask trainOperators
  [
    let ownOperatorID 0
    set ownOperatorID my_ID
    let competitorsBaseFares get-competitors-baseFares ownOperatorID

    if not is-list? competitorsBaseFares ;i. e.: there is only one other competitor
    [
      set my_competitorsBaseFareMemory1 lput competitorsBaseFares
my_competitorsBaseFareMemory1
      set my_competitorsBaseFareMemory2 "only_one_competitor"
      if length my_competitorsBaseFareMemory1 > 10 [set
my_competitorsBaseFareMemory1 but-first my_competitorsBaseFareMemory1]

    ]

    if is-list? competitorsBaseFares ;i. e.: there are two competitors
    [
      set my_competitorsBaseFareMemory1 lput item 1 item 0 competitorsBaseFares
my_competitorsBaseFareMemory1
```

```
      set my_competitorsBaseFareMemory2 lput item 1 item 1 competitorsBaseFares
my_competitorsBaseFareMemory2
      if length my_competitorsBaseFareMemory1 > 10 [set
my_competitorsBaseFareMemory1 but-first my_competitorsBaseFareMemory1]
      if length my_competitorsBaseFareMemory2 > 10 [set
my_competitorsBaseFareMemory1 but-first my_competitorsBaseFareMemory2]
    ]
  ]
  if ticks mod 5 = 0 AND ticks > 0
  [
    ask one-of trainOperators
    [
      if my_priceStrategy = "ignore" AND NUMBER_TRAINOPERATORS != 1 [];show "I
ignore the collected data from my competitors."]

      if my_priceStrategy = "follow"
      [
        ;show "I follow my competitor(s)."
        if NUMBER_TRAINOPERATORS = 2 ;there is only one competitor
        [
          ;print "1 competitor scenario..."
          if my_competitorsBaseFareMemory1 != []
          [
            let my_price 0
            let others_price 0
            let others_railcard false
            let ID_number my_ID
            ask one-of trains with [my_operator = ID_number] [set my_price
my_baseFare]
            ask one-of trains with [my_operator != ID_number ] [ set others_price
my_baseFare ]
            if RAILCARD = true [ask one-of trains with [my_operator != ID_number ]
[ if railCardAllowed = true [set others_railcard true ]]]
            if others_railcard = true
            [
              set others_price others_price * [strategic value] ;for instance, a com-
petitor may only follow to a price level defined by a railcard.
                let input_fare others_price
                set others_price get-roundFare input_fare
            ]

            let difference my_price - others_price
            let ratio my_price / others_price
            let step 0

            if ratio > 1 [set step ceiling ((-1 * (1 - (1 / ratio) ) * 100))]
            if ratio < 1 [set step ceiling ((1 - ratio) * 100)]
            if step > 90 [ set step 90 ] ;maximum move of 90%
            if step < -90 [ set step -90 ] ;maximum move of -90%
            if my_ID = 1 [set operator1_railPrice operator1_railPrice + step]
            if my_ID = 2 [set operator2_railPrice operator2_railPrice + step]
            if difference < 0 [];print word "I'm cheaper than my competitor: "
difference]
            if difference > 0 [];print word "I'm more expensive than my competi-
tor: " difference]
            if difference = 0 [];print "I have an equal base fare level with my
competitor."]
          ]
        ]
```

```
        if NUMBER_TRAINOPERATORS = 3  ;two other competitors on the market
        [
            ;print "2 competitors scenario..."
            if my_competitorsBaseFareMemory1 != [] AND my_competitorsBaseFareMemory2
!= []
            [
```
;build an average difference to the competitors
```
            ]
            if my_competitorsBaseFareMemory1 = [] AND my_competitorsBaseFareMemory2
= [] [print "No observation point(s) yet."]
        ]
    ]


    if my_priceStrategy = "punish"
    [
```
This strategy is subject to possible specific experimental designs in the field of price war gaming.
```
    ]


    if my_priceStrategy = "experiment"
```
This part of the code is a preparation for a possible model extension with inductive reasoning behaviour
```
    [
        Strategy subject to experimental design
    ]
    ]
  ]
end


;---------------------------------------------------------------------------
to-report get-competitors-baseFares [ownOperatorID]

  let otherOperatorID 0
  let otherOperatorID_2 0
  let otherBaseFare 0
  let otherBaseFare_2 0
  let competitorsBaseFares 0
; if only 1 operator, no observation necessary
  if NUMBER_TRAINOPERATORS = 1 [report "no_competitors" ]
; case of 2 operators
  if NUMBER_TRAINOPERATORS = 2
  [
    ifelse ownOperatorID = 1 [set otherOperatorID 2] [set otherOperatorID 1]

    ask one-of trains with [my_operator = otherOperatorID]
    [
      set competitorsBaseFares my_baseFare
      ;print word "Single competitor's base fare: " competitorsBaseFares
    ]
    report CompetitorsBaseFares
  ]
; case of 3 operators
  if NUMBER_TRAINOPERATORS = 3
  [
    if ownOperatorID = 1
    [
      set otherOperatorID 2
      set otherOperatorID_2 3
    ]

    if ownOperatorID = 2
```

```
  [
   set otherOperatorID 1
   set otherOperatorID_2 3
  ]

  if ownOperatorID = 3
  [
     set otherOperatorID 1
     set otherOperatorID_2 2
  ]
  ask one-of trains with [my_operator = otherOperatorID]
  [
     set otherBaseFare my_baseFare
     print word "1 out of 2 competitor's base fare: " otherBaseFare
  ]

  ask one-of trains with [my_operator = otherOperatorID_2]
  [
     set otherBaseFare_2 my_baseFare
     print word "1 out of 2 competitor's base fare: " otherBaseFare_2
  ]
  let input1 list (otherOperatorID) (otherBaseFare)
  let input2 list (otherOperatorID_2) (otherBaseFare_2)
  let helpList []
  set helpList fput input1 helpList
  set helpList lput input2 helpList
  set competitorsBaseFares helpList


  report competitorsBaseFares
 ]
end

;-------------------------------------------------------------------------------
to align-referencePrices
```

This function allows for interaction between consumers in the realm of their price experience. Technically, items in the consumer memory record are exchanged.

```
  ask passengers
  [
    let otherLinkEnd_LastCarPriceExperience 0
    let otherLinkEnd_LastRailBasePriceExperience 0
    let otherLinkEnd_LastRailSpecialPriceExperience 0
    let otherLinkEnd_Railcard false
    ;individuals chat about their last transaction
    if count my-links > 0
    [
    ask one-of my-links
    [
      ask other-end
      [
        ;print (word "I'm " who ", the link of the passenger stated above.")

     ;random selection with a pre-set 99% probability to share
         let r random-float 100
         ifelse r > 0.01
         [
          if my_transactionsCar != [] [set otherLinkEnd_LastCarPriceExperience
last my_transactionsCar]
```

```
            if my_transactionsRail != [] [set other-
LinkEnd_LastRailBasePriceExperience last my_transactionsRail]
            if my_transactionsRailSpecials != [] [set other-
LinkEnd_LastRailSpecialPriceExperience last my_transactionsRailSpecials]
            if RAILCARD = true AND my_railcard = true AND my_railcardValidity <=
350 [set otherLinkEnd_Railcard true] ;the other consumer agent has not just recently bought a
railcard.
          ]
```

In order to avoid confusing different categories of prices among individuals, consumers do not share their reference prices in case a recently bought railcard is involved.

```
          [ ];print "No price sharing in this case." ]
      ]
    ]
```

Share car price experience

```
      ;print word "My transactions car before sharing: " my_transactionsCar
      if otherLinkEnd_LastCarPriceExperience != 0
        [
        set my_transactionsCar lput otherLinkEnd_LastCarPriceExperience
my_transactionsCar
          ;print word "My transactions car after sharing: " my_transactionsCar
        ]
```

Share rail base fare experience

```
            if otherLinkEnd_LastRailBasePriceExperience != 0 AND RAILCARD = false
;railcard is not relevant
          [
          set my_transactionsRail lput otherLinkEnd_LastRailBasePriceExperience
my_transactionsRail
          ]

          if otherLinkEnd_LastRailBasePriceExperience != 0 AND RAILCARD = true
          [
          if my_railCard = true AND otherLinkEnd_Railcard = true ;both have a railcard
          [
            set my_transactionsRail lput otherLinkEnd_LastRailBasePriceExperience
my_transactionsRail
          ]
          if my_railCard = false AND otherLinkEnd_Railcard = false ;both do not have
a railcard
          [
            set my_transactionsRail lput otherLinkEnd_LastRailBasePriceExperience
my_transactionsRail
          ]
```

Ignore the information in case one end owns a railcard, while the other end doesn't.

```
        if my_railCard = true AND otherLinkEnd_Railcard = false ;other link-end without
railcard
          [
          ;print "I have a railcard, but my link doesn't - I can't compare the
prices."
          ]
          if my_railCard = false AND otherLinkEnd_Railcard = true ;only the other link-
end has a railcard
          [
          ;print "I don't have a railcard, but my link has - I can't compare the
prices."
          ]
```

```
        ]
            ;print word "My transactions rail (base fare) after sharing: "
my_transactionsRail
```

Share rail special fare experience

```
            ;print word "My transactions rail (specials) before sharing: "
my_transactionsRailSpecials
        ifelse otherLinkEnd_LastRailSpecialPriceExperience != 0
        [
            set my_transactionsRailSpecials lput other-
LinkEnd_LastRailSpecialPriceExperience my_transactionsRailSpecials
            ;print word "My transactions rail (specials) after sharing: "
my_transactionsRailSpecials
        ]
        [
            ;print "No sharing occured because my link did not have any rail special
price experience."
        ]
```

re-setting values to zero for the next link

```
        set otherLinkEnd_LastCarPriceExperience 0
        set otherLinkEnd_LastRailBasePriceExperience 0
        set otherLinkEnd_LastRailSpecialPriceExperience 0
        set otherLinkEnd_Railcard false
    ]
    ]
end
```

```
;------------------------------------------------------------------------------
to monitor-referencePrices
```

This function calculates the average reference prices for rail and car transportation to be displayed in the observer interface.

```
let helpSum 0
let counter 0
ask passengers with [my_referencePriceRailBase != 0]
[
  set helpSum helpSum + my_referencePriceRailBase
  set counter counter + 1
]

if counter != 0 [set globalReferencePriceRailBase precision ( helpSum / counter
) 2]
;print word "GlobalReferencePriceRailBase: " globalReferencePriceRailBase

set helpSum 0
set counter 0

ask passengers with [my_referencePriceRailSpecials != 0]
[
  set helpSum helpSum + my_referencePriceRailSpecials
  set counter counter + 1
]

if counter != 0 [set globalReferencePriceRailSpecials precision ( helpSum /
counter ) 2]
;print word "GlobalReferencePriceRailSpecials: " globalReferencePriceRailSpe-
cials

set helpSum 0
```

```
  set counter 0

  ask passengers with [my_referencePriceRailMix != 0]
  [
    set helpSum helpSum + my_referencePriceRailMix
    set counter counter + 1
  ]
  if counter != 0 [set globalReferencePriceRailMix precision ( helpSum / counter )
2]

  set helpSum 0
  set counter 0
  ask passengers with [my_referencePriceCar != 0]
  [
    set helpSum helpSum + my_referencePriceCar
    set counter counter + 1
  ]
  if counter != 0 [set globalReferencePriceCar precision (helpSum / counter ) 2]

end
;-------------------------------------------------------------------------------
to calculate-referencePrices

  ask passengers
  [
    let who_number who
    set my_referencePriceCar get-referencePriceCar who_number
    set my_referencePriceRailBase get-referencePriceRailBase who_number
    set my_referencePriceRailSpecials get-referencePriceRailSpecials who_number
    set my_referencePriceRailMix get-referencePriceRailMix who_number ;generating a
mixed reference price according to Thaler (1985)
  ]
end


;-------------------------------------------------------------------------------
to-report get-referencePriceCar [who_number]
```

Together with the following ones on reference price calculation, this reporter uses an exponential smoothing approach both to reflect historic prices and the most recent price experience made by the consumer.

```
  let referencePriceCar 0
  let i 0
  let helpSum 0
  let helpTransactionsList my_transactionsCar

  ;historic price experience less last price experience
  ifelse length helpTransactionsList > 0 [set helpTransactionsList but-last help-
TransactionsList] [];print "list my_transactionsCar void, no last item deleted."]
    while [i < length helpTransactionsList]
    [
      set helpSum helpSum + item i helpTransactionsList
      set i i + 1
    ]
    if length helpTransactionsList > 0
    [
      let alpha priceLearningParameter
      let oldReferencePriceCar (helpSum / length helpTransactionsList)
      let lastTransaction last my_transactionsCar ;most recent price experience
```

```
      set referencePriceCar precision (oldReferencePriceCar * (1-alpha) +
(lastTransaction * alpha)) 2
    ]
    if length helpTransactionsList = 0 AND length my_transactionsCar = 1
    [
      set referencePriceCar last my_transactionsCar
    ]
  report referencePriceCar
end
```

```
;-----------------------------------------------------------------------------
to-report get-referencePriceRailBase [who_number]
```

This function collects the reference price for base fares as a first step to calculate the consumer's overall reference price for rail transportation.

```
  let referencePriceRailBase 0
  let i 0
  let helpSum 0
  let helpTransactionsList my_transactionsRail

  ;historic price experience less last price experience
  ifelse length helpTransactionsList > 0 [set helpTransactionsList but-last help-
TransactionsList] [];print "list my_transactionsCar void, no last item deleted."]
    while [i < length helpTransactionsList]
    [
      set helpSum helpSum + item i helpTransactionsList
      set i i + 1
    ]
    if length helpTransactionsList > 0
    [
      let alpha priceLearningParameter
      let oldReferencePriceRailBase (helpSum / length helpTransactionsList)
      let lastTransaction last my_transactionsRail ;most recent price experience
      set referencePriceRailBase precision (oldReferencePriceRailBase * (1-alpha)
+ (lastTransaction * alpha) ) 2
    ]
    if length helpTransactionsList = 0 AND length my_transactionsRail = 1
    [
      set referencePriceRailBase last my_transactionsRail
      ;print (word "Only one transaction with rail base fare" referencePriceRail-
Base)
    ]
  report referencePriceRailBase
end
```

```
;-----------------------------------------------------------------------------
to-report get-referencePriceRailSpecials [who_number]
```

```
  let referencePriceRailSpecials 0
  let i 0
  let helpSum 0
  let helpTransactionsList my_transactionsRailSpecials

  ;historic price experience less last price experience
  ifelse length helpTransactionsList > 0 [set helpTransactionsList but-last help-
TransactionsList] [];print "list my_transactionsCar void, no last item deleted."]
    while [i < length helpTransactionsList]
    [
      set helpSum helpSum + item i helpTransactionsList
```

```
      set i i + 1
    ]
    if length helpTransactionsList > 0
    [
        let alpha priceLearningParameter
        let oldReferencePriceRailSpecials (helpSum / length helpTransactionsList)
        let lastTransaction last my_transactionsRailSpecials ;most recent price experi-
ence
        set referencePriceRailSpecials precision (oldReferencePriceRailSpecials *
(1-alpha) + (lastTransaction * alpha) ) 2
    ]
    if length helpTransactionsList = 0 AND length my_transactionsRailSpecials = 1
    [
        set referencePriceRailSpecials last my_transactionsRailSpecials
    ]
  report referencePriceRailSpecials
end


;---------------------------------------------------------------------------
to-report get-referencePriceRailMix [who_number]

  let degree degreeOfMentalAccounting / 100
  let referencePriceRailMix 0
  if my_referencePriceRailBase != 0 AND my_referencePriceRailSpecials != 0
      [
        let length1 length my_transactionsRail
        let length2 length my_transactionsRailSpecials
        let length_sum length1 + length2
        let input_base my_referencePriceRailBase * length1
        let input_specials my_referencePriceRailSpecials * length2
        let input_baseAndSpecials (input_base + input_specials ) / length_sum
        set referencePriceRailMix (my_referencePriceRailBase + (in-
put_baseAndSpecials * (1 - degree))) / (1 + (1 - degree))
```

The result of this calculation is a weighted reference price according to length of transaction lists and influence of specials (=degree of Mental accounting) to the mixed reference price.

```
      ]
      if my_referencePriceRailBase != 0 AND my_referencePriceRailSpecials = 0 [set
referencePriceRailMix my_referencePriceRailBase]

  report referencePriceRailMix
end


;---------------------------------------------------------------------------
to-report get-travelTimeRail [chosen_train]
```

All trains in the simulation model can have distinct scheduled travel times which are collected by this reporter.

```
  let travelTimeRail 0
  ask one-of trains with [my_number = chosen_train]
  [
    set travelTimeRail my_travelTime
  ]
  report travelTimeRail
end
```

```
;--------------------------------------------------------------------------------
to set-trainDetails
```

Travel time of specific groups of trains can be set here by the observer. Travel time affects utility if a consumer compares different transport offers available for her/him.

```
  let operator1_categoryA_travelTime [number]
  let operator1_categoryB_travelTime [number]
  let operator2_categoryA_travelTime [number]
  let operator2_catgeoryB_travelTime "void" ;not implemented
  let operator3_categoryA_travelTime [number]
  let operator3_catgeoryB_travelTime "void" ;not implemented
  ask n-of ([quantity] * count trains with [my_operator = 1]) trains with
[my_operator = 1]
    [
      set my_category "A"
      set my_travelTime operator1_categoryA_travelTime
    ]
    ask trains with [my_operator = 1 AND my_category != "A"]
    [
      set my_category "B"
      set my_travelTime operator1_categoryB_travelTime
    ]
    ask trains with [my_operator = 2]
    [
      set my_category "A"
      set my_travelTime operator2_categoryA_travelTime
    ]
    ask trains with [my_operator = 3]
    [
      set my_category "A"
      set my_travelTime operator3_categoryA_travelTime
    ]
end
```

```
;--------------------------------------------------------------------------------
to-report get-roundFare [input_fare]
```

This reporter generates a rounded fare according to railway nominal price standards.

```
  let workFare int (input_fare * 100) ;calculating in cents because of the floating point inac-
curacy issue
  while [ workFare mod 10 != 0 ]
    [
      set workFare workFare + 1
    let roundFare workFare / 100
    report roundFare
  ]
end
```

```
;--------------------------------------------------------------------------------
to calculate-occupancy
```

Within this function, trains automatically renew their current average occupancy rate.

```
ask trains
[
  let i 0
  let helpSum 0
  while [i < length my_occupancyRecord] ;occupancyRecord is only filled if ticks>10
```

```
    [
      set helpSum helpSum + item i my_occupancyRecord
      set i i + 1
    ]
  ifelse length my_occupancyRecord > 0
  [
    set my_averageOccupancy helpSum / length my_occupancyRecord
    set my_averageOccupancy my_averageOccupancy + [out-of-model occupancy value]
  ]
  [
    set my_averageOccupancy 0
  ]
]
end
```

;---
```
to calculate-personalDiscount
```

Please note that this feature has only been implemented for a 1-operator-scenario.

```
ask passengers
[
  let helpsum 0
  let i 0
  while [i < length my_transactionsRail]
  [
    set helpSum helpSum + item i my_transactionsRail
    set i i + 1
  ]
if helpsum != 0
 [
   if helpSum <= [value1] [set my_personalDiscount x1]
   if helpSum > [value1] AND helpSum <= [value2] [set my_personalDiscount x2]
   if helpSum > [value2] AND helpSum <= [value3] [set my_personalDiscount x3]
   if helpSum > [value3] AND helpSum <= [value4] [set my_personalDiscount x4]
   if helpSum > [value4] AND helpSum <= [value5] [set my_personalDiscount x5]
   if helpSum > [value5] and helpSum <= [value6] [set my_personalDiscount x6]
   if helpSum > [value6] [set my_personalDiscount x7]
 ]
 if helpsum = 0 [set my_personalDiscount 0]
 ]
end
```

;---

Appendix B Market research

Questionnaire "Revenue simulation model for Railcorp passenger division"

Screening

1. Age: _____ years (16-70 years)

2. Place of residence

    1 City A & surroundings
    2 City B & surroundings
    3 City C & surroundings
    4 Other place of residence → **END**

3. No matter the means of transport used – which of the following routes have you travelled in the past 4 weeks?
    Multiple answers

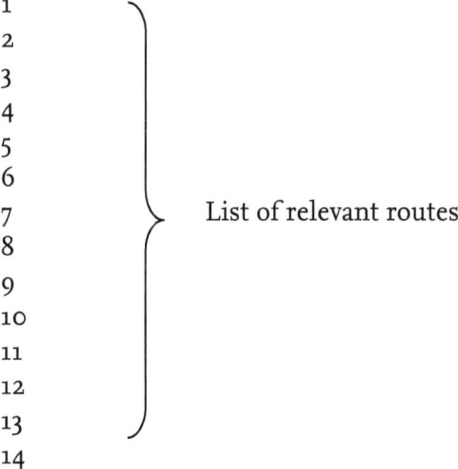

    1
    2
    3
    4
    5
    6
    7   List of relevant routes
    8
    9
    10
    11
    12
    13
    14

    15 None of the listed routes → **END**

4. And how did you travel those routes? If you used different means of transport, please choose the answer of the means of transport you used most.

© Springer Fachmedien Wiesbaden GmbH, part of Springer Nature 2014
N. Kellermann, *Searching for a path out of distance fares*, Edition KWV,
https://doi.org/10.1007/978-3-658-23112-5

Select one answer

1 I took the car (as a driver)
2 I was a passenger in the car of a member of my household
3 by motor bicycle
4 by rail
5 by bus
6 other → **END**

General information

5. Do you own a car?

1 yes
2 no

6. Are there any public means of transport (bus, tramway, underground, urban rail or railways) available close to your place of residence?

1 yes
2 no

Mobility budget

In the following, you will find a couple of questions concerning your expenses for car travel and for travel by public means of transport. We understand **expenses for car travel and expenses for public means of transport** as your payments for petrol, railway tickets (incl. railcards, commutation tickets etc.) and reservations.

Only to owners of a car according to question 5:
7. How much money did you approximately spend (as a single person) for petrol/diesel in the last month?
___ .- Euros

o I don't know / I don't want to specify this

8. How much money did you (as a single person) spend for **railway tickets for single journeys** (this means <u>no</u> railcards or commuter tickets) you used either for private or business trips in the last month?

    ___ .- Euros

    o I don't know / I don't want to specify this

9. Broadly speaking: When you buy a **railway ticket for single journeys** (no commutation tickets), does it happen that you chat about the price you paid with your family, friends or colleagues?

    1 yes
    2 no
    3 I don't buy railway tickets for single journeys

10. **If question 9 is answered with "yes":** How often do you chat with family, friends or colleagues on the price you paid?

    1 after every purchase made
    2 mostly
    3 from time to time
    4 very rarely

Price experience

In the following, you see a couple of questions concerning "long distance trains". Long distance trains are [Product name_1], [Product name_2], [Product name_3].

11. How often did you travel with a long-distance train inside [country] within the last four weeks (a return journey is 2 trips)?

    ___ times (0-999)

12. **If no. of journeys from question 11 = 1:** On which route did you travel? *Select one answer*
    If no. of journeys from question 11 > 1: On which route did you travel most frequently? If you travelled equally often on different routes, please choose the one of your last journey.

Select one answer

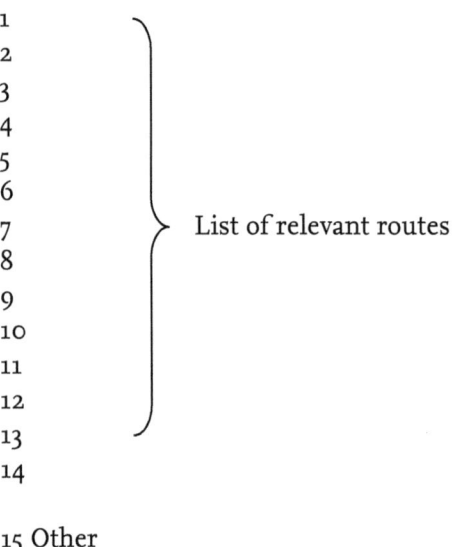

1
2
3
4
5
6
7
8
9
10
11
12
13
14

List of relevant routes

15 Other

13. **If no. of journeys from question 11 > 1:** In [country], there are different railway undertakings with respective prices. Please remember your last trip on the route [answer of question 12], no matter what railway undertaking you chose, how much does a trip on that route **typically** cost?

____. - Euros

o I don't know / I don't want to specify this

14. **If number of trips in question 11 = 1:** Which railway undertaking did you choose for travel?
If number of trips in question 11 > 1: Which railway undertaking did you mostly choose for travel? *Select one answer*

1 [Railcorp A]
2 (only if question 12 is not answered with codes 10-14) [Railcorp B]
3 (only if answer to question 11 > 1 and question 12 is not answered with codes 10-14) [Railcorp A] and [Railcorp B] equally
4 I don't know

15. **If number of trips in question 11 = 1:** How much money did you pay for this one-way trip?

If number of trips in question 11 > 1: How much money did you pay for your last one-way trip on the route?

_____. - Euros

o   I don't know / I don't want to specify this

16.   **If number of trips in question 11 and [Railcorp] in question 13:** Was the ticket you bought a permanent special offer?
If number of trips in question 11 > 1: Was the ticket you bought a permanent special offer of [Railcorp]?

1 yes
2 no
3 I don't know

17.   **If number of trips in question 11 > 1:** Please estimate how many of the tickets you bought in the last four weeks (tickets for one-way trips) were permanent special offers of [Railcorp]?

1   all tickets
2   more than half of the tickets I bought
3   exactly half of the tickets I bought
4   less than half of the tickets I bought
5   none

18.   **If question 17 is answered 1-4:** [Railcorp's] permanent special offers are available at different price levels and restricted in number of seats. Therefore, not all prices are available at all times. How much did you pay on average for a [Railcorp] permanent special offer on route [answer of question 12]?

_____. - Euros

o   I don't know / I don't want to specify this

Restrictions and utility

To all respondents:

19. Not everyone can exactly plan all trips in advance. And not everyone likes to commit to a certain train. Do you agree with the following statements?

Rotating presentation of items!	Fully agree	Tend to agree	Not sure	Tend to dis- agree	Fully disa- gree
I am planning in advance if I get a financial advantage from that.	1	2	3	4	5
Flexibility is worth a higher price.	1	2	3	4	5

20. How do you agree with the following questions?

Rotating presentation of items!	Fully agree	Tend to agree	Not sure	Tend to dis- agree	Fully disa- gree
If others pay for my travel expenses, price doesn't play a role for me.	1	2	3	4	5
If I can only use a restricted number of trains with my ticket, fare prices should be reduced.	1	2	3	4	5
[Fare name] special offers are rarely available.	1	2	3	4	5
Anyone who wants to save money should book early in advance.	1	2	3	4	5
Elaborate search for special offers doesn't pay off.	1	2	3	4	5
A railcard is amortised after approximately 10 trips.	1	2	3	4	5
The most important choice factor for me is the lowest price for getting from A to B.	1	2	3	4	5
I avoid crowded trains.	1	2	3	4	5
There should be a full refund for cancelled reservations.	1	2	3	4	5
I don't like to commit myself to a specific train.	1	2	3	4	5
I get annoyed if I have to pay different prices for an identical product.	1	2	3	4	5

21. Generally, train tickets are open tickets and you can flexibly choose the specific train to travel with. If you have to **commit yourself to a specific train when buying a ticket**, how much lower do you expect the price to be compared to a flexible ticket?
Select one answer

1 At least 10% less expensive
2 At least 25% less expensive
3 At least 50% less expensive
4 At least 75% less expensive

22. Generally, train tickets are open tickets and you can flexibly choose the specific train to travel with. Thus, an open ticket is generally available for all [Railcorp] trains. Assuming that a ticket would only be valid for half of all [Railcorp] trains, how much lower do you expect the price for such a ticket to be?
Select one answer

1 At least 10% less expensive
2 At least 25% less expensive
3 At least 50% less expensive
4 At least 75% less expensive

STATISTICS

Sex:

    1 Male
    2 Female

Place of living:

    1 Up to 2,000 inhabitants
    2 Up to 5,000 inhabitants
    3 Up to 20,000 inhabitants
    4 Up to 50,000 inhabitants
    5 Up to 50,000 inhabitants

Occupation:

    1 Self-employed, executive employee   5 Pupil/student
    2 Civil servant, clerical worker   6 Housewife
    3 Worker   7 Pensioner
    4 Cultivator   8 Unemployed

Education: What is your highest level of education?

    1 Secondary school
    2 Vocational school, technical college
    3 College
    4 School examination qualifying for university
    5 Graduated

Household income: If you sum up the earnings of all members of your household members, what is the total monthly income of your household? Please estimate if you don't know the exact number.

    1 less than 1,199 Euros
    2 1,200 to 1,799 Euros
    3 1,800 to 2,399 Euros
    4 2,400 to 3,299 Euros
    5 3,300 Euros or more
    6 I don't know, I don't want to specify this

Marital status:

  1 Single   3 Divorced
  2 Married / in a registered relationship   4 Widowed

How many people, including yourself, are living in your household?

  1 1 person   4 4 persons
  2 2 persons   5 more than 4 persons
  3 3 persons

Do you currently possess a railcard?

  1 yes
  2 no

Which tickets do you normally use when travelling by rail? Which commuter ticket of [Railcorp] or of a transport association, -if appropriate - which type of railcard do you currently use for rail travel?

Multiple answers

  1 Base fare ticket
  2 Special offer
  3 Flat-rate offer
  4 Regional transport special
  5 [special local offer]
  6 Promotional ticket
  7 Railcard discount
  8 International ticket
  9 Free ticket for pupils and apprentices
  10 Week ticket
  11 Commuter ticket valid for one year or one month
  12 Other ticket
  13 None
  14 I don't know

Appendix C Abstract

Abstract

This dissertation reconstructs the path of fare policy in the European passenger railway industry and integrates behavioural pricing theory into an agent-based simulation model for railway revenue management. Representing supply and demand on a transport market and calibrated with empirical data of an incumbent European railway, the model is employed to conduct artificial experiments on fare innovations. Explaining the emergence of a persistent pricing pattern in railway history and analysing the effects of alternative fare options, this work contributes to the theory of path dependence as well as to marketing and operations research.

Kurzfassung

In dieser Dissertation wird der Pfad der Eisenbahntarifierung im europäischen Personenverkehr rekonstruiert. Weiterhin werden verhaltenswissenschaftliche Ansätze der Preispolitik in einem agentenbasierten Simulationsmodell für die Anwendung im Erlösmanagement umgesetzt. Das Modell basiert auf Daten eines europäischen Eisenbahnverkehrsunternehmens und dient zur Durchführung von künstlichen Experimenten zu innovativen Tarifmaßnahmen. Diese Arbeit leistet durch die Erklärung eines persistenten Musters der Tarifgestaltung in der Eisenbahngeschichte einen Beitrag zur Theorie der Pfadabhängigkeit. Durch die Untersuchung der Effekte alternativer Tarifoptionen liefert sie außerdem einen Beitrag zur Marketingforschung und zum Operations Research.

© Springer Fachmedien Wiesbaden GmbH, part of Springer Nature 2014
N. Kellermann, *Searching for a path out of distance fares*, Edition KWV,
https://doi.org/10.1007/978-3-658-23112-5